Conversations with
Coach Wooden

ON BASEBALL, HEROES, AND LIFE

BY GARY ADAMS
UCLA HALL OF FAME BASEBALL COACH

FOREWORD BY ERIC KARROS

PRAISE FOR
CONVERSATIONS WITH COACH WOODEN

"Long before I became a Bruin, I learned all about the legend of John Wooden—eighty-eight consecutive victories and ten national championships speak for themselves. His Pyramid of Success became the blueprint for how I lived as an eighteen-year-old boy and, today, as a thirty-six-year-old husband and father of three. Thank you, Coach Adams and Coach Wooden, for the lifelong lessons I now will pass along to my children."

—ERIC BYRNES, UCLA All-American outfielder
and twelve-year major-leaguer

"I had the blessing of not only playing for Coach Gary Adams, but also coaching against him at the college level later in life. I knew he was a man I wanted to follow when I was one of his players. Now, having been a college head coach for thirty years, I can honestly say he is one of the finest human beings I have ever known—a great teacher of the good, but more importantly, a great leader of young men!"

—ANDY LOPEZ, University of Arizona Head Baseball Coach,
three-time NCAA Coach of the Year,
and two-time national championship winner

"Coach Adams changed my life by taking my average bat and slick fielding glove away from me during my senior year at UCLA and telling me I was only going to be a pitcher. He was honest with me—and from what I know about Coach Wooden, it was something he would have done, too."

—CASEY JANSSEN, Toronto Blue Jays closer
and UCLA All-American pitcher

"Though he long stood at the top of college basketball's pyramid and is revered for teachings that went far beyond the sport, Coach John Wooden had a little secret—a grand affinity for baseball. As a student of the game, he enjoyed discussing strategy and tactics with other knowledgeable enthusiasts, most notably an individual who's been around the bases a few times himself. That conversational partner, former UCLA baseball coach Gary Adams, has captured the essence of both Wooden the man, and Wooden the fan, in this book. Two coaches, working their magic in distinctly different circumstances, bonded by America's pastime. My thanks to Gary for bringing to life musings so powerful that I can almost smell the pine tar."

—DAN GUERRERO, UCLA Athletic Director
and former Bruin Baseball Hall of Fame player

"When I first heard Coach Adams say, 'Be quick, don't hurry,' I knew exactly where it came from. Coach not only enriched my UCLA experience, he also made me a better man. That is how Coach Wooden and Coach Adams were so uniquely similar; they felt it was their responsibility to make eighteen-year-old freshmen into upstanding young men who could function in life beyond the playing field."

—TOREY LOVULLO, Boston Red Sox bench coach,
UCLA All-American second baseman,
and eight-year major-leaguer

"Gary Adams is the best coach I have ever had. He not only made me a better ball player, but also a better man! The confidence he had in me was the single reason I believed I could one day be a big leaguer. I am grateful to have played for him for four years, and I am proud to call him a friend."

—DAVID ROBERTS, first base coach for the San Diego Padres,
UCLA outfielder, and ten-year major-leaguer

Published by: Santa Monica Press LLC
P.O. Box 850
Solana Beach, CA 92075
1-800-784-9553
www.santamonicapress.com
books@santamonicapress.com

Printed in the United States

Santa Monica Press books are available at special quantity discounts
when purchased in bulk by corporations, organizations, or groups.
Please call our Special Sales department at 1-800-784-9553.

ISBN-13 978-1-59580-076-3

Library of Congress Cataloging-in-Publication Data

Adams, Gary.
  Conversations with coach Wooden : on baseball, heroes, and life / by Gary Adams ;
foreword by Eric Karros.
     pages ; cm
  ISBN 978-1-59580-076-3 (hardback)
  1. Wooden, John, 1910-2010. 2. Basketball coaches—United States—Biography.
  3. Coaching (Athletics)--Philosophy. 4. Conduct of life. 5. Wooden, John,
  1910-2010—Friends and associates. 6. Adams, Gary. 7. Baseball—Anecdotes.
  8. University of California, Los Angeles—Sports. I. Title.
  GV884.W66A43 2013
  796.323092—dc23
  [B]
                              2013002640

Cover photo courtesy of UCLA Photography, a division of Associated Students UCLA
Back cover photo by Kyrstin Pummill
Cover and interior design by Future Studio

CONTENTS

THE MIDDLE INNINGS
1983-2002

THE LATE INNINGS
2003-2010

Dedicated to John and my players—
thanks for the memories.

FOREWORD
by Eric Karros

My first face-to-face conversation with Gary Adams took place through the right field chain-link fence at UCLA's Jackie Robinson Baseball Stadium. I was still a senior in high school, and having already been admitted to UCLA, I was hoping to convince Coach Adams to let me try out for the baseball team. He listened as I pleaded my case. I tried to assure him that I could play for UCLA, though I knew there was no guarantee.

I played for Gary for three years—1986 through the 1988 season. During that time, we had a couple successful seasons. I improved as a player, but more importantly, I was starting to grow up. Coach Adams played a role in both of these developments. Baseball was the vehicle Gary used to teach his players about life. Many times my teammates and I were showered with praise, and there were also those moments when Coach would get in our face. During those times, I'm not sure I always recognized what Coach was trying to do, but I did always feel like he was on my side.

It wasn't until I had grown older, and perhaps wiser and more mature, that I gained a greater appreciation for Coach and his efforts. Gary isn't a physically intimidating man, nor is he a yeller or confrontational type of person. He is a teacher who uses sport as his classroom. I didn't know it at the time, but his coaching style was impacted by endless conversations he had in the UCLA athletic department. Those talks were with the men's basketball coach, John Wooden, who goes down in history as the greatest college basketball coach who has ever lived. The life lessons he passed on to his players and peers are unparalleled. In his own way, Gary has many of the same beliefs and ideas, especially when it comes to coaching young men.

In the following pages, Gary recounts experiences in which his conversations with Coach Wooden and his interactions with his players intersect. These descriptions represent and define certain qualities and characteristics that are important on the field, but more important in life.

There have been a handful of people and experiences that have significantly impacted my life. My father is at the top of the list, but my three years with Coach Adams at UCLA continue to shape me as I learn and grow. For that, I will be forever grateful.

PREGAME WARM-UP

One April morning in 2010, I hopped into my pickup truck, tossed a book into the passenger seat, and took off from Bear Valley Springs, California, to see my longtime friend. I knew Coach John Wooden's heart was tiring out; what I didn't know was that it would beat for the last time only forty-six days later.

John's devoted friend, Tony Spino, had been keeping me informed about Coach's health. The day before, Tony had told me that John's condition was deteriorating. Those were not encouraging words, since I was used to hearing Tony speak more positively, saying things like, "Coach has slowed down a bit, but he's still strong, and his mind is as sharp as ever."

Because Tony now spoke with some urgency, I told him that I would like to see John, if it was all right with the coach. Not much later, Tony called back and said, "Coach would like to see you. When can you come?"

"How's tomorrow morning?"

The next day, as I began the 118-mile trip to John's home in Encino, my mind traveled back over the journey of our friendship, which had begun thirty-six years beforehand. Even before then, more than fifty years ago, when I was playing varsity

baseball for the UCLA Bruins, I had the rare privilege of seeing in person the man I had heard so much about. I didn't know then that this man and I would become lifelong friends.

—GARY ADAMS

THE EARLY INNINGS
1959-1982

THE FIRST INNING

Hey, you guys, Coach Wooden is watching us!" our ace pitcher, David Weiner, yelled as we sat on the bench in our sunken dugout at UCLA. Following the lead of my fellow benchwarmers, I turned and saw Dave peeking around the corner of our dugout, looking up at Coach Wooden in the bleachers behind us.

It was the spring of 1959, and we were only in the first inning against the mighty USC Trojans, who were on their way to whipping us with a score of 10–6. Our players would soon forget that loss, but the memory of the man sitting in the wooden bleachers would remain with us for the rest of our lives.

We spotted him easily amongst the sparse crowd on that chilly Saturday afternoon. I had seen Coach Wooden on television and in newspaper photos, but never in person, and never up close. I found it hard to believe that John Wooden would want to see me and my teammates play baseball. Sitting in the top row of a set of eight-row bleachers, his posture was the same as I remembered seeing on the television screen—leaning forward on the bench, arms folded and eyes glued to the basketball court—only this time, his eyes were fixed on our baseball diamond on Joe E. Brown Field.

If he noticed us benchwarmers gawking up at him, he showed no signs of it. Coach Wooden focused on the game while we players, with our backs to the game, focused on him. We took turns spying on our celebrity spectator, trying to conceal our actions from Coach Reichle, who was at the other end of the dugout, engrossed in the game.

When my turn came, I ignored the action on the field and studied UCLA's popular coach. This was the coach who consistently got the most out of his players, despite playing some home games in high school gyms that were closer to USC than to our own campus. This was the man whose teams practiced and played most of their games in a cramped campus gym that he shared with the gymnastics and volleyball teams, and with physical education classes. Coach Wooden, not so fondly, called UCLA's gym "the BO Barn," because it reeked with the smell of sweat emitted from the many athletes who trampled its hardwood floor. Even though he and his assistant opened the windows and mopped the floor before each practice, the smell was always there. I know this well, having spent many hours in that stinky gym as a physical education major.

Despite the facilities, Wooden's teams were always competitive and exciting to watch. This was years before he had ever won a national championship, and long before Pauley Pavilion Basketball Arena would be built on the spot where we were playing baseball that day. Although the sports world knew very little about him at that time, Coach Wooden was a hero on the UCLA campus. We were in awe of him.

None of us realized then, as we stared up at this man, that we were looking at a legend—a man who would become one of the most admired and respected men in our nation's history. John Wooden wasn't just *my* hero; he would become *America's* hero.

Hard telling what would have happened that day if we had known what he had yet to accomplish. I'm guessing that we would have jumped over the rail and climbed eight rows of bleachers to ask him if he would autograph our hats, gloves, and baseballs. Knowing him now as I do, Wooden would have gladly signed each and every one—"*After* the game, boys."

Six years earlier, when I was thirteen years old, having just moved from Ohio to Riverside, California, I would tune our family's twelve-inch Philco television set to the local channel and watch Bruins basketball games. During that 1953–1954 season, UCLA had a typical Wooden team, the smaller and quicker Bruins beating up on their bigger, slower opponents. I loved the way Coach Wooden's players hustled up and down the court. Being only five feet four inches at the time, I prayed that I would grow tall enough so that I would have a fighting chance of making his team. I dreamt of the day I would be wearing the Bruins uniform—white with black trim (our television set was black and white, so I didn't know at the time that UCLA's colors were blue and gold).

My favorite player then was Ronnie Livingston, a little left-handed guard who was adept at stealing the ball, leading the fast break, and almost always making his free throws, especially in the clutch. *Oh,* I thought, *if only I could make my dream come true and become the next Ronnie Livingston.*

Although that dream never materialized, I did have the honor of playing *baseball* at UCLA with another leftie basketball player who reminded me of Livingston. In 1962, my senior year, future college All-American and Los Angeles Lakers star Gail Goodrich played first base while I played across the diamond from him at third base. It was the closest I would ever come to playing basketball at UCLA.

As a student-athlete from 1959 to 1962, I often went to the men's gym to watch Coach Wooden's practices. I vividly recall hearing Coach's whistle, shortly after walking through the gym's double doors. All action stopped—the players suddenly stood like statues—as Coach Wooden spoke.

"Be quick—don't hurry!" he would say. This great coach, who preferred being called a "teacher," would tell his pupils:

"You can't do anything with the ball until you catch it first. Don't be in a hurry to shoot. Don't be in a hurry to dribble. Don't be in a hurry to pass. *After* you catch the ball is the time to be *quick*. If you get in a hurry, you'll drop the ball. You can't do any of those things without the ball."

I liked it when he added, "And when our opponent has the ball, it's our goal to make *them* get in a hurry so *they* make mistakes."

My second year at UCLA, I roomed with Ray Smith, a close friend and former teammate of mine at Riverside Poly High who played fullback for the Bruins football team. One night, when I was lying on the top bunk and the two of us had finished talking about our girlfriends, Ray, from the bottom bunk, asked, "Gary, did I ever tell you about how I met Coach Wooden?"

It was an attention grabber. "Uh-uh," I said.

"My speech class prof told us we had to interview a prominent person on campus," he said. "I chose Coach Wooden. Gave him a call. Could hardly believe I was talkin' to him. I asked if I could interview him. Boy, was I surprised when he said he would do it, since it was basketball season and all else he had to do."

Ray said that he had met with Coach Wooden the next day at the "bungalows"—two small modular buildings on campus that housed the coaches' offices. "When I walked into his office," he said, "Coach was sittin' at his desk, and he gave me a smile. I couldn't help but notice all the picture frames on the walls. Coach saw me looking at 'em. Most were filled with words. He stood up and said they were a bunch of maxims— words, I guess—that he liked. Then he pointed to each one and recited them by heart. I was impressed."

So was I, as I listened to Ray—impressed that he was able to get so close to Coach Wooden.

"Coach asked me, 'Ray, now tell me again, why are you interviewing *me?*'" he continued. "I told him that my speech class professor assigned us to interview a prominent person on campus. That's when Coach reached into his pocket and pulled out a newspaper clipping. The thing looked like it was a hundred years old, all wrinkled. Coach said, 'This was in the South Bend, Indiana, newspaper long ago.' The newspaper said, 'Because no one else is available, John Wooden will be our speaker at the end-of-the-year athletic banquet.'"

Ray paused then, and said, "I'll never forget it."

I thought Coach's clever use of the news clipping was a great icebreaker for Ray's interview, and I told him so. But Ray said Coach's easy smile and friendliness from the beginning had already made him feel relaxed.

Lying on my back, staring up at the ceiling, I was thinking how lucky my roommate was to have had a personal meeting with Coach Wooden. I thought of all the UCLA students, besides me, who would have scrambled for the chance to meet Mr. Wooden.

A year later, when Ray became the captain of the UCLA football team, he told me, "Whenever Coach Wooden passes me on campus, he nods, smiles, and says, 'Hi, Cappie.' He even asked me to help him recruit a couple of high school basketball players."

Then Ray told me of Coach Wooden's surprising request. He asked if Ray would like to be a member of the UCLA basketball team.

"I told Coach that I wasn't as talented as the other members of his team," he said. "Coach said, 'Ray, I want you on the team because of your leadership and character.' I declined his offer so I could concentrate on playing football."

I thought Coach's request was the ultimate compliment to Ray, but not unusual for Coach, whose teams were made up of players who had both talent and character.

At the time, to say I was envious of Ray's relationship with Coach Wooden would be an understatement. The closest I had ever come to Wooden was the day he sat in the bleachers during my baseball game, and when I watched his team's practices.

I also saw Coach Wooden in 1963 and '64, when I served as a graduate assistant baseball coach for Art Reichle—but I had yet to meet the man. After I received my master's degree from UCLA, I coached for four years as an assistant at UC Riverside, and five years as the head baseball coach at UC Irvine. Then, in ways I never could have dreamed of as a youngster, the direction of my life turned. How lucky I was that my growth spurt had ended at five foot eight, shattering my youthful dream of playing basketball for UCLA, because later events led to a bigger dream.

This new dream began when our team at UC Irvine won its second straight NCAA College Division championship. Within minutes of winning, J. D. Morgan, UCLA's director of athletics, called me on the phone. I was still in the midst of celebrating with my UCI team at the College World Series site in Springfield, Illinois, when he offered me the head baseball coaching job at UCLA. There was no mention of salary at the time, but one of my first thoughts after hanging up the phone was, *I would be back at my alma mater, and on the same coaching staff as John Wooden.* The salary mattered little to me.

A short time after I was hired, J. D. Morgan introduced me to Coach Wooden. The most surprising part of this event—this dream of mine, of meeting Wooden—was when, as he shook my hand, he said: "You know, Gary, you're coaching my favorite sport."

"Baseball?" I managed to say. I couldn't believe it.

From that moment on, baseball was the common ingredient that cemented our long-lasting friendship. For the next three and a half decades, we rarely talked about the sport *he* coached; he always wanted to talk about the sport *I* coached. And that was okay with me.

A SCARY MEETING

John's last year as UCLA's basketball coach, the academic year of 1974–1975, was my first year as the university's baseball coach. He was winning his last of ten national championships, while I was busy coaching players I didn't know very much about.

We didn't see each other very often, even though we both had our respective offices in the small athletic department building. John's office was on the opposite side of the building, next to head football coach Terry Donahue's office. Two of my offices would have fit into one of theirs. At the other end of the hall from these two major sports figures was the largest office in the building, which belonged to our athletic director, J. D. Morgan.

My office was among those of the other coaches of the so-called "minor sports" (subsequently renamed "Olympic sports.") Each of our tiny offices barely had enough space for Lewis Alcindor to lay down on the floor in any direction, but I did manage to squeeze one small desk, a swivel chair, and a folding chair into mine.

Occasionally, John and I would see each other in the hall-way. He was always pleasant, smiling, and wishing me good

luck in my next game. I would wish him the same. Both of us were guilty of hurrying along, two busy coaches focusing on our teams and little else. That situation changed dramatically in the late spring of 1975, after baseball season ended.

That spring day, I found a note attached to my door. It read, "Gary, J. D. would like to see you."

This was the first time in my entire first year that the athletic director had asked to meet with me. I had no idea why J. D. wanted to see me, but I was uncomfortable with the message. In fact, I poked my head in several of the other head coaches' offices and asked them, "What do you think J. D. wants to see me for?"

My fellow coaches did a wonderful job of reinforcing my worst fears. "Gary, J. D. never meets with us unless it's bad," they replied. "It can't be a good thing!" Grim thoughts raced through my mind: *What did I do wrong?* Even worse: *Will he fire me in my first year on the job?* Our team record wasn't that bad, nor was it that great (thirty-one wins and twenty-two losses). I wondered whether it was good enough for my boss.

After procrastinating as long as I could without causing further aggravation on J. D.'s part, I mustered the courage to walk into his office and face the man who was noted for his tough, abrupt, no-nonsense personality.

"Sit down, Gary," he ordered in his deep voice, pointing at a solitary chair in front of his oversized desk. We coaches often said that J. D.'s tone was less like a human voice and more like a grizzly's growl.

"Yes, sir," I replied meekly, sinking into the chair. A wooden placard on J. D.'s desk stared me in the face. Inscribed in gold letters were the words, WINNING SOLVES ALL PROBLEMS. It was not an encouraging sign.

Showing no hint of pleasantness, J. D. got directly to the point.

"Gary, as you know, Coach Wooden has retired," he growled. "We want to make him feel welcome to come back here to UCLA during his retirement years. I thought that, since you are the rookie coach on our staff, I would ask if you wouldn't mind sharing your office with John whenever he comes back to visit with us."

I sat stunned, frozen in my chair. This was far from what I had feared.

"Gary?" J. D.'s gruff voice awakened me from my stupor.

Suddenly, I was transformed from a trembling, fearful young man to the happiest, most relieved person on earth— so relieved that I lost all sense of who I was talking to. With a smile as wide as my facial muscles could stand, I replied, "How much do I have to pay you, J. D.?"

It was a corny response. There was no laughter or even a hint of a smile on the other side of the desk. But J. D. had my answer. In a second, he was standing up and saying, "Well, that takes care of that. Thanks, Gary."

I left J. D.'s office feeling almost giddy, the way I remembered feeling as a kid when I left the principal's office without the imprint of his paddle on my behind.

My friends and fellow coaches were anxious to hear my story of this scary meeting with J. D. "Well," I said nonchalantly, "he just wanted to know if I would mind sharing my office with Coach Wooden."

Almost in unison, they said, "Of course, you said yes."

Working hard to keep a straight face, I said, "Actually, I told J. D. that I'd like to think about it. I said I'd get back to him."

I took great pleasure in watching their mouths drop and their eyes grow wide. I let them stand in awe of my answer for a painfully long time before I finally smiled and said, "Just kidding. Of course I agreed."

Fate was extremely kind to me. I have always been grateful to J. D. for thinking I would be an appropriate office mate for Coach Wooden. We shared that tiny office until a new building was constructed eight years later, appropriately named "The Morgan Center" in honor of J. D.

COACH'S VOICE

On the basketball court, Coach spoke firmly, strictly, and confidently. I had no trouble hearing him from my position on the sidelines of the gym when, as a UCLA student, I popped in to observe his practices. His players had no difficulty hearing him either, especially when he preceded instructions or criticism with one of his famous Woodenisms: "Goodness gracious." When he wanted to be more adamant, he would exclaim, "Goodness gracious sakes alive!" Upon hearing those four words, his players knew they had better pay attention and listen intently to what would follow.

Those phrases were the extent of his "profanity." His father had made sure of that when John was a young lad working on the family farm in Indiana.

As Coach told me, and as he was fond of telling others, he had learned not to cuss the hard way. "One day," he said, "my older brother and I were in the barn, picking up horse manure with our pitchforks. He decided to pitch his load into my face. I called him the SOB word and charged him. We were tussling on the ground when dad heard the yelling and came running in to break us up. We each gave our side of the story, but dad whipped the both of us. I always felt I got the worst of the whippings because he didn't like my use of the English language. I never cussed again."

Off the basketball court, Coach spoke softly and gently. I often found myself straining to hear him. Sometimes his words would fade, trailing off at the end of his sentences. He often recited poems to me, half of which he wrote himself, but he would speak so rapidly that it seemed he was in a hurry to finish or assumed I already knew the poem and there was no need to speak slowly or loudly.

Many times, I observed his listeners leaning forward in their chairs to hear Coach better. Like Teddy Roosevelt, who was famous for speaking softly and carrying a big stick, Coach Wooden did the same, but his "stick" was not physical; it was the substance and wisdom of his words. Wooden was the master of delivering a meaningful message in a simple sentence— his "be quick, don't hurry" was meant for the athletic fields and courts, while "failing to prepare is preparing to fail" was meant for us all in our daily lives.

I never heard John burst out into boisterous laughter, but sometimes a smile would threaten to blossom, only to emerge as a chuckle. The chuckle was almost melodic, sounding like the alternating purring of a car engine: "Hummmm . . . hummmm." Three "hummmms" or more was his gut laugh. I don't remember him ever bursting forth with more than three or four of these melodic chuckles.

Although his voice may have registered low on the decibel scale, there was no doubt that his use of the English language was impeccable. Possessing an uncommon fondness for English all his life, and having been a high school English teacher for fifteen years, Coach spoke similarly to the way he might write a final manuscript or a college thesis.

When Coach gave speeches, he preferred to say "do not," "did not," or "was not" instead of "don't," "didn't," or "wasn't." When talking to someone one-on-one, he shortened his words with contractions, but he did it much less frequently than the

rest of us.

As a coach and teacher, Coach Wooden was a perfectionist—and he expected the same perfection from himself when speaking. What he may not have expected, however, is that whenever he spoke, everyone listened.

LEWIS ALCINDOR CONSIDERS PLAYING BASEBALL

Only a few people know that UCLA's Lewis Alcindor considered playing baseball for the Bruins—though it was a short-lived consideration.

Lewis was a huge baseball fan while growing up in New York. His favorite team was the Brooklyn Dodgers, and his hero was former UCLA four-sport star Jackie Robinson. Lewis mostly pitched when he played ball. With his seven-foot-two-inch frame and those long limbs, his potential as a pitcher would be enticing to any college coach or pro scout.

On March 1, 1968, UCLA pitching coach Glenn Mickens and I were walking down the hallway of the athletic department when we spotted Lewis ahead of us. We caught up with him and congratulated him on a great season so far, wishing him luck in their game against Stanford later that evening.

Coach Mickens (most people called him "Mick") did most of the talking, as I was not yet the UCLA baseball coach—at the time, I was still the assistant coach at UC Riverside. Our team was in Westwood that afternoon to play a game against the Bruins. Before our game, Mick had invited me to go over to the campus with him.

I listened as Mick and Lewis talked about basketball, but

soon Mick turned the conversation around to baseball, talking mostly about the team he once pitched for: the Brooklyn Dodgers. Just when I thought the conversation was ending, I heard Mick say, "Lewis, when your basketball season is over, how about coming out to pitch for our baseball team?"

My first lightning-bolt thought was, *What would Coach Wooden think of Mick's question?* My answer: *Not much.* He probably wouldn't want his star player distracted with the thought of playing baseball, especially since the basketball team was going into the NCAA playoffs in a couple of weeks.

I was also concerned that Coach Wooden would be upset with Mick for asking Lewis to play baseball, since he might be injured—Lewis still had one more year of basketball left at UCLA. However, knowing that Mick is a man who always speaks his mind and is as honest as any I have ever met, his question did not surprise me that much.

"Well," Lewis replied, "I have a good arm and can throw a hard fastball—I just don't know where it's going."

Lewis's answer reminded me of the time I overheard two old-time baseball scouts talking about a prospect's strong arm. The one scout said to the other, "Boy! That kid sure has a God-given arm to throw a baseball." The other scout replied, "Yeah, and only God knows where it's going."

Encouraged by Lewis's words, Mick pushed further. "I can help you find the plate," he said. "We'd love to have you out there pitching for us, Lewis."

I looked away, pretending I wasn't that interested in the conversation—and hoping that Coach Wooden wouldn't suddenly turn up.

Lewis finally said he would think about it. It seemed like he really meant it.

After we parted ways with Lewis, Mick was on a high. "Can't you just see him out there on the mound, Gary?" he said. "He'd be intimidating to any hitter. Heck, the ball would be almost halfway to the plate before he ever let go of it!"

I just nodded, saying, "You're right," and let Mick dream on.

"If Lewis pitched for us, that would be the best thing that could happen to our ball club," he continued. "Think of it, Gary, everybody would want to see him pitch—we'd pack 'em in!"

I did not ask Mick if he had checked with Coach Wooden before asking Lewis to play baseball, because I knew he hadn't. But several years later, after Lewis had graduated and changed his name to Kareem Abdul-Jabbar, I asked Mick if he ever told John what he did.

"Oh, heck yeah, Gary. I told him right after I talked to Lewis."

"So, what did Coach say?"

"He said, 'Mick, if you can find a pair of size twenty-two baseball spikes for him, it's okay with me.'"

I don't know if Mick ever looked for a pair of spikes that size, but I do know Lewis Alcindor never showed up for baseball.

COACH'S FIRST LOVE

In the tiny office that Coach Wooden and I shared, a single photo hung on the wall—a gift from Coach to me. The photo was a headshot of Wooden wearing a bright smile and a basketball net around his neck, which his players had placed there immediately after cutting the nets down when they defeated Kentucky in the 1975 national championship game. It was Coach's tenth NCAA championship, and the last game he would coach.

I hadn't asked him for his permission to hang the photo, which I framed myself. I'm sure he thought I would take it home and maybe put it on a shelf or paste it into my scrapbook. If I had asked for his permission, I believe he would have said something like, "No, Coach Gary, we don't need it in our office."

I wasn't in the office when Wooden walked in and first noticed it, so I don't know how he reacted to seeing it framed and on the wall. He said nothing about it to me for several months. Finally, one day in the middle of our conversation, he looked up and pointed to the photo. He quietly, but firmly, said, "Coach Gary, I wouldn't mind my picture being on the wall so much if it were joined with some others—at least, one of you, too."

I didn't know what to say for a while. He waited. Finally, I said, "I understand, Coach. I'll do that."

A few days later, next to his photo, I hung a single photo of my assistant, Coach Mickens, and I together. I knew Coach would be especially pleased that his good friend, "Mick," would also be alongside his photo.

Coach's gift was special because, at the bottom of his picture, he had written a unique note:

> For Coach Gary Adams, who teaches my favorite sport,
> with best wishes always, John Wooden

His words were almost identical to what he had said to me when we first met, although this time, he wrote "*teaches* my favorite sport" rather than "*coaches* my favorite sport."

So, why was baseball Coach Wooden's favorite sport?

In time, I learned that John had many reasons for his love of baseball, some of which he had no control over—such as the weather.

Growing up in Indiana, John experienced weather more suitable for an indoor sport, so one would think it was a no-brainer for him to like basketball more. But that's not the way John looked at it. Playing baseball always meant being outside in the fresh, *warm* air. Playing basketball meant harsh, freezing cold winters.

For a farmer's son in Indiana, there was no greater season than summer. Besides the satisfaction of watching his father's hard labor reward him and his family with lush crops, John could finally spend most of his days outdoors, playing baseball.

I also grew up in a small midwestern town in Ohio, only forty miles from John's home state of Indiana. I once told him, "My favorite sport in the fall was football, my favorite in the winter was basketball, and my favorite in the summer was baseball." He replied, "My favorite sport in *all* seasons was baseball, even though I could only play it in the summertime." That was true love.

I admitted that a big reason I loved baseball was because it meant school was "out" and summertime was "in." This confession produced a wry smile from John.

One of my favorite pitchers, Johnny Vander Meer of the Cincinnati Reds, once fondly said of baseball, "Kids are always chasing rainbows, but baseball is a world where you can catch 'em." When I told Coach what Vander Meer had said, he shook his head dreamily. "That's how I felt, Gary."

John was a good baseball player in his youth. Many locals claimed that baseball was his best sport. He was a shortstop from elementary school throughout his time at Martinsville High School, and also played on the town team that competed against the Kansas City Monarchs, the touring Negro league team that Jackie Robinson would eventually play for.

John was good enough to play baseball at Purdue University his freshman year, but when a pitcher's fastball plunked him on his throwing shoulder, Coach said, "my rifle arm became a slingshot arm. That ended my thoughts of ever playing professional baseball."

Many years ago, Coach took out his wallet, unfolded an old newspaper clipping, and handed it to me. The article told of the Pittsburgh Pirates general manager, Joe L. Brown, offering John the field manager's job. As I read it, I thought of how ironic it was that the ball field I played on at UCLA was named after Joe's father, Joe E. Brown.

With a bashful grin, Coach told me how he had responded to Joe's offer. "Joe," he had said, "if I should take you up on this, and we lost too much, who do you think they'd fire first, you or me? If I were the owner, I'd fire you first for hiring me. Then I'd fire me."

Years later, I asked John if he still had the clipping in his wallet. He grinned again, this time not bashfully, and said, "Yes, Gary, just for fun."

That says a lot about John's feelings for baseball—the *fun* part, that is. Whenever John and I talked about his years playing baseball "in the olden days," his eyes grew bigger, his hands moved quicker, and the pitch of his voice grew higher. The fun he used to have playing baseball showed as visibly as a batter's face lights up when he sees a fat pitch coming down the middle of the plate. For John, having fun with sports was huge, especially after playing pressure-packed basketball in the basketball-crazy state of Indiana and then coaching under even more pressure in college. I believe John's boyhood memory of a relaxed game of baseball—a game where he felt no pressure— is why John told me, more than once, "Baseball is my first love."

One morning in our office, I had the chance to see Coach's face light up again when I asked him, "What do you think is the most exciting play in baseball?"

"Coach Gary, I doubt my most exciting play is the same as most people's, which is either the triple on offense or the triple-play on defense. Yet, I will admit that the three-base-hit is more exciting than watching someone trot around the bases on a ball hit over the fence."

Coach paused as he looked up from his desk with that same bright face. "You may not agree with me, but I believe the most exciting play—and sometimes the most comical—is the hit-and-run. Think about it, Gary. The hit-and-run, when executed perfectly, is baseball at its best. I like to watch the second baseman trying to reverse his direction to chase down the grounder before it gets to the right fielder, and I like watching the runner trying to make it to third before the outfielder can gun him down."

Then John's face grew even brighter as he described the hit-and-run play when baseball was played at its worst. He could hardly keep from smiling as he detailed it for me: "The runner takes off from first base. Sometimes he just runs with his head down, without ever looking to see if the batter hits the ball. He keeps on running when he hears the crack of the bat. He has no idea where the ball is, so he takes a look at his third base coach—who's yelling like crazy and waving his arms to tell

his runner to get back to first base. The ball is headed on a fly straight to the right fielder, and the runner can't slow down until after he's rounded second base. Now, it's a race between him and the ball to first base." At this point, Coach smiled and said, "How often do you see a base runner going full speed, running the bases backwards?"

Coach smiled even broader as he added, "It's really exciting when the runner doesn't re-touch the base because he doesn't know the rule."

"You actually saw this happen?" I asked.

"Once, when I played on my old town team in Indiana," Coach replied. "One of our players got almost to third base before he ever spotted our coach yelling to get back to first."

Coach chuckled as he relived the play that had happened over a half-century ago. "He put on the brakes about a dozen feet in front of third base—broke into a mad dash across the diamond. I can still see him running up, over, and down the pitcher's mound. He made a head-first dive into first base, just as the ball arrived. We all thought he was out, but the hometown umpire called him safe—I think because his dive was so desperate. The umpire felt sorry for him."

"Didn't the umpire know the rule?" I asked.

"I think so, because the coach of the other team came out and had his shortstop take the ball and tag second base. The umpire called the runner out—which was the right thing to do."

I asked, "Did you know the rule at the time?"

"No, I didn't. I was only fifteen or sixteen at the time, but because of that play, I never forgot it. What do you think? Exciting?"

I had to admit that, the way he described the action, it was more exciting than any triple or triple play I'd ever seen.

John not only loved *playing* baseball, he loved *coaching* it. From 1935 to 1948, he coached baseball. His first year of coaching the diamond sport came in Dayton, Kentucky. When he talked about his Dayton High School baseball team, I was amazed at how he could remember his players' names and the positions they played; but, as he admitted with a sly smile, "Remembering the names was the easy part because, except for our right fielder, the rest of our starters were Polish, and their last names all ended in "ski."

In his first year of coaching, John had a winning record in baseball and a losing record coaching basketball—his only losing season in his coaching career. After coaching in Kentucky, he returned to Indiana the following year and coached high school baseball again for the next eleven years, along with tennis and basketball. His final baseball coaching days came at Indiana State Teachers College (now called Indiana State University). After that, it was all about basketball, although he admitted that he missed and loved coaching baseball.

John praised baseball for not "messing with the rules"—rules that are mostly the same today as they were when he played as a youngster. John said, "Pitchers still stand sixty feet six inches from the plate, the bases are still ninety feet apart, and it's still three strikes and you're out." He didn't hide his dislike for the changes made in basketball over the years. "Basketball officials allow players to travel and carry the ball almost like running backs in football."

His face grew a shade redder when he talked about the football mentality of basketball. "Goodness gracious, Gary," he would say, "the way the players push and shove each other out on the courts today, I would not be surprised if someday they started tackling each other."

He didn't like the "entertainment" aspect of pro basketball, either. "Those fancy behind-the-back passes and showmanship slam dunks do not make the execution of the game any better. They are only done to entertain the fans. Well, it does not entertain me. If you ask me, I would rather watch the ladies play in college—sound fundamental basketball that emphasizes good old-fashioned teamwork."

"Look at baseball, Gary," he continued. "Baseball still

applauds the well-executed sacrifice bunt, while a home run, no matter how far it goes over the fence, is still counted as only one run." He added, with a wink, "Not *three* 'runs,' like the *three*-point long shot in basketball."

I had to chuckle when he told me how much he disliked the slam dunk. "In my opinion, they should only award *one* point for the slam dunk. What's so difficult about dropping the ball down through the rim? If you ask me, I would raise the baskets a foot higher because players are getting bigger and bigger. The slam dunk may be good for entertainment, but it's not good for the game."

John talked about baseball being a mind game. "I love to sit in the stands and try to read the mind of the managers," he said. "What will he do next? Will he sacrifice bunt, hit-and-run, or steal to get the tying or winning run on second? And what will the other manager do to combat his opponent's strategy? Will he pitch-out to stop the steal? Will he charge his first and third baseman to field the bunt quickly, so he can force the runner at second? Will he guard against the hit-and-run by having the shortstop cover second base, leaving the second baseman in position to field the grounder on the right side?"

When Coach talked about these things, I was impressed by his knowledge of the game. Usually, he would end his "lessons" by saying, "Baseball is simple, yet you have to be thinking all the time." With that comment, he sounded almost like Yogi Berra, but I agreed with him.

I will never forget the day Coach offered a revolutionary way of looking at pitching. He started the conversation by saying, "Gary, sometimes the 'thinking game' surprises you. Take the strategy of pitchers, for example. What do pitchers try to do when the best hitter on the opposing team comes to bat?"

"Try harder?" I said.

"That's right. They bear down on the tough hitters. But Warren Spahn, the great Braves pitcher, had a different strategy—he tried harder on the *weaker* hitters. He did not believe in wasting time and energy with the great hitters—like Mays, Musial, and Clemente—because the great hitters are going to get their hits no matter what you do, anyway."

I had never heard of this strategy before, and Coach seemed to notice.

"Yes," he continued, "Spahn believed there were only one or two great hitters on every team—usually only one. Get the weak hitters out, and the great hitters can go four for four but they can't drive in any runs if the bases are empty."

"What about home runs, Coach? They could drive themselves in."

"Yes, Spahn gave up his share of home runs, but relatively few with men on base. That's why he won more than three hundred games. Those great hitters occasionally got their home runs, but more often they got singles on Spahn's purposely-thrown bad pitches. He knew all great hitters like to swing the bat—they aren't up there to walk—so he could get them to swing at non-strikes and make it more difficult for them to get their hits—especially home runs. So what if he walked them? He knew the next batter would be a weaker hitter, maybe even hit into a double play."

"Coach, are you saying that, if you coached baseball, you would teach your pitchers the same strategy Spahn used?"

With a sliver of a grin, he said, "Gary, that all depends on if I thought my pitchers were good enough to get the weaker hitters out." Then a big smile broke out as he added, "You know what Satchel Paige always said: 'If a man can beat you, walk him.'"

"Coach, did you ever see Satchel play?"

"No. But I sure heard enough from other people who did see him play. I also know that Joe DiMaggio faced him in an exhibition game and said Paige was the best pitcher he ever went up against. I think Joe got a hit off of him, but Satch got him out three other times. Satchel's philosophy on pitching was quite similar to mine . . . so simple. He always said, 'You gotta keep the ball off the fat part of the bat.'"

"That's tougher than slam-dunking a basketball, don't you think?" I joked.

Though John always appreciated the pure athleticism of basketball, it's true that baseball was his favorite sport. Yes, baseball—not basketball—was his first love. But there was never any doubt in John's mind of what sport required the superior athlete. That's why, whenever he told me that baseball was his favorite sport, he sometimes added, "But basketball is the harder game to play." That was before Michael Jordan, arguably the best basketball player his sport has ever seen, failed in his attempt at playing professional baseball in 1994. I never did broach that argument with Coach.

THE REMARKABLE
BILLY KILMER

During one of my first office chats with Coach Wooden, the subject of Billy Kilmer came up. Most UCLA fans don't remember that Billy played one year of basketball for Coach Wooden in the 1959–1960 season—probably because he didn't play enough to earn a letter. Fans *do* remember him as one of UCLA's all-time great football players. In the season after he played basketball for Coach, Billy was an All-American tailback and finished fifth in the Heisman Trophy voting.

Despite Billy's lack of playing time, Coach was quick to praise his basketball skills. I was just as quick to add that Billy was an All-State baseball player in high school and an All-Conference selection in his only year of baseball at Citrus Junior College. At that time, I was playing against Billy in the same league for Riverside Junior College. I told Coach, "Billy deserved the honor of making All-Conference. He was a great athlete."

"I disagree, Gary," Coach replied. "Billy was *not* a great athlete. He was a smart athlete who competed intensely. He was not gifted with the skills that most great athletes possess."

I think Coach noticed the surprised look on my face. "Now, Rafer Johnson," he explained, "who played on our basketball team the year before Billy, *was* a gifted and superb athlete. Billy

could not run fast, nor could he jump high—skills that Rafer and most great athletes possess—but, as I said before, Billy was a savvy athlete who also possessed that rare characteristic I placed at the top of my pyramid: competitive greatness.

"In basketball, he was excellent at rebounding because of his court intelligence. He always seemed to show up where the ball showed up. Most others jumped higher than Billy but no one could predict better where the ball was going after it hit the rim. Now, I will say, Billy had athletic hands—they were strong and sure. Once he got his hands on the ball no one was able to take it away from him. I don't ever recall him losing the ball once he touched it—whether it was catching a pass, rebounding, or dribbling. That was also because of his competitive nature. His attitude was, 'That ball belongs to me, and I'm not going to let go of it.'"

Coach ended his praise of Billy, saying, "He sure wasn't afraid to shoot the ball. Most of the time, he was on target."

I guided our discussion back to baseball. "Coach, do you realize that you and Billy have two things in common when it comes to baseball?"

Coach shook his head.

"Well, the Pittsburgh Pirates wanted to sign you as their manager, and they also offered Billy $50,000 dollars to play baseball for them. Who knows, you might have ended up coaching Billy in baseball—not just basketball."

"What was the second thing we had in common?"

"Like most great athletes," I replied, smiling, "Billy played shortstop—just like you did."

Coach smiled back, pointed his finger at me, and said, "I get it." It was the only time I ever came close to winning a debate with Coach.

I asked Coach if he had time to listen to my Billy Kilmer story. He nodded. I began by telling him that I attended UCLA at the same time Billy did. In the fall of 1959, Billy and I were in the same three-unit baseball class that was required of all physical education majors.

"Our class of about twenty met out on the UCLA baseball field," I said. "It was mid-morning. We were warming up, when Professor Moore yelled for us to gather around him while he explained the day's drill. Our assignment was strictly an offensive one. He wanted us to learn the importance of hitting the ball where it was pitched. As he said, 'If the pitch is an inside strike, you should pull it. If it's outside, hit it to the opposite field. Don't ever try to pull an outside pitch.'

"This would have been a simple task for the three or four of us who played varsity baseball at UCLA, but not so easy for those who were in other sports like gymnastics, swimming, or track.

"Professor Moore wanted to make the drill more 'game-like,' so he divided the class into two teams. My team hit first, and the batting order was arranged according to the alphabet, making me, Adams, the first hitter. My twin brother, Gene, would be hitting second, but he never came to the plate that day.

"Professor Moore was the pitcher, as he wanted to control the drill and get a better look at how the hitters executed his assignment. Standing on the infield grass, directly behind the pitcher's mound, was Billy Kilmer.

"Coach Moore never required Billy to compete in any of the activities on the ball field, for fear that he might be injured. This was football season. Everyone in our class knew that head UCLA football coach Bill Barnes had instructed Professor Moore to protect his star tailback from injury. But on this day, Moore asked Billy to call balls and strikes, safely behind him and the pitcher's mound.

"Professor Moore's first pitch to me was way outside. Billy called, 'Ball one!'

"Moore's next pitch was not outside, but neither was it inside. The pitch was right down the middle of the plate. I did what I was always taught to do—I hit the ball up the middle.

It was a shot—a 'frozen rope'—that whistled past Professor Moore and slammed into Billy Kilmer's right shin. The sound was something like a bowling ball striking a single ten-pin, and Billy dropped like he was that ten pin.

"I don't remember hearing Billy scream, but he probably did. I don't remember if Professor Moore screamed—he probably did. For me, all I heard was silence. I stood paralyzed at the plate, bat still in my hands, watching this silent movie in front of me. Professor Moore rushed to Billy's aid, hunched over him for a brief moment, then fell to his knees."

Coach Wooden leaned back in his chair and said, "Goodness gracious, Gary! He was probably praying." We both chuckled.

"No, Moore wasn't praying. He was trying to grab Billy's leg to inspect the injury. Billy was clutching his leg, writhing on the ground in agony. He wouldn't allow anyone to touch his leg."

Coach kept smiling. "Well, if he wasn't praying, he was probably already thinking about what he would say to Coach Barnes."

I nodded. "I was afraid to leave my post at home plate . . . not only because I believed Billy's leg would look ugly, but because I didn't want to be near Professor Moore. I knew he wouldn't be happy with me. I also knew our UCLA football team was scheduled to play the mighty USC Trojans on Saturday—just three days away. We would have no chance of beating the Rose Bowl-bound Trojans without our star tailback.

"I just kept staring out at the horrible scene behind the mound and thinking about all those who would not be happy with me. Besides Professor Moore, I knew I would not be popular with Coach Barnes, his players, and all of UCLA's students, alumni, and fans. Almost in a trance, I watched two of our bigger players escort Billy from the field, his arms draped around their shoulders and his right leg propped up in front of him by a smaller classmate. Professor Moore was leading the way. Class was over. The players carried him to the athletic training room, where our trainer, 'Ducky' Drake, quickly examined the injury and placed an ice pack on Billy's ankle and shin. Ducky didn't waste any time; he drove Billy over to the campus hospital, where X-rays showed a hairline fracture. The next day, Coach Barnes told the press that Billy's injury would keep him from playing against USC.

"Later on, I wondered what Professor Moore had said to Coach Barnes, and how much of the coach's wrath he had to take. Neither Professor Moore nor Coach Barnes said anything to me, because I didn't give them a chance. I laid low for the rest of the week, keeping far away from the athletic and physical education offices.

"It was not a brave three days for me at school. I did a good job of avoiding the players on the football team. It came in handy that I was a twin. I pretended I was Gene. I purposely tried not to be seen with him, because then the hostile students would know that one of us was the villain. I didn't want to have to point to Gene and say, 'He did it!'"

I heard a chuckle from Coach as I continued.

"Fortunately for me—the campus villain—the Bruins beat the Trojans that weekend, even though Billy didn't play the entire first half. But he played in the second half, and ended up being UCLA's gutsy hero. The victory by the Bruins was doubly pleasurable, because it knocked the Trojans out of the Rose Bowl and handed the gift to the Washington Huskies."

Breathing a sigh of relief, I told Coach, "I felt like the weight of all the UCLA buildings had been lifted off of me."

Coach said, "Billy was remarkable. I used to watch in amazement when he was running with the football, and how he was able to shake off the tacklers who got their hands on him but couldn't take him to the ground. He couldn't outrun many of them, but he was a slippery runner for a lot of tacklers." Then, with a sly grin, Coach said, "You brought him down with one swing of the bat!"

"Yeah, and I paid for it," I replied. "I never saw Billy again in that baseball class, so I guess the football coaches got to

Professor Moore. But I heard Billy got an A. As I remember it, I only got a B."

Little did I know, when I finished telling this story, that Coach and I would have a chance to relive the Billy Kilmer saga more than a quarter of a century later.

OUR FRIEND, COACH REICHLE

Coach Wooden and I enjoyed those quiet times in our office, when we did a little reminiscing. In one of our first discussions, Coach talked about his friend, the coach I replaced, Art Reichle.

"Art was the first UCLA coach I met when our family came to California," Coach said. "He was nice enough to help us unpack our things and carry them into my office. He also helped me put in my front lawn. It was like I was with my Hoosier friends back in Indiana. Ever since then, I've considered him one of my dearest friends."

Coach chuckled. "You know what Art used to say to me about winning and losing? He'd tell me, 'The first sign of insanity is a laughing loser.'"

When Coach said that, it brought back old memories of when I played for Coach Reichle. It seemed like he uttered that phrase every time we lost a ball game. I told Coach Wooden about a couple of other "Reichleisms" that we players were used to hearing: "Light the lamps" and "Get the leading lady." At first, we had laughed at those quips, but we learned that he had good reason for yelling them.

When he yelled to our defense, "Get the leading lady!" we

knew that if we did, it meant our opponents wouldn't score as many runs. His phrase got our attention and made our pitcher and our defensive players bear down on that first batter of every inning.

"What about 'Light the lamps?'" Coach asked.

"He usually said that when we came off the field to take our turn to bat. He used it mostly after an inning, when we gave up some runs. I think our players had more than one interpretation. Personally, it reminded me to keep my head steady and my eyes on the ball when I was hitting. I heard other guys say that it meant the same thing, as if someone said, 'Get your head in the ball game.'"

After sharing more affectionate words about Coach Reichle, John looked down and stared at his shoes for a moment. When he looked up and met my eyes, I could see he was troubled.

He brought up a subject that was difficult for him to talk about, one which I had been hesitant to bring up myself. In 1964, Pauley Pavilion Basketball Arena had been constructed practically on top of where home plate used to be located, on Joe E. Brown Field.

John said, "When they took Art's field from him, naturally, I was bothered. I told Art of my concern for him the day I learned they were talking about building the new basketball facility there. But Art told me, 'John, don't worry about me. They will build another ball field somewhere else on campus—probably much better than Joe E. Brown Field.' Even so, I still had concerns for him, but he was confident that it would work out for the betterment of UCLA baseball, in the long run."

I shook my head. "Too bad it didn't turn out that way for Art."

"Yes. Despite all the promises they made to him, he coached the rest of his career on the old Sawtelle Field. I felt bad for him—truly bad. Now *your* teams are playing on it."

As bad as I felt for Coach Reichle and for our baseball program when we lost our field, I now found myself feeling sorry for Coach Wooden. All I could think of to say was, "Well, Coach, you deserved a better place to play your games. Art doesn't blame you. Neither do I. And I never heard Art make excuses because he was playing across the freeway, and I won't make 'em, either."

I smiled at Coach. "You know what I tell my players about playing on Sawtelle Field?" I asked him. I didn't give him a chance to answer. "I tell 'em, 'It's our field, and we love it.' They've taken those words to heart, and I've heard them yell them out to the opponents when the ball takes a dirty hop in the infield, or a gopher hole trips up an outfielder."

All Coach said was, "Thanks."

I decided to change the tone, but not the subject. "Coach Reichle could never tell my brother and me apart, so he'd just call us both 'twin.' That was okay with us. We were used to it, since that's what our friends called us when we were growing up in Ohio. He *did* know that I wore number eight and Gene wore number nine on our uniforms, so he always got us straight during games. Actually, since my brother was a starter and I was a bench warmer our first year, I often thought of switching uniforms with Gene so I could play more."

I told Coach about my first ever ball game at UCLA. It happened at El Camino College, in a scrimmage against their team prior to our official season beginning. I was anxious to prove to Coach Reichle that he had not made a mistake in recruiting me along with Gene. I wanted to be a starter for the Bruins.

"Just before the game was to begin," I told Coach, "I got sicker than a dog. My guts were churning, and I had the trots real bad. I don't know if it was because of my nerves or what, but I was in the head when my brother came running in, yelling, "Gary, the game's starting—you're up to bat!" I was the lead-off man that day, and we were the visiting team.

"'No way, Gene,' I moaned. 'You hit for me. Maybe I can get off this can and be ready when we go out to field.'

"So, quickly, I slipped off my jersey top and gave it to Gene.

I heard his spikes clatter against the concrete floor as he left me sitting with my head bent over.

"Well, Coach, he went to bat for me and grounded out to shortstop. Then, while I was still sitting, hoping for a long inning, he came up to bat for himself as the fifth hitter. He hit a double with the bases loaded. I was lucky that we batted around without any more outs, but I just missed my turn at bat again as I sneaked out of the bathroom in time to watch Gene fly out to center for the second out. We switched uniform tops again and when the third out was made, I trotted slowly out to my position at second base."

"Didn't Coach Reichle know the difference?" Coach asked.

"No. Like I said, he only knew us by our number, and I don't think any of the players knew, either. Remember, my brother and I had just transferred into UCLA. We were all new to each other at that stage of the season."

Coach couldn't wipe the smile off. "That's a good one, Gary. I guess sometimes it pays to be a twin."

"Yeah, except it wasn't *that* good for me. You see, Gene went 1 for 1 in that inning, and I went 0 for 2 without ever coming to the plate."

That little story got John to chuckle again, which brightened the room. Then he asked me a question that most of my friends were probably afraid to ask for fear of hurting my feelings. But I didn't mind at all when Coach said, "So, your brother was a better player than you?"

"He sure was, at that time in our lives," I replied. That's why Coach Reichle gave Gene a full scholarship, and he got me a job bussing dishes in the school cafeteria."

Coach persisted. "Was he *always* better?"

"We were pretty close to the same for most of our lives, but the year we played at Riverside Junior College, Gene made All-Conference and I made All-Nothing. Gene deserved Coach Reichle's scholarship, and I was just thankful for working in the cafeteria. Mom and Dad said they were grateful, too, because it helped pay for my schooling. We weren't poor, but without Gene's scholarship and my job, we'd never have gone to UCLA.

"That year at junior college, I didn't get any better, but my brother did. I sure don't blame Coach Reichle for not giving me any athletic aid—I didn't deserve it. I never blamed him for not playing me much my first year, because I wasn't ready."

"You know, Gary," Coach said, "he was a real gentleman, on and off the field. I really didn't see him argue much with the umpires. But I do know that he was a fierce competitor, because I watched him play handball with his coaching buddies, Ken Moore, Briggs Hunt, and Norm Duncan. They would play doubles regularly, and sometimes I'd go with them just to watch. Handball never appealed to me, but these guys played it like their lives depended upon it. They were all good friends, but not when they were inside those four walls.

"Chasing that little black ball around, they would crash into each other harder than I've seen blocking backs hit linemen. They showed no mercy. And they argued constantly—mainly over the score and the interference rules. They were relentless in their effort to beat each other.

"I admit that I enjoyed watching them play, behind that little window. Sometimes, when someone came along to see what all the commotion and yelling was about in that room, I'd let them take a peek. Usually, after a couple of minutes of watching the show, they'd turn to me and say, 'Should we break it up before they kill each other?' I would just smile and tell 'em, 'Oh, no. They're good friends, just having fun.'

"Art would tell me, after his battles on the handball court, how lucky he was to have buddies who could beat up on each other and still be the best of friends. He once told me, 'If any of them needed it, I'd give 'em the shirt off my back. I'd do it for you, too, John.' You know what, Gary, I knew he would."

"I know he would, too, Coach," I said.

Now it was my turn to tell John how good of a friend Coach Reichle was to me. "Physical education majors," I began, "were required to take a football class taught by Norm Duncan. It was his tradition, on the last day of the class, to hold what we students called the 'Blood Bowl.' We dressed in full football gear and played until the ninety-minute class period ended."

"Yes, I know all about the Blood Bowl," Coach replied. "My basketball players were excused from participating, because we had already started playing games. But Norm required them to be officials for the game."

"Well, then, Coach, you know why they called it the Blood Bowl."

"Yes, I do. But ever since UCLA did away with the P.E.-kinesiology major, there hasn't been a Blood Bowl for at least a decade."

I resumed my story. "In the fall of 1960, my senior year, it was in that blasted game that I tore the medial collateral ligament in my knee. One of the varsity football players, Ron Hull, blocked my teammate and sent him crashing full-blast into my extended left leg." Coach laughed when I told him, "That might have been payback for what I did to Kilmer in our baseball class.

"They carried me to Ducky Drake's training room, and it didn't take Ducky long to figure out that I needed to go to the campus hospital. The next morning, they operated on my knee. When I recovered from surgery, the doctor told me I would be in a cast for six weeks, and the knee would require rehabilitation for at least four more months before I could play ball again. My first thought was, *There goes my baseball season . . . and maybe even my scholarship.*"

"I thought you didn't have a scholarship," Coach interrupted.

"Coach Reichle gave me a scholarship for my senior year because I won the starting second base job my junior year. But I was worried that he might take away my aid, because I would be no use to the team that year. I wondered whether he would even want to continue my aid the following season. I knew that losing the scholarship would deal a big blow to Mom and Dad's budget."

Coach Wooden didn't wait for me to explain what happened to my scholarship concerns. "Art would never take your scholarship away from you because you were injured," he said.

"You're right, Coach. The first visitor I had after my operation was Coach Reichle. He told me that I didn't need to worry about my scholarship—it was mine for the rest of the year, and if I wanted to redshirt, I would have it the next year. That was when I knew that Coach Reichle was more than a coach—he was an honorable man who became a true friend. Because of Coach Reichle, I have never taken a scholarship away from any of my players, and I never will."

Coach Wooden said that he never had, either.

A LESSON IN PATIENCE

At the apex of Wooden's Pyramid of Success is the word "patience." Underneath that word, he inscribed, "Good things take time." I already knew how important he believed this was on the basketball court; he constantly reminded his players to be patient for the *best* shot. What I didn't know then was that he considered patience to be a quality in people that should be utilized off the court as well.

After Coach retired, he made frequent appearances on the UCLA campus and spent much of his time in the tiny office we shared. The "ins and outs" of coaching was a popular topic of conversation, but, sooner or later, John would always turn the topic to baseball, be it college or pro.

Whenever Coach offered his pearls of wisdom, it was hard to resist the urge to reach for a pen and scribble his words down. But I resisted, because it would not have been the right thing to do in front of Coach. I felt that he should be as comfortable and free in our conversations as possible. I feared that taking notes in front of him would have been insulting and would diminish the quality of our friendship to a lower, less personal level.

What I *did* do, however, was grab my pen and pad after he left our office, to jot down his words as accurately as I remembered them. The years I spent with Coach and the notes I took in that office inspired most of what I have written in this book.

On October 28, 1978, my family's house burned to the ground in a raging fire that spanned sixteen miles, from the 101 Freeway to the Pacific Ocean, and destroyed 206 homes. Unfortunately, I had been keeping my Coach Wooden notes in my home. They became nothing but ashes. Luckily, a few notes that I had slipped into a desk drawer at my UCLA office were saved, and I have a memory which serves me well. Shortly after the fire, Coach was one of the first to hand me a check to help our family recover. I was truly grateful for his thoughtfulness and generosity, as were my wife and three young daughters.

I didn't have to jot down one particular question he asked me one day in our office; his words stuck in my mind for the rest of my coaching days. "Gary," he said, "would you have the confidence and the patience with your players to let them play their games without you being in the third base coach's box, or on the bench coaching them?"

"Uh, I don't think so, Coach."

"Well, I never did it," he said, "but I often *thought* of doing so just to prove to myself and to my players that they could manage just fine without me during games. You see, I always believed that if my practices went well—if they were organized and I effectively prepared my players for games—I could just go up in the stands on game nights and watch them play."

When John said that he didn't do much "strategizing" from the bench during games anyway, it started me thinking. Up until that time, I had looked at myself as sort of a controlling coach. I decided to trim back my control and let my players play. No, I never went up in the stands to watch them during games, but I did give the players more liberties to be themselves. I gave my runners the green light to steal on their own; my hitters had permission to swing the bat on counts of two balls and no strikes or even on 3 and 0; and pitchers had the freedom to pitch the pitch they and their catchers selected, not the pitch

I chose. In other words, I wanted my players to learn the game well enough that they would have the confidence to play it without having to look over their shoulder to see what their coach's next move would be. I did not want them to play the game as if they were robots or puppets on strings, controlled by their coach. To me, that takes the fun out of playing the game—and it *is* a game.

I knew this change in my coaching would take a great deal of patience, but, in the long run, I felt it would be the best way for my players to learn and have fun at the same time. I often explained this philosophy to them quite simply: "Our practices belong to me; the games belong to you."

Like I said, patience was important to Coach off the court, too. He felt patience was a quality we should master in our everyday living. One day, in our office, he taught me the lesson of patience.

I sat at our desk, working diligently on my baseball budget, which was due the following day. Absorbed in getting it done, I wasn't paying any attention to the activity around me. I didn't even hear the office door open.

It was my custom to be on the lookout for Coach Wooden, so that I could move from the desk over to the folding chair against the wall, and leave the desk and swivel chair for him. But on this day, he surprised me.

When I saw him, I erupted from my chair and scrambled to get all my budget notes off the desk to make room for him. But he had already sat down in the folding chair next to the wall. He told me to keep my things on the desk and stay right there.

Noticing the mess on our desk, he asked, "What are you working on, Gary?"

"It's my baseball budget," I said. "J. D. wants it by tomorrow. The budget he's handed me isn't enough to do what I want to do for my team next year. I'm frustrated."

"Have you talked to him about it?"

Of course, being the rookie coach (as J. D. had once

reminded me), I answered Coach with a simple, "Never thought to do that."

Then Coach told me about his experience with J. D. and his basketball budget. "In 1964, I was in my office preparing my budget, just like you are doing today. J. D. walked in and asked what I was doing. When I said, 'The budget,' J. D. replied, 'You leave that to me. You have a basketball team to coach.'"

Coach looked at me, as if he expected J. D. to do the same thing for me. Knowing I was no John Wooden, I didn't expect J. D. to sympathize with me or with my sport, which didn't come close to producing the income that basketball produced. Asking J. D. to increase my budget would certainly be enough dynamite for J. D. to blow his top. I didn't want to go through that.

J. D.'s historic temper was all I needed to know about. I did not want a confrontation with my boss. I had heard the story about him and his booming voice getting a technical foul while he was sitting on the team's bench, watching the Bruins play basketball. The PAC-8 Conference even made a special rule forbidding all athletic directors from being on the bench. They used the word "all," even though they knew that J. D. was the only one who ever caused trouble. The rule came to be known as "the J. D. Rule."

I also observed J. D.'s behavior at one of our games during my first year. His favorite spot to watch the games was down the right field line, where he would stand alongside a small gate that only our players used. Sometimes, especially when things got exciting, he would venture ever closer to the foul line and, with that imperious voice of his, blast the umpire's calls that went against his Bruins. Even the people sitting in the bleachers over three hundred feet away could hear J. D.'s booming voice.

I'll never forget the time an umpire had had enough of J. D.'s yelling. The umpire called timeout and came over to me in the dugout. "Get that man off the foul line, Gary!" he ordered.

"Do you know who that man is?" I asked.

"I don't care if he's the pope," he said through gritted teeth.

"Get him off the field!"

"You'll have to tell him yourself," I said firmly. "That man's my boss. That's J. D. Morgan."

The umpire's head snapped around in the direction of J. D. Then he turned back to me and said sheepishly, "Oh, why didn't you say so?" He walked back to his spot behind home plate, put his mask back on, and yelled, "Play ball!" Clearly, J. D.'s reputation was widespread.

Sitting in the office that morning, I must have looked just as sheepish as that umpire. "I'm sorry," I told Coach, "but I can't go see J. D. I'm new here."

Coach was persistent. "Gary, what is it that you want the additional money for?"

I told him that we needed to pay for one extra night of lodging for the players on our upcoming trip to the Bay Area to play Cal and Stanford. This would also mean extra expenses for a team's breakfast.

"When I played ball for UCLA in the early 1960s," I told Coach, "it was hard on the players to get out of bed at 5:30 AM, put on slacks, coat, and tie, go without breakfast because the dorms and fraternities didn't serve until 7:00, then walk to the campus to meet the bus at 6:30, in time for departure to the airport. By the time the plane landed in San Jose or Oakland and we rode another bus to our hotel, there was no rest for our team. We rushed to check into our hotel rooms, we rushed to eat lunch, and then we hurried to meet another bus to head for the Cal or Stanford ball parks for a 2:30 PM game. When we finally arrived at the field to take batting practice and our pregame infield-outfield practice, we were a tired bunch of players—and just as tired on Saturday, when we had to play a double-header.

"I felt sorry for Coach Reichle. He tried to pep us all up, but it was a tough assignment under those conditions. I couldn't do it this year with my team, either."

"How did you do against those teams in the Bay Area this year?" Coach asked.

"We lost two of three games on each trip."

"Well, Gary, sounds to me like you have a good reason for asking to travel the night before your first game, so your players will be as rested as your opponents. No reason at all not to talk to J. D. and ask him to increase your budget."

I had to admit that Coach's words were encouraging. I felt better that *he*, at least, believed my request was a reasonable one. Still, I did not want to face my boss.

"Mind if I make a suggestion?" Coach asked.

"Of course not."

He folded his arms and crossed one leg over the other. "Gary, it is my opinion that J. D. wants to do all he can to help his coaches, especially if he believes it is needed and in the best interest of the team. You should meet with him and tell him the story, as you just told me. At the end, just say, 'J. D., we *need* to do this, in the best interest of the team.' And, Gary, remember—emphasize the word '*need*.'"

Coach wasn't finished. "Be prepared for J. D. to rant and rave. Listen to him attentively and wait *patiently* for him to finish. When he is done talking, just repeat, 'But J. D., we *need* to do this in the best interest of the team.'

"J. D. will again argue against your idea, but not as aggressively as before. You just sit there and continue to listen *patiently*. Then, when he is finished, you say once again, "But J. D., we *need* to do this in the best interest of the team."

Having finished his instructions, Coach said, "Gary, if you remain patient, I believe J. D. will grant your request."

Thanks to Coach, I found the courage to reach for the phone, dial J. D.'s extension, and ask Ellen, his secretary, if it would be possible for J. D. to meet with me sometime that day.

"How's 1:15 sound, Gary?" Those words still ring in my ears today, although I was half-hoping that J. D. would be too busy, meaning no such meeting would ever occur.

It's funny what one remembers about times like these. When I walked through the doors to J. D.'s office at 1:15 and

saw him sitting at his desk, working busily, a picture appeared in my mind—a sign I once saw in a tavern that read, EVERY-BODY IS ENTITLED TO *MY* OPINION.

"Sit down, Gary," J. D. said in his familiar growl.

I sat in the chair in front of his desk and noticed that same wooden placard staring at me once again: WINNING SOLVES ALL PROBLEMS.

Finally, he looked up from his work. "What can I do for you, Gary?" he said impatiently.

"Well, J. D., the budgets are all due tomorrow and I was wondering if it would be possible for baseball's budget to be increased so the team could fly up to the Bay Area the night before we play."

I proceeded to deliver the same speech I had given to Coach earlier in the day, making sure, as he instructed, to conclude with, "J. D., we *need* to do this, in the best interest of the team."

J. D.'s response was very close to what Coach had predicted, but it was much louder and livelier. He shot straight up from his chair like a jack-in-the-box, his face strawberry red. No profanity escaped from his mouth; none was needed. His expression, demeanor, and imperious way of speaking were enough to get his message across without having to resort to profanity. He ranted on and on, sometimes yelling in my direction and sometimes yelling up at the ceiling. "Do you know how much it costs to run your baseball program? Do you know how little income your program brings into our department?"

I was already regretting my decision to appeal my case to the boss, but I tried my best to do what Coach had suggested. When J. D. had finished shouting, I said, "But, J. D., we *need* to do this, in the best interest of the team."

Again, J. D. took off on a tirade, although it wasn't as loud as the first one. I'd say that the first one was a ten on the Richter Scale, while this one was a milder six or seven. Nevertheless, J. D. kept talking with the authority, confidence, and deliberation that had led him to becoming a commander on a torpedo boat during WWII, and the man who had coached UCLA's tennis teams to seven national championships. I listened *patiently*. When he had finished, I thought of quitting right then. If anyone else besides Coach Wooden had recommended that I stick with our plan, I wouldn't have kept going, but I followed Coach's suggestion, repeating, "But J. D., we *need* to do this, in the best interest of the team."

I was hopeful that this time, J. D. would give me the good news, as John had predicted. But J. D. was relentless and continued the onslaught. As he talked (at least he wasn't yelling anymore), I stopped listening because he kept saying the same thing over and over again.

Everything inside me was saying, "Surrender . . . give up." But how could I concede, after the wise Coach Wooden had been kind enough to make his suggestion, which could lead to a budget that clearly was best for our team? So, I maintained my *patience*. Once again, I repeated those words: "But J. D., we *need* to do this, in the best interest of the team."

Finally, there was a long and scary silence. I wondered, *Is he catching his breath and preparing for another barrage?* I waited patiently for his turn to speak. Then, J. D. looked straight at me and, with an unusual softness in his voice, said, "You know, Gary, I always wondered why Art never wanted to go up there the night before."

Coach won! Coach Wooden had just won another game, but this time, the sport was baseball and it was played in an office.

I give Coach and J. D. much of the credit for what happened that next season, as the Bruins beat Cal and Stanford two out of three in both of the trips to the Bay Area. Without those wins, we would not have won the conference championship in 1976.

I understand well why Coach Wooden placed "patience" at the top of his Pyramid of Success. It is needed in times of challenge. I am grateful for Coach's patience in taking the time to teach me that lesson.

Looking back on that morning with Coach, and then with J. D., I learned something else besides patience. It came after a few more years of observing the actions of J. D., my fiery athletic director. I watched as he supported all of his sports teams and coaches with a vigor and energy that was rare. He represented UCLA and all of college athletics in battles with the NCAA and television companies for more rights and increased payments. I watched as he fought for his teams to position themselves in the NCAA playoffs. I watched as he struggled, with an uncommon perseverance, to build great facilities on the campus for all sports. I suffered with him when he lost the battle to build an on-campus baseball stadium, but afterwards won a semi-victory by getting a modern stadium built off-campus in his former schoolmate's name. Jackie Robinson Stadium became a reality. I learned to truly respect J. D., not only as my athletic director, but also as a person.

I also learned that Coach Wooden, as much as any other coach in our department, was just as appreciative of our athletic director. Being a great competitor, Coach respected that same quality in J. D. In fact, I still remember Coach shaking his head and telling me, "You couldn't argue with J. D. . . . he'd always win." Coach said it twice to me, and added, "That's why it was best to listen to him until your argument became his idea."

Coach was absolutely right when, back in his coaching days, he told everyone, "J. D. is the best athletic director in the country."

It took a little patience, but I learned it, too.

RECRUITING THE WOODEN WAY

Long ago, John told me, "Don't mistake activity for progress." His words soon became famous after he said them often when speaking publicly. Wooden's recruiting style reflected his philosophy, and sharply contrasted with that of Pepper Rodgers, who was in his second year of coaching UCLA football when I was in my first year of coaching Bruins baseball.

Pepper once said, "Recruiting is like shaving—miss a day, and you look like a bum." John probably missed more days recruiting than any major college basketball coach in the nation. But he never looked like a bum.

Keith Erickson, who was one of the stars on UCLA's first NCAA championship team, is a prime example of Coach Wooden making the best use of his recruiting time. Keith admitted to me, "Coach Wooden had never seen me play. My El Camino Junior College coach [George Stanich] had played for Coach Wooden, and told John, 'I have somebody that could help you . . . maybe.' Coach Stanich told Wooden that I also played baseball and was young—I skipped third grade—and had potential."

Keith said, "Coach Wooden went to Art Reichle and told him the same story—young, potential, good baseball player—

and asked if he would consider a half-and-half scholarship deal, so that if I was a bust in one sport, the other might get lucky, and if a bust in both, they each only lost a half a scholarship."

The rest is history. Keith played both baseball and basketball his first year at UCLA, leading the basketball team to a conference championship. He never played baseball at UCLA again, because Coach Wooden had seen enough—he rewarded Keith with a full basketball scholarship from then on, and Keith led the Bruins to two national championships. I always wondered what Pepper Rodgers would say about his shaving-recruiting philosophy if he had witnessed the less than half an hour Coach Wooden spent recruiting blue-chipper Keith Erickson.

Coaches are known as promise makers—and promise *breakers*. Not John. He made a single promise that every recruit, if he applied himself, would get a great education at UCLA and reap the benefits of that education. It was a promise he believed would come true, if the recruit applied himself.

He knew that other rival coaches often embellished or enhanced their school's qualities, but John kept it plain and simple. He never wasted time on a recruit who didn't want to come to UCLA. He wanted to coach the player who wanted to be a Bruin.

He spent little time recruiting another of UCLA's all-time greats, Gail Goodrich. Even though Gail and Coach Wooden lived in the same city, John only watched Gail play basketball twice. That was all John needed to see of Goodrich to know he wanted Gail to play for UCLA. The fact that Gail's dad went to USC and Gail had grown up rooting for the Trojans did not discourage John.

Gail had played baseball since he was eight years old, and had played every year in high school. He asked John if he could play baseball during his freshman year at UCLA. "Coach Wooden told me it was okay," he said, "as long as my academics and basketball took priority. He reminded me that I was on a basketball scholarship, not a baseball scholarship."

Some coaches, wanting desperately to land a player like Goodrich, would have been tempted to give in, without condition, to a player's requests. Not Coach Wooden. Honest recruiting was the only method Coach knew.

Gail played baseball for two years at UCLA—the freshman team in 1961, and the varsity in 1962. I wondered if Coach Wooden had forbidden him from playing after 1962. "Oh, no," Gail told me, "Coach never made that decision for me. He probably would have let me keep on playing."

What Coach had said to Gail when recruiting him stayed with him. "I wasn't a great student," Gail said. "My grades were not up to par, so I figured I'd better concentrate on my studies. I believed my future was in basketball, not baseball. I learned that in my only year on the varsity baseball team. I couldn't hit left-handers' curve balls."

Recruiting can become so competitive at times, coaches are tempted to make all sorts of promises they know they can't keep. I remember a time in 1975 when I felt that kind of pressure in a heated recruiting battle with Stanford for the talents of a particular high school phenom. Luckily for me, I had an office-mate who helped me see the honorable way to recruit.

John sat at our desk in the office after answering some fan mail, while I sat in the folding chair against the wall and complained about the ugly college recruiting game. Mainly, I was fretting over the rigors of trying to out-do the Stanford coach so I could land a prospect we both wanted.

John finally had heard enough of my lamenting. "Gary," he said, "it is my opinion that a coach should not worry about what another coach might say about *his* school. You just need to be honest in what you say about *yours*. Let me tell you my favorite recruiting story. I think you'll like it."

Coach spun his chair around to face me, crossed his legs, folded his arms, and with a trace of a slight grin, he began.

"The devil and God were in competition to recruit a deceased star athlete to come to their respective places—heaven

or hell. The athlete paid a visit to God's heaven first. He was welcomed with open arms by God and his angels, as a lady played a harp for background music. The athlete was impressed with the overall peacefulness and happiness of the place. There was no war, no famine, no poverty, no disaster, and no sickness anywhere. When the recruit finished his tour, he told God that he enjoyed the visit but he had promised the devil a visit also. God was understanding and bid the young man a warm farewell with the hopes that he would return to heaven.

"The athlete was greeted by the devil on earth in front of an elaborate elevator, which proceeded to take them both down to hell. The recruit was greatly impressed with the music he heard in the air-conditioned elevator on the way. The devil had done his homework, and knew the favorite songs and recording artists of his recruit.

"When the doors of the elevator opened, the athlete walked out and stood at the top of a hill overlooking a golf course. He was in awe of the beauty enveloping him. The devil handed him some golf clubs, knowing this was his favorite recreational sport, and asked him if he would like to play.

"The devil and the athlete had a very competitive game, in which the athlete won by a single stroke. After the game, the devil took him to dinner, where the recruit sat next to a beautiful young lady whom the devil said had won the Miss Hell Beauty Pageant. The young lady and the athlete hit it off wonderfully.

"When the visit to hell was finished, the athlete told the devil, 'This is where I want to be.' He committed to hell, but told the devil that he must return to heaven and give God the news.

"After the athlete told God he had chosen hell, the athlete returned to the spot in front of the elevator where, once again, the devil met him. They hopped onto the elevator—a *hot* elevator—with no music. When the doors opened again, the athlete saw nothing but people with pointed ears and forked tails in ugly red costumes, running from the numerous scattered fires. When the young man felt all the intense heat and saw the gruesome site, he turned to the devil and said, 'This is not what you showed me before.'

"The devil replied, 'We were recruiting you then.'"

When John finished the story, he leaned back and smiled. I got it.

As things turned out, I didn't land the recruit. He decided on Stanford, but it was by my own choosing, not his. Recruiting is a two-way street. The player has a choice of attending the school or not, and the coach has the choice of wanting him or not. In this particular case, after taking the recruit to the Bat Rack, a fancy steakhouse on Wilshire Boulevard near the UCLA campus, I decided that he would not be the kind of person I would enjoy coaching. I also believed that my players wouldn't enjoy him, either.

I realized it was a judgment call I made on just one meeting with the recruit, but I didn't think he would be a good *team* player. Before, during, and after dinner, he only talked about himself and boasted all night long about how good he was. I still remember him saying, after looking at a framed picture of Babe Ruth on the Bat Rack's wall, "Someday my picture will be next to his." I like confidence, but I thought this was going a bit too far for a lad who had only pitched in high school. Not once did he mention the word "team"—not even the school team he played for.

My pitching coach, Glenn Mickens, also noticed this, but didn't say anything to me. Mick and I had decided *before* the recruit arrived that we would offer him a full scholarship. But at the conclusion of the evening, when it came time for me to present the offer, I just couldn't make myself do it.

When the recruit drove off, Mick asked, a bit surprised, "Gary, why didn't you offer him the scholarship?"

"He might be a good guy," I said, "but I don't think I'd enjoy coaching him for four years. Would you? Would our players?"

As it turned out, the Stanford coach lost him, also. He signed a big bonus after high school with my favorite team, the Cincinnati Reds, and pitched in the big leagues for six or seven years.

Another coach who would appreciate John's funny recruiting story is Phil Mathews. Phil played basketball at the University of California, Irvine when I coached baseball there. After he graduated from UCI, he became Irvine's assistant basketball coach. He is well known in California, because he also coached at Cal State Fullerton and the University of San Francisco.

Phil had a reputation for being a good recruiter. When he was the head coach at the University of San Francisco, he coached the son of a good friend of mine. Anthony Naylor told his dad that, on their first day of practice, Coach Mathews had told the team, "I *kissed* your ass when I recruited you. Now, when I coach you, I'm going to *kick* your ass." My friend told me that Phil was half-joking, but his players got the message.

John and I agreed that there were two essential ingredients that influenced a recruit's decision to attend a college. First was the school itself—its reputation for academics, its location, and its all-around campus activities. We felt blessed to be coaching at a place like UCLA, which appealed to the best student-athletes.

Second, the coach had to be a man they respected and wanted to play for. We agreed that the best way to earn their respect was to be honest in recruiting and try to show them that we cared about them not only as players, but also as human beings.

John admitted to me that he chose to go to Purdue University mainly because of basketball coach Piggy Lambert. "Maybe Piggy reminded me a lot of my first coach, Mr. Warriner, who was also my principal in grade school and who I admired. Lambert and Warriner both were excellent baseball players in their day. Maybe part of the reason I went to Purdue was because Piggy loved baseball as much as I did."

If college coaches were asked what they disliked more than any other facet of coaching, most of them would answer, "recruiting." UCLA's great football coach, Terry Donahue, told me after he retired that there were three things he did *not* miss about coaching: "First, recruiting; second, recruiting; and third, recruiting."

When I told Coach Wooden what Terry had said, John sighed and said, "Amen; amen; amen."

oach wasn't a fan of choosing captains for his teams. In fact, in his twenty-seven years at UCLA, he only personally selected three captains prior to the season—Eddie Sheldrake (1950–51), Mike Warren (1968–69), and David Meyers (1974–75). Each player was a senior who had outstanding leadership skills and, in all cases, Coach felt a need for a captain because his teams were young and inexperienced. Coach didn't want his players voting for a captain before the season began because, he said, it became a "popularity contest." At the end of the season, however, a captain or sometimes co-captains were chosen by the players and announced at the year-end banquet.

Before I played baseball at UCLA, I had never been on any sports teams that had captains. Coach Reichle had always had captains, in all of his thirty years of coaching baseball at UCLA. He had his players vote for a captain, and he always made sure to say, "I don't want this to be a popularity contest. Pick the best leader." Coach Reichle must have talked to his good friend, John.

In 1961, the year I redshirted due to a knee injury, my twin brother, Gene, was elected captain. In 1962, at the beginning of my senior year and a couple of days prior to our first official game, Coach Reichle announced to our team that we would be electing captains the following day. He wanted us to think about who we should vote for. I resolved to not vote for myself. I did not want to be captain if it depended upon my single vote. The next day, Coach Reichle said there was a tie between Ezell Singleton and me. I had voted for Ezell. I was pleased that Coach Reichle made us co-captains.

It was an honor to be elected as one of the captains by my teammates. I believe that is one reason I continued the practice of voting for captains during my coaching years. But it was not the main reason. Sometimes players just can't talk openly to the "head man." They have an easier time making their voice heard by going to one of their peers, the captain. Then it is up to the captain to decide if he should go to the head coach. Most of the time, however, the captain can satisfy the player with some words of wisdom and avoid a confrontation with the head coach.

I remember an instance when I had to make a decision on my own that I believed was the best thing for the team. I had been the starting second baseman in my junior year. Ray Zak, a sophomore, had become the second baseman while I sat out during my redshirt season. The two of us had both been playing second base during intra-squad games—I played for the starting unit, and he played for the second string. On the practice day before our first official game—and the day I was elected one of the captains—Coach Reichle ordered the infielders to take our positions. He wanted to hit us ground balls. What I did next surprised all of our infielders, and especially Coach Reichle. Instead of going to second base, where I had been playing, I ran out to the third base spot. Had I not been a captain, I would never have made such a bold move.

It might not have been the right thing to do in the eyes of the two other third basemen, but neither of them had "won" the spot up to now, and I believed Ray Zak was better than both of them. We needed Ray in our lineup. I knew I could make the adjustment to move to third base easier than Ray, who was only a junior. I was the senior and captain—it was up to me to make the change.

Just before Coach Reichle prepared to throw the ball up in the air and hit a grounder to his third baseman, he hesitated. I can still see his furrowed eyebrows as I crouched in my ready position, waiting for him to hit me the first grounder. I didn't know if he would go through with his intention, or send me over to my regular spot at second base.

He decided to hit me the ground ball, and I fielded it and threw the ball as hard as I could to our first baseman to show my coach that I had the arm to play this position. He never said a word to me about it, then or ever. But I was the starting third baseman for every game the entire season, and Ray Zak started every game at second.

Years later, in the privacy of our office, I related this story to Coach Wooden. When I finished, he didn't say anything. I knew, by the look in his eyes, that he didn't approve.

I didn't want Coach to think I had disrespected Coach Reichle. I said, "I had been thinking of talking to Coach Reichle before that practice and I probably should have, but I didn't have the nerve. I had always respected and followed my coach's decisions. I didn't want him to think I was questioning his judgment."

I looked at Coach Wooden for a hint of approval, but he only said, "You were right when you said you should have talked to him before the practice."

Shortly after I told him this story, Coach recited a rhyme that struck home with me, although when he said it, he was talking about himself . . . I think.

> *I'm not what I ought to be;*
> *Not what I want to be;*
> *Not what I am going to be;*
> *But I'm thankful I am not what I used to be.*

THE GAME

I have always envied Coach Wooden's ability to treat people—
all people—with a consistent kindness, whether it was oblig-
ing them with an autograph or flashing a friendly smile. He
welcomed everyone into his life and made them feel right at
home. This was a man who had accomplished so much, and was
admired by everyone. However, there was one time I felt he
showed a glimpse of envy for me. It was one of those times we
spent in our office, just chatting about baseball. When the topic
turned to Sandy Koufax, I told Coach that I was a spectator at
"the Game."

The Game was played on September 9, 1965, in Dodger Stadium. Sandy Koufax and the Chicago Cubs' Bob Hendley were
locked up in one of the greatest pitching duels of all time. This
was a game made for Coach Wooden, low-scoring and perfect
in every way except for one questionable throw by the Cubs'
catcher.

The box score tells most of the story. The Dodgers had only
one hit that had nothing to do with their only run. Their winning run had scored off Hendley without the benefit of an *official* at bat. Koufax struck out thirteen Cub batters on his way
to pitching a no-hit, perfect game. Old-time Dodgers fans have

referred to this as "the Game." Since then, *young*-time Dodgers fans have referred to Kirk Gibson's 1988 World Series home run as "the Game." Both groups, young and old, are correct.

When I told Coach that I watched the Game from a box seat directly in line with first base, he looked at me like a little boy looks at another boy licking on an ice cream cone. He had relied on Vin Scully's voice through his home radio for his vision of the Game. I told him that I had also listened to Vin—in the stands—along with everyone else in Dodger Stadium. By the fifth inning, Vinny's voice was heard on every transistor radio in the ballpark. *This* game was special, and Coach wanted to know every detail from someone who had witnessed it in person.

Coach asked, "Why did you go to *this* game, Gary?"

"My best friend, Chris Krug, was the catcher for the Cubs," I said. "He got tickets for me, my wife, and our parents. When the six of us walked into the stadium, we noticed that Chris was *not* throwing batting practice. That meant we would get to see him play, because Chris always threw batting practice on road games if he was not in the starting lineup."

"Why did the manager have his catcher throw BP?" Coach asked.

"Good question. I guess it's because catchers get plenty of practice at throwing strikes because they've been returning 'strikes' back to pitchers their whole lives—only in the reverse direction."

Coach said, "I never thought of that before, but it sure makes sense."

I told Coach that Chris threw BP because of what had happened a year later, when I went to see the Cubs play. "A few of Chris's friends and I arrived early, and as we walked into the nearly empty stadium, we noticed that Chris was on the mound, pitching batting practice to the starting lineup, which meant he would *not* be playing that night.

"I yelled down to Chris from high on the second deck, just to let him know we were there. Chris looked up and surprised us all when, from the mound, he wound up and launched a high arching throw that I caught in my bare hands."

Another purpose in telling Coach this story was to let him know just how good of an arm Chris possessed, and that he was a fun-loving sort of guy. I had played high school ball with Chris, and his arm was the strongest and most accurate of any catcher I had ever played with, and better than most of the catchers I ever coached.

"When Chris and I discussed his long throw to me," I said, "I told him he was lucky that his no-nonsense manager, Leo Durocher, didn't see him do it. He might have fined him."

Coach smiled and said, "I might have, too. He could have injured his arm throwing the ball so far and high into the stands." That was Coach—always the sensible one.

I described the Game to Coach, starting in the top of the third inning, when Chris led off. "Koufax had already struck out three of the first six batters he faced, so Chris felt pretty good about his line drive straight to Willie Davis in center field, which turned out to be the hardest hit ball in the entire game.

"Going into the bottom of the fifth inning, Bob Hendley had matched Koufax pitch for pitch, until 'Sweet Lou' Johnson led off the inning with a base on balls that spoiled the Cubs lefthander's chance of a perfect game.

"The next batter, Ron Fairly, laid down a sacrifice bunt that moved Johnson to second base. On the first pitch to Jimmy Lefebvre, Sweet Lou surprised all the Cubs, except for Chris, who had a clear view of Johnson taking off in an attempt to steal third base.

"Chris threw a rifle shot throw toward third baseman Ron Santo, but the ball ended up in left field. It was scored E-2 [error on the catcher], as Sweet Lou waltzed home with the only run of the game. Chris's miscue might have been the most talked-about error of the baseball season."

Coach was quick to comment. "Not talked about more than Fred Merkle's."

I cocked my head and raised an eyebrow.

"You don't know about Fred 'Bonehead' Merkle?" Coach asked.

"No, never heard of him."

Coach seemed delighted. "I'll tell you the story as I heard it told to me by the older players I played ball with in Martinsville. In 1908, the Giants and the Cubs were in a close pennant race. In one of their last games against each other, it was tied in the last inning. The Giants were the home team and had a runner at third base, and Fred Merkle was on first base. The batter hit a base hit to the outfield to score what everyone thought was the winning run. But Merkle never touched second base as he joined in the celebration with the Giants fans and players. Meanwhile, a Cubs player noticed Merkle not touching the bag, and he retrieved the ball after a long search for it. No one's ever been sure if they found the actual ball that was hit, but they grabbed the base umpire and tagged second base with a ball in their hand. The umpire called Merkle out."

Coach paused long enough for me to ask a question. "Did they continue the game then?" I said.

"Yes, but not until the next day. They started from the beginning. This time, the Cubs won. At the end of the season, the Cubs won the pennant by one game. Fred Merkle was blamed for the Giants not going to the World Series. From the day he failed to touch second base, he was given the nickname 'Bonehead.'"

"You're right, Coach," I said. "Chris's error wasn't *that* big. But if it weren't for Chris, the game could have gone extra innings, and Koufax might not have even won his perfect game."

Then, in defense of my buddy, Chris, I said, "Coach, not many people know this, but there's another side of this story. Quite possibly, it was not Chris's fault at all. There was some controversy over Chris's throw being off-target. Sweet Lou told Chris, 'The throw was good—the ball got there first, I got there second, and Santo got there third—too late for him to catch the ball.'"

"Too bad, Gary, but if that was the case, it would still be an error on your friend," Coach said.

"Yes, but Chris had another version of what happened. He said that Johnson got such a great jump on Hendley that his slide cut down Santo before the ball ever got to third base. Hendley agreed with Chris. A photograph that appeared in only a few newspapers seemed to confirm that version. It shows the ball still on its way to third, and Santo sprawled on top of Johnson. Santo was in no position to catch the ball that went on its merry way to left field. Whenever I was in company with Chris and his friends asked about this play, I backed him up . . . sort of. I said, 'Chris's throw was a great testimony to the strength of his arm—a hard one-hopper right to his left fielder.'"

Coach grinned and said, "I had to get out of my chair in the top of the ninth, listening to Vinny describe that game. I was pulling so hard for Sandy to get his perfect game, that I found myself pacing the floor. I never did any pacing when I coached on the basketball court. I think I was more nervous than Sandy."

"I was nervous, too, Coach, as I sat only a hundred feet from home plate and watched my friend walk into the batter's box to lead off the ninth inning. I wasn't rooting for Koufax. I was rooting for Chris to spoil his perfect game."

After I said this, I saw more white than blue in Coach's eyes. "Goodness gracious, Gary," he exclaimed. "How could you be thinking that?"

"He's my best friend, John."

Coach didn't say a word; he just stared at me, as if I didn't know that Koufax was his favorite player at the time.

I tried to bend the subject slightly. "You and I weren't the only ones who were nervous. Scully described the feelings of the 29,000 fans in Dodger Stadium as having a million butterflies, but I might have been the only one nervous for Chris."

"Well, Gary, Chris struck out. Now, who were you rooting for?"

"No contest, Coach, I was pulling for Sandy all the way."

John smiled. I had my friend back.

Lou Johnson's bloop double down the right field line in the seventh inning was the only hit of the game, and Sandy had struck out the last six batters he faced to finish his perfect game.

But after listening to my description of the Game, I could see that Coach wished even more that he had witnessed it in person . . . perhaps so he could have made a judgment call on the E-2 play.

COACH SAVES THE DAY

oach Wooden once told me, "Gary, I will often give you my opinion, but rarely will I give you my advice." His opinions had already come in handy at the beginning of my second year on the job, when he taught me the best way to ask J. D. Morgan for an increase in my budget. And how could I forget his opinion and that funny recruiting story that helped me put things in the proper perspective?

In 1976, Coach offered a couple of his opinions regarding on-the-field strategy that made a big difference in the outcome of a crucial game.

On Thursday morning, May 13, 1976, I walked out of the house and picked up the *Los Angeles Times* on our driveway, then went back inside, anxious to turn to the sports page. It didn't take long to find what I was looking for. A headline in bold black print read, "Suddenly, UCLA's Magic Number is 1."

Times sportswriter Bob Cuomo's first two paragraphs were not news to me. "UCLA has an opportunity to accomplish something no team has managed since 1969—wrest a conference baseball title from USC. All the Bruins have to do is win one game of their regular season-ending, three-game series with the Trojans to take the California Intercollegiate Baseball

Association championship."

Later in Bob's story were some facts regarding the baseball history between UCLA and USC—impressive, if you were a Trojans fan. USC had won thirty of the last thirty-five games played. USC had won five national championships in the past six years, and the Trojans, in total, had won ten national championships, more than any college team in history—all under the leadership of Hall of Fame coach Rod Dedeaux.

Cuomo quoted me in the article: "I'd give us the edge in hitting. Fielding and team speed are about equal, and USC may have a pitching edge. But the coaching advantage is USC's, because Rod has been involved in so many of these situations." I was referring to the always competitive and pressure-packed games Rod had to manage in the NCAA Playoffs and the College World Series.

Early that afternoon, I drove to UCLA, needing to stop by the office to pick up my lineup cards for the three games. Coach Wooden sat at "our desk" when I walked in. He was in the middle of answering fan mail, a common sight.

He looked up and said, "Three big games, Gary. All you need is one, right?"

"Yeah, Coach . . . easier said than done, though." I must not have sounded too confident, because he asked, "Well, you're going with Cowan tonight, aren't you? He's pretty good."

"Yeah, I'll probably pitch Ed. He's our ace. But I haven't announced it yet."

"Who are they pitching?" Coach asked.

"They're going with their ace, John Racanelli. He beat us earlier this year. We only got one run off him."

John only nodded.

"Racanelli will be tough on our hitters," I continued. "Under our dim lights, his fastball will be even tougher to hit. Cowan doesn't throw as hard as Racanelli, but Ed has a great slider. I wish we were playing in daylight—it would help our hitters track the fastball better, and Ed's slider would still be effective."

John rubbed his chin and said, "Sounds to me as if you don't like tonight's match-up between Cowan and Racanelli. Have you given any thought to saving Cowan for the second or third game? You only need one win. It doesn't matter which game it comes in."

"Well, Coach, that might be a slap in the face to Ed. Besides, the players might think I'm surrendering the first game to the Trojans."

With a flicker of a grin, John said, "They won't care, and you shouldn't care, as long as whatever plan you come up with works."

"I don't know, Coach," I mumbled, shaking my head. "I'll have to think about it more. I've got a few more hours before I have to announce the pitcher."

"Gary, you're the head coach. You know what is best for your team. You have good, sound reasons for saving Cowan for the second or third game. It seems to me your reasons for pitching him tonight aren't based upon logic—it's based more on compassion and how your decision might look to your players."

Coach was not *telling* me what to do. He was just giving his opinion. Yet, in his unique way, he was making me think. I asked him, "If I didn't pitch Cowan in the first game, which game would *you* pitch him in, the second or the third?"

"Well, Gary, that second game is being played at their place, and what I know about USC is that they are awfully tough to beat on their own field. The percentages of winning over there aren't as good as winning the third game on your own home field. Who would you want to pitch in the third game if you would happen to lose the first two?"

"Cowan," I quickly answered.

"Why?"

"Because Ed is a senior and is the best competitor on the staff. He may not be the most talented, but he has proven to be the toughest when things get tough."

"Who would he be pitching against in the third game?"

Coach asked.

"Rod Boxberger, a freshman. He's a major league prospect."

"But he's a *freshman*," Coach said. "Sounds to me like that's a pretty good match-up for you."

When Coach said that, I no longer felt the need to delay my decision. Cowan would pitch the third game.

I told Coach of my decision and thanked him for helping me think logically.

As I walked toward the door to leave, he complimented me on what he had read in the school newspaper that morning. I hadn't read it yet. "You told your players about USC's great tradition in baseball and that they should respect that, but you also told them that 'tradition' is only a word. I believe your quote was something like, 'Tradition doesn't beat you unless you let it.' I liked that, Gary."

"Thanks, Coach, but my words were meant for me as much as for my players. USC's tradition has always been quite intimidating."

"Gary, if you don't mind me offering an opinion . . ."

"Of course not, Coach."

"Well, in my opinion, it's best you don't let your players see that you are intimidated."

I turned around to face him. "Coach, were you ever scared before a game?"

"Oh, I don't think that 'scared' would be the right word—'nervous' is more like it." He smiled. "But I did my best to give the *impression* that I wasn't. I wanted my players to believe that I was always under control, so that *they* stayed under control."

I smiled back at Coach as I shut the door. I felt good about our discussion and having arrived at a decision on my pitching rotation. That night, however, I did not carry all of Coach's wise words with me to the playing field.

We lost the first game at home on Sawtelle Field by a score of 6–3. The Trojans jumped out in front with a three-run first inning off of our starter, Curt Peterson. The loss wasn't solely his fault; we had two errors in the infield, unlike our usual stellar defense, which accounted for most of their runs. Racanelli pitched a complete game and only allowed one earned run. He dominated our hitters, who appeared as fidgety at the plate as I was in the dugout. I attributed the errors and the meek hitting to our head coach. I had coached "scared."

The next night, we played at USC in front of 2,237 fans, mostly Trojans. Our number two pitcher, freshman Tim O'Neill, was pitching against their number two, sophomore Ernie Mauritson. After five and a half innings, it was all tied up, 3–3. But in the bottom of the sixth, the Trojans scored four runs and ended up beating us, 7–3.

Once again, we played scared, with two more errors by our infielders on plays they had routinely made all season long. I was the infield coach as well as the head coach. My infielders had made four errors in two games, in part because their coach pacing back and forth in the dugout like a caged tiger was not the kind of picture that sent a message of confidence and trust to his players.

Certainly, if that had been my style all season long, it probably would not have had a detrimental effect on our team. Coach Mark Marquess of Stanford constantly paces up and down in his dugout during the game, and his players think nothing of it. They are used to their coach's back-and-forth trips, and they have had great success over the years. But my players were not used to seeing me so jittery. The old saying, "Like father, like son," applies to the coaching fraternity, also: "Like coach, like player." Our four errors should have been recorded as "E-13" to correspond with the number on my back.

I hardly slept the night after our second loss. I tossed and turned until I finally got out of bed at 5:30 AM on Saturday and drove the thirty-five minutes to Sawtelle Field. Game time was not until 1:00 PM. I still had about six hours to prepare for the game that would decide the conference championship.

Walking has always helped clear my mind. I decided to walk across Sepulveda Boulevard from our ball field to the quiet serenity of the Los Angeles Veterans' Cemetery.

At the beginning of my walk, all I could think about was how bad it would be for all of our fans, friends, and players if we were to lose today, after coming so close and so far. After my first half mile or so, I decided that this kind of thinking was not productive. I needed to be looking forward and figuring out how best to win today's game.

Coach Wooden's words from two days ago finally hit home: "Gary . . . don't let your players *see* that you're intimidated."

The key word in his message was *"see."* I had spent the last two days *telling* my players there was nothing to be scared of, but I was not doing a good job of *showing* them. The impression I gave was a poor example of what I preached. I decided that the best thing I could do for the team was to *show* them. But it had to be genuine, not artificial.

I began looking back on our season, which was filled with many positive events. We had won more than twice as many games in conference this year than we had won last year, and all eleven seniors on the squad had contributed significantly to our winning season. I knew the seniors felt good about themselves, and, of course, I wanted them to end their college careers on a high note. They deserved it, and I didn't want to let them down.

I was determined to show them that I had had a great experience in coaching them. In short, it was a fun year, not only for the seniors but for all the players and coaches. I made up my mind that I would *show* them today how much fun I had by coaching the same way I did all year. I was determined to be loose and enjoy the game of baseball as it was meant to be enjoyed.

I still remember the comfortable and relaxed feeling I had when I returned to our off-campus field. I had a plan, and I couldn't wait for our pregame preparations to begin.

I chose to do several things differently than I had done in the previous two games. First, instead of Coach Mickens throwing the entire batting practice, I would pitch the first half hour, and he could do his usual good job of polishing up the hitters in the final ten minutes. Another change I made was to use my best friend and former Chicago Cubs catcher Chris Krug as our batting practice catcher.

I knew that having Chris behind the plate would keep me loose. He had been my catcher when I pitched in Pony League baseball, when we were both fourteen years old. We have always had fun ribbing each other, and he had always been a source of laughter and smiles for me. I actually felt like I was back in Pony League, pitching again with my best pitch, the "knuckle-drop." On occasion, I challenged the hitters to hit my sinking drop into the air—a difficult feat for the fourteen-year-olds I had faced a long time ago. I was having fun, and the players could see it.

I always made sure that the hitters finished on a good note. I grooved the last couple of pitches in their "sweet zone," while they hammered the ball over the fence. The more I pitched, the more all of us relaxed and enjoyed the game of baseball, as we had all year.

The third thing I changed had to do with my infielders. Usually, while Coach Mickens did the pitching during batting practice, my other assistant, Mike Gerakos, and I would hit ground balls to the infielders. But today, for the first half of batting practice, Coach Mickens and I switched duties. While I pitched, he hit grounders to our infielders along with Coach Gerakos. I felt that these two were a better fit to relax my infielders. When Mickens came out to pitch the last ten minutes of batting practice, instead of me hitting ground balls, the job went to Krug. Chris is a strong, six-foot-four man who can hit powerful grounders. I believed that anything the USC hitters would hit in this game would be routine compared to what my team fielded for ten minutes from Chris.

Perhaps the last change I made was the most critical, though quite subtle. I did not give the players my usual pep talk. Coach Wooden was never a big fan of pep talks, and since neither one of mine before the first two games had done any good, I kept my mouth shut—except when we huddled to take the field in the first inning. I only said, "Men . . . enjoy the competition." Coach Wooden would have been proud.

The wooden bleachers of Sawtelle Field sit less than a thousand people. Every seat was filled at the start of the game. Those fans arriving after the umpire yelled, "Play ball," had to stand behind chain-link fences along the foul lines and the outfield. On that Sunday afternoon, it seemed to me that there were more USC fans than UCLA fans, but maybe that was because the Trojans band was making the most noise, playing "Fight On for USC." (Most UCLA fans believe that is the *only* song they know how to play.) I remember thinking that some of our fans might be embarrassed to attend today's game for fear of USC sweeping the series. Trojan fans are noted for rubbing victory in the faces of the Bruins, but I have to admit, UCLA fans don't balk at doing the same thing whenever the Bruins beat the Trojans.

I learned early in my playing career at UCLA how crucial it was for the Bruins to beat USC in any sport. Football's only coach to win a national championship for the Bruins, Red Sanders, put it quite distinctly: "Losing to USC is not a life-and-death matter. It's worse than that."

Coach Wooden had predicted that USC's freshman pitcher, Boxberger, might struggle, and he was right. Boxberger gave up three runs on three hits, and four bases on balls in only one and two-thirds innings. The Trojan players were playing tight, because they had three errors by the fourth inning. Meanwhile, our Ed Cowan allowed base runners every inning, but the Trojans could not take advantage and only scored one run up to the fifth inning. Our defense also made some sparkling plays to back up Ed. Our ace was pitching like he had all year—tough in the clutch and limiting USC to scratch singles.

The Trojan hitters came alive in the middle innings and soared to a 6–3 lead. Our hitting had stalled when USC junior leftie Charlie Phillips relieved Boxberger. In the bottom of the seventh inning, our catcher, Dennis Delany, got us a little closer with a home run. It was a sign that we could score off of Phillips.

Although the Trojans roughed up Cowan in the middle innings, I stuck with him. In the ninth inning, he pitched with the bases loaded and one out. I heard some fans yelling, "Take him out, Adams!" But all season long, Ed had been strong in the late innings. Also, I did not want to show any sign of panic to our team or to the Trojans. Ed was our ace, and he was the best one to pitch in a close and crucial game. I am sure there were many Bruins fans doubting my strategy.

Ed proved the yellers wrong. With the bases loaded, he jammed the next hitter, who hit a routine grounder to first baseman Brian Viselli, who threw to catcher Delany at home to force the runner. Delany completed the double play by throwing back to first. With only three outs left for us to win, the score remained 6–4.

When we came off the field to take our turn at hitting, I was thinking of what Coach Wooden had said about not letting my players see that I was scared. All day, I had showed my players a positive outlook. I clapped my hands and kept my enthusiasm for all the players to see. I reminded them that there was no time limit in baseball. "Be patient at the plate. We're going to take this game away from them." When I spoke those words, I really did have a good feeling. I was speaking from the heart, and I think they could see that.

In that historic ninth inning, freshman Jim Auten started things off with a single to left field. UCLA's star basketball guard, Raymond Townsend, who had played on Coach Wooden's last national championship team in 1975, was the next hitter. This lean and wiry shortstop followed Auten with a sharp

single to center field. I felt Phillips was tiring and we would do some more hitting before the inning ended, but Coach Dedeaux made a brilliant move. He brought in his ace, John Racanelli, to finish the job for USC.

I thought, *I'm glad it's daylight. Our hitters can see the fastball better than they could two nights ago.* But still, I was not happy with Rod's move as I stood in the third base coach's box, listening to the cheers from the USC fans for Phillips's fine effort and, mostly, for the entrance of their ace, Racanelli.

I remember thinking, *Do I sacrifice bunt with Delany, even though he had hit a home run his last at bat?* I gave him the sac bunt sign. There was no way I wanted to give the Trojans a chance to get a ground ball double play on our less-than-average running catcher. I wanted to get the tying run on second base, with one out. But the Trojans were ready for the bunt, and they managed to nip our runner at third base.

Dennis made it safely to first. Then David Penniall, our fleet-footed center fielder, hit a grounder in the hole at short. But their shortstop ranged far to his right, and used his momentum to make a smart play by throwing to third base for another force out.

We were down to our last out, and had nothing to show for it. Runners were still on first and second base, where they had been perched two outs ago. The USC band began playing "Taps." I thought, *The Trojans band does know how to play more than one song!* I felt good that I could see some humor in such a critical time. I also knew that most of their fans were beginning to make plans for another NCAA run to the College World Series. I wanted, more than anything, to ruin those plans.

Our next hitter was Bobby Dallas, a stocky little five-foot-seven second baseman. When I talked to our hitters about being patient at the plate, I never dreamed that Bobby would take it so far. The box score will merely say that he received a base on balls, but it was the best-executed base on balls I have ever witnessed.

After Racanelli got his sign from the catcher and was preparing to go into his stretch, Bobby raised his right hand to the umpire and asked for a time out. The umpire obliged. Bobby wears glasses, and apparently, he felt they were dirty. He calmly stepped out of the batter's box and reached into his back pocket for a handkerchief. With great deliberation, he wiped off his glasses in front of 1,603 anxious fans (at the time, the largest crowd to ever witness a UCLA baseball game).

Meanwhile, Racanelli was becoming impatient. He stepped off the mound and stared at Bobby. He didn't look pleased. He seemed anxious to get the third out and begin the celebrations.

I was in the third base coaching box, thinking, *Good idea, Bobby . . . make sure you can see the ball.* But what he did next was comical—at least in my eyes.

Bobby stepped back into the batter's box and appeared ready to hit. Racanelli stepped back on the mound and went into his stretch to pitch. But, once again, before Racanelli made his move to deliver the pitch, Bobby raised his hand to the umpire and asked for time. I could hardly believe it when the umpire raised both of his hands and granted Bobby his request as he yelled, "Time out!" Once again, Bobby reached into his back pocket for his handkerchief, and calmly wiped off his glasses.

Racanelli did not hide his frustration, pacing back and forth and slamming the resin bag down. The players in the Trojans dugout began hollering insults to our little right-handed hitter, and the Trojans fans did a good job of heckling. Bobby didn't appear to mind.

I knew Bobby did not do this as a trick. He confirmed it afterwards, saying to me, "Coach, my glasses were all fogged up. I couldn't see. Then, when I stepped back in again, I saw that I'd missed a spot. No way was I going to hit with a smudge on my glasses like that."

Regardless, Bobby's patience had a detrimental effect on Racanelli. With his adrenalin flowing, he made the mistake of over-throwing his fastball. He threw four straight balls that

didn't come close to the strike zone—and now the bases were loaded.

I decided to pinch-hit for our next hitter, Tommy Parma, with another left-handed hitter, freshman Steve Splitt. Steve had played mostly for our junior varsity team that season and would not have even suited up for the game, had it not been for a rule that permitted an unlimited number of players when cross-town rivals played each other. Although Steve was a freshman, he was the best fastball hitter I had remaining on the bench. I liked the match-up with Racanelli.

Racanelli's first pitch was a fastball high for ball one. The next pitch was another fastball that Steve swung at so late, the ball appeared to be in the catcher's glove before he even started his swing. It looked to me like he was looking for an off-speed pitch—not a fastball.

In the midst of this battle, I found myself thinking about what Coach Wooden had told me two days earlier. Maybe I thought of Coach because I had overheard one of my players say, late in the game, that Coach Wooden was sitting in the bleachers. If he was, I never saw him. Anyway, when I saw how badly Steve Splitt was fooled, I called time out and *calmly* walked toward the batter's box.

I simply said, "Steve, you won't be seeing anything except a fastball. Look for it, and give us that good swing of yours."

"Okay, Coach," he said.

The next pitch was a fastball, and Steve was ready for it. He hit a hard line drive to center field—almost too hard. Their center fielder got the ball on one quick hop as Dave Penniall, our fastest runner, came running full speed from second base toward me in the third base coach's box. I had no intention of stopping this potential tying run, and started waving my arms like an airplane propeller (my friends told me later—exaggerating a bit—that I was waving so hard, my feet weren't touching the ground). Dave rounded third at about the same time that the center fielder threw the ball. I was amazed at how quickly he got rid of the ball, but it was too late to stop the speeding Penniall. The ball got to the catcher slightly ahead of Dave, but with an expert slide to the outside corner of the plate, he slid around the catcher's tag. When I saw the umpire's safe sign, I fought hard to stay under control. Yes, I did pump my fist once, because we had just tied up the ball game—but we had yet to win it. In the meantime, the Bruins fans were going wild, and the cars that were parked beyond the chain link fence in center field were honking loudly.

Bobby Dallas, who went to third on the throw home, stood at the base with the potential winning run. The next hitter was junior Brian Viselli, who wasted no time at the plate. He promptly hit Racanelli's first pitch over the left fielder's head. I watched as little Bobby Dallas did a "cannonball-landing" on top of home plate to score the winning run and win us the conference championship.

I was dazed for a moment until I heard a familiar voice behind me say, "Congratulations, Gary." It was Coach Dedeaux. What a gentleman—the greatest coach in college baseball history. In fact, he is to college baseball what Coach Wooden is to college basketball. He shook my hand as I said, "Thanks, Rod. Good game."

The next thing I knew, I was celebrating with my players. The fans had spilled from the bleachers, and were now jumping and running around the field. It was a wonderful feeling to get rid of the adrenalin that had been building up these last three days. The players carried me to the clubhouse and sat me down under one of the most refreshing showers I ever had—with my uniform on.

As Marc Dellins wrote in the first line of his story that appeared in the school newspaper the following Monday, "Miracles do happen." In my mind, I have Coach Wooden to thank for that miracle, and for helping me keep my poise throughout the last game.

When I returned to my office on Monday, there was a yellow

sheet of paper lying on the desk that John and I shared. On that paper was a hand-printed message from my office-mate.

> *Coach Gary—*
> *Tremendous!*
> *Congrats #1!*
> *Congrats #2!*
> *Congrats #3!*
>
> *J.W.*

People have asked me what the numbers one, two, and three stood for. I always knew what John meant by them, and never felt a need to ask him. Number one meant it was a good decision to save Cowan in Game One. Number two meant it was a good decision to save Cowan in Game Two. Number three meant it was a good decision to *start* Cowan in Game Three.

I placed Coach's note in the top drawer of my desk, and left it there for safekeeping. I kept his note in that top office drawer as a reminder of what Coach had taught me, and as a fond memory of the games it represented.

When I saw Coach in our office not too long afterwards, I said, "Thanks, Coach, for all your advice . . . uh, I mean, your opinions. You saved the day."

A COACH'S PLAYER

Every college baseball coach in the country looks for the position player who is not afraid to get dirty diving for a fly ball or a grounder, who battles pitchers as if his life depended on it, and who competes with all his effort on every pitch, every out, every inning, and in every game. We coaches call this type of player—regardless of his God-given talent—a coach's player.

Most of the time, this kind of player is not blessed with all of the physical tools to make himself a star. Occasionally, though, a player comes along who also possesses the athletic talent *and* the qualities of a coach's player.

The year after we had won the conference championship, I was fortunate to land a recruit that came close to fitting the mold described above. After seeing him play in two games with his junior college team, I agreed with most professional scouts that this recruit possessed the potential to become a big league ball player.

In the early summer of 1976, I was telling Coach Wooden about this center fielder, who "could run like a deer, hit for power, hit for average, and could even hit from both sides of the plate."

Coach grinned. "Sounds like Mickey Mantle, Gary."

John seemed pleased. He knew we needed a good center fielder to replace our graduated senior captain, David Penniall.

Not long after that conversation, I flew to Alaska to coach a team in America's premier summer collegiate league. I took twelve Bruins with me. I also took my highly prized recruit to play center field.

It didn't take long for this switch-hitting, five-tool player to demonstrate his "fire" on the ball field. I admired his competitiveness from the start, but I did *not* admire the quick and fiery temper that accompanied his competitiveness. It surfaced whenever things didn't go his way. If Coach Wooden had witnessed his playing, I'm sure he would have said, "He needs to learn the art of self-control."

I knew where Coach stood on this matter, because of what he had said in one of the first serious talks we ever had in our office. His words at that time were so profound that, as soon as he left, I jumped out of my chair into his vacated one to scribble his words on a notepad. I wrote:

> *Life is not about winning, as most people define the word*
> *. . . life is about trying to be the best you can be, and when*
> *your best doesn't quite cut it, how quickly you can recover*
> *from it and overcome it.*

His words became my creed for coaching young men who hadn't yet learned to cope with the many failures they would meet in baseball—a sport designed for the hitter to fail at least twice as much as he succeeds.

This creed was put to the test by my new recruit in Alaska, during the first game I ever coached him in. While he was batting in the last inning of a tight ball game, the umpire called him out on strikes—a pitch my player believed was a ball. I admit that the last strike could have been a ball, but that didn't matter to me. It mattered greatly to my hitter, however.

The fans and the players on both sides watched in amazement

as my newly recruited Bruin took his helmet off after taking a couple steps out of the batter's box and flung it as hard as he could at our dugout. That was a bad enough decision, but what made it worse was the fact that I was standing exactly where the spinning projectile was headed. Luckily for me, my footwork had not yet deserted me at the age of thirty-five, and I hopped over the skipping helmet before it could slice my legs off.

Sporting a face colored red, my star recruit came stomping past me and into the dugout, where the other players sat quietly, as if in silent prayer.

What do I do now? I thought. I chose to do nothing at that moment. I waited until we made the third out to end the game, and then I announced to the team, "We'll meet down the right field line."

My speech was brief and featured only one topic—controlling your temper—or, more positively, the importance of keeping your poise and self-control when playing baseball. I ended my talk by saying, "Win or lose, I am going to coach the rest of the summer. And I'm going to coach a team that keeps its poise under all circumstances." Then, without mentioning any names, I said, "If you can't play the way I ask, then quit this team now and don't plan on ever playing for me at UCLA—transfer to another school." Most of the players knew who I was talking about, and I was certain that *that* player knew.

Fortunately, the season went without further major incidents; yet, I did on occasion notice our center fielder on the edge of losing it when things went poorly for him and the team.

When the short-season Alaska League ended, this superb player led our team in home runs (eight), runs scored (thirty-five), and stolen bases (fifteen). I felt confident that I had recruited an outstanding player, but I had some concerns about how he and his temper would handle the long college baseball season.

When I returned to UCLA in early fall, Coach Wooden asked how my summer had gone, and we ended up talking about the

new recruit. I told Coach, "He is a sensational player, and he wants to do his best for the team. But . . . " I stopped at that point, and wanted to leave it at that, but Coach wouldn't allow it.

"But what, Gary?"

I stammered a bit when I answered. "Well . . . it's just that he has a temper. I'm not sure how it's going to work out."

From there, I told him about the helmet-throwing incident. I confided in Coach, and asked him what he would do.

As he often did, Coach answered my question with a question. "Is his problem something you can live with and your team can win with, or is it so big that you'd rather lose without him?"

Coach's question put everything in perspective. I thought to myself, *Of course I want him on the team, and so do the players. His problem is not as big as I'm making it—that's my problem. I should be grateful that I have a player like him, who wants to compete as hard as I do. So what if he throws his helmet or bat or glove? I'll run him. He'll get the message.*

Sitting against the wall in our office folding chair, I had been fiddling with my hands and keeping my head down while in deep thought. John, meanwhile, sat patiently at our desk, waiting for my answer.

"It is way more important that he be on the team than me worrying about what *might* happen because of his temper."

Coach nodded and went back to writing letters.

In the 1977 season, we finished in second place to the USC Trojans. Our center fielder made sensational catches, and threw out plenty of runners trying to take the extra base. He led our club in stolen bases and bases on balls, and was among the top three hitters in most offensive categories. He didn't throw any tantrums, nor any helmets or bats. At the end of the season, I told Coach Wooden that he had done a splendid job of maintaining his self-control.

After his junior season, he was drafted in the first round by the Dodgers. A bright future lay in front of Ron Roenicke. Ron went on to have an eight-year big league career, playing for six different organizations. Then the Dodgers and the Giants gave him a chance to manage in the minors, and he worked his way up the ladder to become Mike Scioscia's bench coach with the Angels. He coached the Angels for eight consecutive years before being named the manager of the Milwaukee Brewers and becoming the first Bruin to ever manage a big league team. In 2011, his first year on the job, Ron Roenicke's Brewers were champions of the National League Central Division

I saw Ron several times after he played at UCLA—the evening he was inducted into the UCLA Baseball Hall of Fame, and at UCLA alumni games. It was at one of those alumni games that I asked him if he remembered his helmet-throwing incident in Alaska, and what I had said after that game.

He smiled and nodded. "Oh yeah, I remember," he said quietly.

"I've always been curious to know what you were thinking after I said that," I said.

Ron's smile broadened. "I was thinking, 'What school should I transfer to?'"

That's Ron—a mixture of honesty and dry humor. At the time, I hoped he would say, "I was thinking, 'Coach is right and I need to learn to control my emotions better.'" But his answer gave us both a chance to laugh at that long-ago event.

From what I hear, since he became a manager—and I have to smile whenever I hear it—his players and the baseball media describe him as a calm and mild-mannered skipper.

I know that Coach Wooden would have liked Ron's quote that appeared in the *MLB Insiders Club Magazine* when he became the manager of the Brewers: "I've worked hard in the minor leagues, I've worked hard in the major leagues, not just preparing for this job, but trying to do things right."

I'm proud to say that I coached Ron Roenicke. Coach Wooden, in his wise way, made me think and do the right thing for Ron, a coach's player and, now, a players' coach.

THE BENCH

When Coach Wooden spoke at coaching clinics, he was often asked, "How do you discipline your players?" His patented answer was, "I put them on the bench. The bench is a coach's best ally." Sometimes he would add, "The bench is a coach's best motivator."

Coach learned that lesson early in life, when his grade school coach, Earl Warriner, made him sit on the bench for the first half of a basketball game because John had left his jersey at home. That wasn't the worst thing he did, though. Being the star of the team, John asked a benchwarmer to go back to his house to get the jersey for him, believing himself to be more important for the team's chances of winning.

When John told Warriner that they would lose without him in the lineup, the coach didn't care. He wanted John to learn a lesson. His team did lose, but Coach Warriner stuck by his principles. He knew that John wanted to play, so sitting him on the bench would be the most useful punishment he could dole out. John learned his lesson. That's why, as a coach, he never punished his players by making them run laps, do push-ups, or perform any physical exercises. He knew players wanted to play more than anything else.

Coach Wooden always had a strong and deep bench, but he was famous for only playing seven or eight players in an entire game. That meant there were four or five unhappy benchwarmers.

Gail Goodrich, except for his first few games at UCLA, started in the rest of them. He told me about an incident he witnessed while listening to Coach Wooden speak at a basketball coach's clinic. "You only play seven or eight players in a game," a young coach had asked John. "I don't know who to choose for my eighth player—they are equally good. What should I do?"

John had answered, "Pick one. You can't be wrong."

Wooden never referred to his own players as "benchwarmers" or "subs"; he was keenly aware of their importance to the team. He tried his best to make them understand that they contributed to the team's success.

"Gary," he once said to me, "don't ignore those players who aren't playing much. They are the ones who make your starters better."

Coach had the relatively unheralded Jim Milhorn push Gail Goodrich and Walt Hazzard during their first years at UCLA.

"Sometimes, the non-starters give up hope and stop working to improve," Wooden said. "Then, when they are called upon to play, they only reinforce in the coach's mind why they should be sitting on the bench."

He always warned his non-starters to be ready to play in case they were needed. I made it a habit to tell my players a phrase Coach had taught me: "Better to be prepared and *not* be called upon than to be called upon and *not* be prepared."

Coach admitted to me that when it came to playing non-starters, his job as a basketball coach was easier than mine as a baseball coach.

"I can put a non-starter into a game which we are leading comfortably, and if the lead gets a little too close, take him out and put my starter back in. In baseball, you can't bring your starters back."

Despite Coach's easier job of substituting, he was not without his critics, especially from the parents of his players. He always said that the parents of his starters *loved* him, the parents of his sixth, seventh, and eighth men *liked* him, and the rest of the players' parents *disliked* him.

I remember Coach shaking his head and saying, "I realize parents are going to be biased regarding their sons. I just wish they would be more reasonable."

One time, when I told John that I was having problems with a dad who thought his son should be playing more, Coach told me about an experience he had with one of his player's mothers. He called the mom "Mrs. Jones," which he confessed was not her real name. John was always careful about saying anything negative behind someone's back—a lesson his father had taught him long ago.

"Mrs. Jones was so troubled about her son's lack of playing time that she paid a visit to my office to complain," Coach said. "She told me that she believed the boy playing ahead of her son was not as good as her son. She said, 'My son can dribble faster, jump higher, and shoot better than the other boy . . . even the players on the team have told him he is a better athlete than the other boy.'"

John told me that he had listened patiently to the mother. When she finished, he told her, "You are so right, your son can do all those things better, and he *is* a better athlete. That's why I believe it is such a shame that he is letting the other boy beat him out."

The UCLA athletic department invited Coach Wooden to speak to their coaches and athletes on occasion. On one of his visits, he recited a poem that made a lasting impression on me and probably every coach in the audience:

> *No written word, no spoken plea*
> *can teach our youth what they should be.*
> *Nor all the books on all the shelves,*
> *it's what the teachers are themselves.*

He was telling us that we, as coaches, are teachers first, and the best way to teach our student-athletes is by our own example—not just our example on the fields or courts of play, but also outside of them.

After Coach had finished his speech, I approached him and asked, "What are some ways a coach can teach by example?"

He answered me with a question. "Gary, do you have a rule for your players to be well-groomed—clean and neat—when the team is in the public eye, such as when you travel on the airplane?"

"Yes. They are to be clean-shaven. No beards, no long hair, no sandals, no tank tops, and no ball caps." I rattled the rules off and noticed a hint of a smile from Coach.

He said, "Well, you have a mustache. Do you allow mustaches?"

"Yes, I do, as long as the mustache doesn't creep down their face lower than mine does."

"That's good, Gary. That is one way to show your players, by example, that you are serious about your rule."

John surprised me with his next point. "Do you still run your players long and hard to teach them a lesson?"

"Yes," I replied.

"Do you run with them?"

"Most of the time. I do it so that I can determine when they've had enough. I'm only 38, so I'm still in good shape for running. When I get tired, I know they're tired."

"Well, Gary, that's one way to set an example. But, as I've told you before, I believe there is a better way to discipline—use your bench." John gave me a half-smile. "One of these days, you may be too old to keep up with your players, and you might need to use the bench method *all* of the time."

I expected that I might need to start using Coach's bench method when I reached the age of fifty; however, unexpectedly, it became necessary before then.

I n Coach's Pyramid of Success, the "Loyalty" block appears in the very center of the foundation. John and I agreed that the most essential quality in our assistant coaches is loyalty to their head coach.

"Gary, I don't mean that they needed to agree with everything I said or did," Coach said. "I wouldn't just want yes-men on my staff. I wanted people who were not afraid to speak up and give their opinions. Why have an assistant if they are going to agree with everything you do or say?"

In 1981, one of my assistants, Mike Gerakos, was hired to be the head baseball coach at the University of California, Irvine. I turned to Coach for his opinion of my candidates to replace Mike. It did not surprise me when he answered my question with one of his own, something he often did when I asked for his opinion.

"What were Coach Gerakos's best assets, Gary?"

"Loyalty. I never doubted Mike's loyalty."

I think he expected that answer, because he quickly said, "What else?"

"Mike was knowledgeable about baseball, and he was a hard worker."

Only then did Coach offer an opinion. "Look at your list of candidates in those three categories, and see which one scores the highest marks. That should give you your answer."

Following his suggestion, I chose Chris Krug, former major league catcher for the Chicago Cubs. He won in a landslide. Until I had my conversation with Coach, I had hesitated in hiring him, because he was also my best friend. I was concerned for two reasons. First, I was afraid of how it would look to others—was it bordering on nepotism? Secondly, after hearing so often that "friends and business don't mix," I didn't want to jeopardize our friendship. Nevertheless, I hired Chris because he fit Coach's requirements best. Besides, without him I probably never would have been able to recruit catcher Todd Zeile, who chose to attend UCLA partly because of Krug's catching expertise.

I remember Coach telling me, "You don't want an assistant you can't trust—a coach who doesn't support you behind your back, be it with your players or the media. You certainly wouldn't want someone who would be disloyal when things are going bad."

"That's easy for you to say, Coach," I replied. "I don't remember you ever coaching when things were bad."

"Gary, I think it's just as difficult keeping your assistants loyal during the good times—maybe even tougher, because jealousy creeps into the picture. I tried to give credit to my assistants when credit was due, not just to the media, but mainly to their faces. I probably didn't do it enough, but I do know this: I *never* blamed my assistants for anything they may have suggested that ended up failing. Loyalty is a two-way street. You can't expect your assistants to be loyal to you if you are not loyal to them."

One of the best maxims Coach ever told me, and one that I said to my coaches often, was this: It's amazing how much you can get accomplished when you don't care who gets the credit.

I don't know if that was Coach's original saying, but he did remind me that it applied to the head coach, as well as to his assistants and his players.

A good example of Wooden giving credit to his coaches is told in one of his books, *They Call Me Coach*. John wrote: "Every assistant made a contribution . . . but probably the most famous one came from Norman [Jerry Norman, who coached with John from 1958 to 1968]. That was in the 1967–68 NCAA championships . . . "

John described how Coach Norman recommended that they use a box and one defense against Houston's Elvin Hayes, who had practically destroyed the Bruins earlier that season. John and his assistants discussed Norman's recommendation and, with a slight variation of Norman's suggestion, the Bruins contained the "Big-E" and clobbered Houston, 101–69.

I was fortunate enough to have had Coach Norman as a professor in a physical education class, Basketball 371B. He was an excellent teacher who displayed a true passion for the game in his classroom, and also on the basketball court. It was easy for me to understand why Coach Wooden respected his assistant's skills as a teacher and as a coach.

In my forty-one years of coaching college baseball, I have been fortunate, like John, to have had outstanding assistants. They have taught me more than I ever taught them, and I do not say that to sound humble—it is simply the truth. But what I appreciated most from them was their loyalty to me, through the best of times and the worst of times.

FATE

When Coach enlisted in the navy in 1942, he didn't know that fate would be on his side and save his life. But there was a catch—fate traded his life for another.

John was assigned to the ship USS *Franklin* in the South Pacific, but just before he was to leave, he needed an emergency appendix operation. A close friend and former classmate from Purdue University, Freddie Stalcup, replaced John. That friend was killed by a Japanese kamikaze plane, as he manned the same gunnery position where Coach would have been. Instead of John Wooden's name being on the casualty list, it was Freddie Stalcup's.

How ironic that Coach's encounter with fate was one that brought the two of us closer. On Monday, September 25, 1978, I was scheduled to appear as a witness in a trial being conducted in San Diego. One of my players, Kevin Stevens, had been injured in a hit-and-run accident as he was walking along a roadway on Halloween night. He had played ball at UCLA his freshman and sophomore years, but this accident ended his baseball career. I was called to testify in his favor for a lawsuit claiming damages for the accident, which prevented him from signing a professional contract and losing out on substantial income. Kevin's attorney made arrangements for my ticket on a flight from Los Angeles to San Diego on the morning of the trial. I was set to go.

However, in the early evening prior to the next day's morning departure, I decided to drive my car instead, so that I could stop at my parents' home in Oceanside. I could visit with them and spend the night there, then drive the rest of the way to the San Diego courthouse.

The next morning, as I woke up and began to dress, Mom and Dad's television blasted shocking news: "Planes collide, all 135 passengers perish!"

It was *my* plane. Mom and dad kept telling me how lucky I was to be alive. But there is also a downside to being lucky *in this way*. It left me with a feeling of guilt that was difficult to shake. That feeling carried over to the trial, where I failed Kevin miserably. I wasn't sharp in my answers, and many times, as I sat on the witness stand, I said to the attorneys on both sides, "Please repeat the question."

I felt numb. The world meant nothing to me, because nothing was important—except for the questions that were running through my mind: *Who took my seat? Who was the lucky-unlucky person on stand-by who, at the time he heard his name announced, could hardly hold back his delight in front of those whose names were not called? Was he elated because he could return to his job sooner? Or return to his home and his family earlier than expected? What if he was a she? A mom? Oh no, please don't let it be a mom.*

Those were the thoughts and questions that were in my head that day—not the comparatively meaningless ones asked by the defense and prosecuting attorneys. Yes, I was numb inside as I sat on the witness stand, because no questions mattered except these: *Who took my seat on that plane? And why wasn't I sitting in it?*

Those thoughts and feelings of guilt kept reappearing for a long time. Even today, they will pop up out of nowhere. It's a form of guilt that is borne from the type of question I most dislike—the hypothetical kind. It's even worse when I am the one asking the question, *If I could replay it, would I trade places with the one who traded places with me?*

My answer was a cowardly one. *No, I would not. I am not that brave—not that courageous—not that good.*

I have tried rationalizing it, saying, "It was God's plan. Only he knows why he had someone take my place on the plane. I must not fret over it." But sometimes those feelings of guilt, which I thought I had tossed away, reappear out of nowhere, and I can find no reason why the one who took my place was any less deserving of life than I am.

Coach Wooden had read the headlines of the disaster in the newspapers, and had also heard the story of how fate had "saved" me. While sitting in our office shortly after the tragedy, he asked me how I was handling it.

"Oh, okay, I guess. I try not to think about it."

"Sometimes, nothing is fixed in our memory more intensely than the wish to forget it," Coach said gently. "I think it best to just go on with your life without trying so hard to forget things. Focus on the present, Gary, because you can do nothing to change the past."

He examined his hands, then slowly glanced up and looked at me compassionately. "I believe I know how you feel. I have similar feelings about a couple of incidents that happened in my life."

I thought he would tell me the story I had heard before—his war story of when his friend took his place at the artillery and was killed. But that wasn't the story he told.

"I was scheduled to speak at a basketball clinic at Campbell College in North Carolina," he began, "but because of another commitment, I canceled my plane ticket from Atlanta." His voice was barely above a whisper. "I postponed it to the next day. The flight I was scheduled to be on crashed. No one survived.

"For a time, I felt guilty, too. Why was I any more worthy to be alive than the person who took my seat on that plane? In time, I realized I should be grateful to God. I learned to cope with it by just trying to live my life in a way that was worthy of God's mercy for me. Gary, I believe he had plans for you and me to complete."

John's words were soothing, and helped—though they did not entirely wipe away the guilt I was feeling. Guilt has a way of lingering, then showing itself at unwelcome times. Why does one live, while another dies in his place? Is it fate? Luck? The hand of God? Coach Wooden had his own answer, perhaps the best one I could accept.

THE WOODEN-BROWN CONNECTION

Joe E. Brown, the comedian-actor our UCLA campus baseball field was named after, and John Wooden were closely connected—but neither one ever realized it.

In the previous chapter, I wrote about how fate played a huge role in Coach Wooden's life. The same can be said for Joe. One morning, he was driving past the UCLA campus along Sunset Boulevard, where he proudly canvassed his "baby," the Joe E. Brown baseball field. Unfortunately, his car couldn't make the bend in the road and somersaulted down a steep embankment.

As he lay at the bottom of the hill in a twisted pile of metal, his back broken in two places, with a collapsed lung and a bloody body, he kept saying, "I don't want to die."

At the hospital, on the operating table, surgeons worked furiously to keep Joe alive, but eventually, his heart stopped. The main surgeon shook his head, took off his gloves, and started to walk away. But fate interfered. An intern made the surgeon shoot some oxygen into Joe's body, and he returned to life, after being dead for forty seconds.

Joe always said that it wasn't the oxygen that saved him— it was his will to live.

Coach Wooden, like Joe E. Brown, possessed that same

quality—an intense desire to live. Without it, Coach would never have made it through almost a hundred years of life.

There were other connections between Coach Wooden and Joe E. Brown, one being Joe's son, Joe Leroy Brown, whom I mentioned in a previous chapter. He was the general manager of the Pirates, and had offered Coach the field manager's job, which John declined.*

But the real capper to the Wooden-Brown connection was in the way they lived their lives. In his book, called *Laughter Is a Wonderful Thing,* Joe admitted, "I have always loved baseball more than any other sport." Coach said almost the exact same thing to me the first day we met.

Like Coach, Joe started playing organized baseball when he was only fourteen years old, becoming the youngest player on a town team. Not much later, he played on a semi-pro team in the Trolley League. Even when he was doing comedy acts, he played ball with St. Paul in the summer.

Joe was offered a contract to play baseball for the New York Yankees when he was in his early twenties. John was offered a contract to play for two clubs, the Reds and the Cubs, when he was one year away from his twentieth birthday. Both young men turned down these professional offers for similar reasons. John declined to play professionally so that he could continue his education at Purdue and pursue his dream to teach. Joe refused to sign so that he could continue acting on Broadway and pursue his dream of being a star actor. Despite a growing acting and comedy career, Joe kept playing baseball in the summers in Baltimore and made three dollars per game—and sometimes, as much as twenty dollars a game.

Even when he was one of the most popular movie stars in Hollywood, Joe kept up his intense love for baseball—just like John, who, throughout his coaching career, kept following college and pro baseball. Joe's movie contract had a clause in it

---

* Joe E. Brown's son, Joe L., passed away only a couple months after John passed. He was ninety-one years old.

that gave him a baseball team: the Joe E. Brown All-Stars. He traveled with that team all over the United States, playing exhibition games. At the peak of his movie career, he couldn't leave baseball alone as he became part-owner of the Kansas City Blues Pro Baseball Club. Joe, at times, even anchored baseball games on the radio during his Hollywood career.

Joe sent his two sons to UCLA eight years prior to John being hired by the Bruins. But, to top off the similarities between Joe and John's love for baseball, there was another freakish similarity.

Lou Gehrig was both of these men's all-time favorite player. Lou was a good friend of Joe's, and when Lou broke Major League Baseball's consecutive game streak, Joe wrote to him and asked if he could have the glove he used in all those games. Joe wanted it for his sports collection, which he called in his autobiography "the finest privately-owned sports trophy collection in the world." In fact, it grew so large that he gave part of his collection to UCLA. I remember spending some time at the entrance to UCLA's Kerchoff Hall, admiring all the sports memorabilia Joe had donated.

Lou refused Joe's request, saying that he could have anything else instead—his favorite bat, or even his whole uniform—but he couldn't part with his glove. One fall day, after Lou had played in his 2,130th game, Joe went to Yankee Stadium to watch the World Series and sat next to their dugout. Lou spotted Joe just before the game started and sent the bat boy to ask Joe to meet him inside the dugout. It was there that Lou handed Joe his glove.

John and Joe were both also devoted to their religious principles—John, a Christian, and Joe, a Jew—but neither of them wore their religions on their sleeves. John never pointed to the sky after a ball game, and never mentioned Jesus in any postgame interviews, but he witnessed to Christianity by the way he lived.

Joe never used profanity, and John had only used a "bad"

word once. When Joe was asked to do a movie that had dirty words in it, he declined because he had made a rule that he would never tell a story that he wouldn't want his mother to hear.

John never dated anyone except his wife, Nell. Joe only dated one other girl—and that was only once—besides his wife of fifty-eight years, Kathryn McGraw. John and Nell were married for fifty-three years, until she died in 1985.

Both men believed in helping others in any way that they could. Joe traveled all over the globe to entertain United States service men during World War II. John traveled throughout the U.S. to give speeches to young people and coaches at high schools and colleges, and even to men and women at their businesses and corporations.

John was not a quitter, and neither was Joe. John believed that quitting was too easy. He respected those who did not give up, and teased people who thought of quitting anything, even if it was leaving a game early. When John went to a ball game, he stayed until the end. He liked Yogi Berra's quotation: "It ain't over till it's over!" Joe E. Brown always said, "As far as I'm concerned, no game is ever over until there are three men out in the ninth inning."

Joe thought it was a fine thing to be able to say after a game that you'd given your best. Coach often told his players the same thing, before and after games. It was the basis of his coaching philosophy. In 1933, Joe wrote in his book, " . . . If you felt in your heart that you'd given everything you had, then there wasn't any more you could do." Familiar words?

John and Joe never met. But, in so many ways, they were like two peas in a pod. Those peas were planted on UCLA's Joe E. Brown Field, grown and cultivated by their love for baseball.

AN OPEN MIND

Most basketball and football coaches in high school and college prefer that their players stick to one sport—some coaches demand it—hoping their players choose the sport they coach. Coach Wooden never had a problem with his basketball players playing baseball. His mind was open to it, and he even encouraged it.

"Let them try other things, as long as they have fun doing it," he said. "Too much basketball can make players stale. I want them to be fresh." Coach said this to his friend, Art Reichle, who coached baseball for twenty-five of John's twenty-seven years at UCLA. When I took over after Art retired, one of the first things he told me was, "Don't worry about recruiting John's basketball players to play baseball. He doesn't mind at all." He also told me not to expect the same thing from the football coaches. But, as it turned out, more football players showed up for baseball than basketball, because their seasons did not overlap.

It was extremely difficult for UCLA basketball players to play baseball, especially when they qualified for the playoffs. Twelve of John's last fourteen years were spent in the NCAA Finals. Sometimes the last championship game wasn't played

until a few days into April, and by then our baseball season was three-fifths done. It could be a real challenge for a basketball player to break into the lineup at that late date, but some tried . . . with mixed results.

Gail Goodrich, who played freshman and varsity baseball for two years, said to me, "Coach is not going to tell you what to do. He wants you to make your own decision. He was smart that way."

In Coach Wooden's first couple of years at UCLA, he didn't hesitate to let two of his basketball players, George Stanich and John Matulich, play for Reichle's ball club. Each player made a significant impact on the baseball team, with Stanich going on to play pro baseball and eventually being inducted into both UCLA's Athletic Hall of Fame and the UCLA Baseball Hall of Fame.

Stanich and Matulich contributed to Coach Wooden's 1949–1950 team, winning UCLA's first ever Pacific Coast Conference championship. Matulich is the only Bruin basketball player to give up basketball to play baseball at UCLA. Matulich told me, "After playing for Coach Wooden's second team at UCLA, I was aware that Coach had recruited some very good players for the following season. I asked him what my chances were of playing much my second year. He was very honest with me and said, 'I doubt you will see much playing time, John. You would play more on the baseball team. I would welcome you back if that is what you decide. It's your decision.' I decided then to concentrate on baseball."

Matulich became a star first baseman on the Bruins varsity team and served as Coach Wooden's graduate assistant coach for a couple of years. Talk about a small world—John Matulich became the head basketball coach at Riverside Junior College, and coached my brother and me for one and a half years there. He is the man who contacted Coach Reichle and told him about the Adams twins, which eventually led to the two of us getting into UCLA.

During my playing years at UCLA, Gail Goodrich joined our 1962 UCLA baseball varsity team after basketball season was over, and eventually won the first baseman's job. My locker was close to his, and I remember quite vividly the picture of Gail putting on his back brace before every practice. I asked him, "How do you even bend over for ground balls, wearing that thing?"

"It doesn't bother me," he said. "I just bend my knees more. I wore it the whole season I played on the frosh basketball team."

At the time, I questioned how this skinny and frail-looking kid—*maybe* six feet tall and not much more than 160 pounds—could ever last through a rigorous varsity basketball season. Little did I know then that he would lead UCLA to two national basketball championships, earn All-American honors, and be an All-Star in the NBA. His teammate on the Lakers, Elgin Baylor, handed him the nickname "Stumpy" because of his relatively small size. In his NBA career, Stumpy led the Lakers to a championship, made five All-Star teams, and played for fourteen years. Gail proved to many basketball experts and non-experts (like me) that he wasn't too frail for the NBA.

Coach Wooden was the exception. Early on in Gail's pro career, he said to me, "Just watch, Gary. He's going to surprise a lot of people. He has quickness, and he can shoot accurately from anywhere on the court. But, best of all, he's left-handed. There aren't many in pro ball, so he will be tough to guard. Gail will drive right past them and they won't be able to stop him from going to the basket."

Gail was an agile, rangy, sure-handed first baseman for our 1962 UCLA team. But there was a play at Cal—not his fault—I wish he could have made that cost us the game. It occurred in the bottom of the ninth inning, and we were winning 3–2. Cal had runners on second and third. All we needed was one more out, and the victory would be ours. I was playing third base when a routine grounder was hit my way. I fielded it easily, and then made my throw to Gail. I watched as the ball kept tailing

away from him. Gail stretched as far apart as his legs would allow and his gangly arms could reach, but my wild throw missed his glove by several inches. It was the final play of the game, and a victory for Cal as both runners scored on my throwing error. I felt horrible, and sat gloomily by myself on the bus trip back to our hotel. I had let the whole team down.

Despite what they say about time healing all wounds, that error still haunts me and remains one of my lowlights as a player. Coach Wooden always said, "You win as a team, and you lose as a team." Nevertheless, it's difficult to forget an error that made the difference between a win and a loss.

One day, when Coach and I were talking about Gail Goodrich, he remarked, "Gail wasn't tall, but he had long and gangly arms." I thought back to my wild throw at our game against Cal. "Not long enough, John," I replied.

Years later, when Gail and I talked on the phone, I reminded him of the error I made at Cal. He didn't remember it. I also told him that I had told the story to Coach Wooden, and that Coach had mentioned his long arms. Gail did acknowledge that his arms were more suited for an over-six-foor-four body. "I think that's one of the reasons Coach Wooden recruited me," he said. "I could play better defense for my size, stealing balls, blocking passes and shots, and rebounding like a taller man who had normal-size arms."

I told him that I always wished his arms were longer, so that he could have caught my throw and I wouldn't have to live with the memory of that error. I was serious, but Gail's reply was blunt. "I think it's time to move on, Gary," he said, laughing. I tried to laugh, too.

Offensively, Gail had a sweet, smooth swing. But after coming out from basketball so late, his timing was not as it should have been. Hitting is all about timing, and that does not come overnight, even for the greatest of athletes. Gail hit over .400 for the freshman team and, in his only year on the varsity, hit close to .200. That was more than a hundred points higher than another UCLA basketball player who played baseball in 1940—a young man named Jackie Robinson.

In 1963, when I was assisting Coach Reichle with the varsity, our starting shortstop was Keith Erickson. As mentioned previously, it was partly due to Coach's open mind—allowing Keith to play both basketball *and* baseball—that brought Keith to UCLA.

Keith's basketball teammate, Walt Hazzard, came out for the team that year as well. I hit Keith and Walt ground balls, and both displayed outstanding footwork. I didn't have to tell them to be quick with their feet—that had already been ingrained in them by Coach Wooden.

For some reason, Hazzard stopped showing up after only a couple of weeks of practice, but Erickson stuck it out. If Keith had concentrated only on baseball, I believe he could have made it to the major leagues. He possessed all the ingredients that professional scouts look for in a shortstop. He was rangy, fluid, and quick of hand and foot, with a strong and accurate arm. If he didn't cut it at shortstop, I felt he could have easily adapted to the outfield, especially center field, where he would have had tremendous range. His swing needed some polishing, but I'm sure that professional hitting coaches and Keith's determination would have been enough to iron it out in due time. He had enough "pop" in his bat to be more than just a singles hitter.

In Keith's only season of baseball, he hit a respectable .250 and had a home run on Joe E. Brown Field, where the fences were a long way from home plate. He was the most athletic player on our team. It was no wonder that Coach Wooden put him in the spot where athleticism was needed most in UCLA's famous zone press.

"Coach Wooden was never against me playing baseball," Keith told me. "I didn't play baseball after my sophomore year because we ended up winning the NCAA championship in the 1963–1964 season. Our season went so long, going all the way to the final four, that too much of the baseball season was gone

for me to join that late. It was just our success in basketball that kept me from playing any more baseball."

Keith was an excellent example of what Coach Wooden meant when he said he wanted his players to have fun trying other things besides basketball in the off-season. Keith not only tried volleyball in the summers, but he was also one of the most talented players in all of Southern California, and had fun playing on the sandy beaches of Santa Monica and Venice.

"I played on the USA Olympic Volleyball team in Tokyo, Japan," Keith said. "I believe I missed a little bit of school at that time, but [Coach] was not opposed to that, either. He was mainly concerned that I get to class when I was supposed to be there, as he was with all of his players. What a great blessing to have played for him."

In my thirty years as UCLA's head baseball coach, Raymond Townsend is the only basketball-baseball player I coached. Raymond played four years of baseball at UCLA (his first year was with the freshman team, in which he batted .400 in only fourteen games). He played for Coach Wooden's last NCAA championship team in 1974–1975, a team that Coach once said had given him "the greatest satisfaction of coaching, since no one expected us to win, and I never had a problem with a single player the whole year long."

Townsend was a switch-hitting infielder who had a UCLA career batting average of .319. Known for his superlative defense on the basketball court, he also played outstanding defense on the ball diamond. Except for catcher, he played every defensive position in the infield.

After Raymond's senior year at UCLA, he was drafted in the first round by the NBA's Golden State Warriors, and also drafted in the sixth round by Major League Baseball's Cincinnati Reds.

Raymond also played high school baseball and wanted to go to a college, where he would be permitted to play both basketball and baseball. "Coach Wooden won the recruiting battle for me when he said, 'Raymond, you can play basketball *and* baseball at UCLA.'" Gene Bartow, who coached Raymond the next two years, and Gary Cunningham, who coached him his senior year, both followed up on Coach Wooden's promise and permitted Raymond to play baseball.

A sportswriter for the *Los Angeles Times,* John Strege, wrote an article about Raymond's participation in dual sports during his sophomore year. Raymond was quoted in that article, saying, "I don't think [Adams] expected me to come out for baseball. I'd see him on campus and say, 'Hey, Coach, I'm coming out.' He would say, 'We'd like to have you.' But that's all he said."

Strege quoted me, too: "I'd been hearing the same thing from [UCLA quarterback and highly drafted baseball player] John Sciarra for two years." Sciarra never did turn out for baseball.

As challenging as it was for Raymond to play both sports, he would never have been successful at it without his positive attitude and a strong belief in his God-given talent. Just as Coach Wooden had told Coach Reichle in the late 1940s, he permitted his players to try other things, as long as they had fun doing it. Raymond had fun playing baseball at UCLA. "I'm just out there, having fun," he told the *Times*. "I'm thankful God gave me enough talent to play both sports."

I truly believe that every time Coach Wooden asked me, "How's Raymond doing out there, Gary?" he mostly wanted to know if he was having fun. That's why I usually answered, "He looks like he's having fun, Coach."

I'll always be grateful to Coach because, if it were not for his open-mindedness, I would never have had the pleasure of coaching or playing with his basketball players— Hazzard (briefly), Goodrich, Erickson, and Townsend.

A RARE BASEBALL INTERVIEW

In the spring of 1980, I received a phone call from John Herbold, the highly successful coach of perennial baseball power Lakewood High School, in California. Coach Herbold also served as a reporter for *Collegiate Baseball*—a newspaper we coaches referred to at the time as "the bible of college baseball." Herbold wanted me to do him a favor.

"Gary, would you ask Coach Wooden if he'd grant me an interview for our paper?"

"Of course," I said, knowing Coach Wooden would be happy to talk about his favorite sport to a baseball man for a baseball-only publication.

When I informed Coach about Herbold's request and told him about the sterling reputation of the newspaper, he responded exactly as I had expected. The arrangements were made, and Herbold and Coach Wooden carried the ball from there.

Although I had told Herbold about Coach Wooden's fondness for baseball, I don't think he was prepared for John's first statement in that interview: "Baseball's my favorite game—always has been." Herbold opened his story with those exact words, and wrote two articles that appeared in the *Collegiate Baseball* newspaper on April 4 and 18, 1980. The Stanford cum laude graduate's two-part series was the first public notice of Coach Wooden's love for the game of baseball.

Below are some snippets from John's quotes in the interview:

"Had I been born in a baseball state like Texas or California instead of a basketball hotbed like Indiana, I might have become a professional baseball player or college baseball coach because, not only did I love to play baseball, but I love to coach it, too. . . . I loved to coach baseball . . . but the weather in California is so much better than the Midwest . . . when you're inside so much. One reason, I guess, that I loved baseball is that it meant we finally could get outside. . . . Baseball's strength is that it hasn't changed too much, and it's shown great consistency in its rules, thus allowing the fans to keep up with the game."

At the time these articles appeared, Coach Wooden and I had been sharing our tiny office for five years. One morning, when I arrived at the office, there were some newspaper clippings lying on the desk. Attached to those clippings was a note in Coach's handwriting.

> *Gary—*
> *I thought you might be interested in these.*
> *J.W.*

He had cut out the articles from *Collegiate Baseball*, and wanted me to have them. Although I had heard that the articles had been published, I had yet to read them because my subscription to the newspaper was always mailed to my parents' home in Oceanside, where I had not been able to visit since baseball season started. I sat down at the desk and read the articles for the first time.

I think Coach wanted to be sure I read the articles so that I could see in print what he had been telling me in our previous chats. Although I was hesitant about writing this next bit, lest

I appear self-important, I chose to include it because it speaks of a budding friendship in those early innings.

I was flattered by Coach's mention of me in the articles. "I also attend as many UCLA games as I can," he had said, "because I like to watch Gary Adams, of whom I'm very fond. In my younger days, I would have liked to help him if he'd asked me, but I hurt my back years ago; so I can't handle a fungo bat anymore, and I have been away from baseball a long time now."

Imagine that—Coach Wooden, my assistant coach, fungoing ground balls to our infielders! I had never even thought of asking him, figuring he was too busy with other things. Goodness gracious, I would have been thrilled to have him just sitting in the dugout as our bench coach!

Coach went on to tell Herbold how he used to watch UCLA ball games from the time he arrived at UCLA. "I was always just a UCLA fan who spent many of my spring afternoons watching Art Reichle's teams play at the old Joe E. Brown Field."

Late in the interview, Coach said, "There's no one way to coach. You have to be yourself. That is what I tell Gary Adams, who's done such a great job at UCLA because he's good on fundamentals."

When I finished reading the clippings, I was overwhelmed and humbled by the complimentary words from one of the greatest—if not *the* greatest—coach in history. I appreciated his words as much as I treasured those times when a player, at the end of his career, looks me in the eyes and says, "Thanks for everything, Coach." That is a coach's greatest reward, worth more than trophies on shelves or anything money can buy.

John's thoughtfulness in sharing those clippings with me is a lasting memory of the man I grew to admire and love.

TWO SIMILAR COACHES

As often as Coach Wooden and I shared our thoughts and feelings in that tiny office for eight years, I tried my best to avoid pestering him all the time with questions or my team's problems—though whenever I did, he didn't seem to mind. Maybe it was my imagination, but at times, he even looked pleased that I "bothered" him with such things.

It was at those times that I would see, in his deep blue eyes, a look of understanding. At other times, those eyes appeared determined to send a message without uttering a single word. Always, he really *looked* at me. That look was very familiar—reminding me of my first coach when I was just ten years old.

Until I was ten, I had never played baseball on an organized team. Little League hadn't arrived in our small town in Ohio yet, but the Knothole League was the biggest and best thing going in the summertime for youths up to twelve years of age. I played with the Hammond Bulldogs. None of the teams in the league wore uniforms, like they all do in Little League today, but I wore my Levi's and my green Bulldogs T-shirt with pride.

The Bulldogs coach was Dick Kaiser, my uncle, who was a firm disciplinarian. We players felt lucky to have him as a coach, and believed that he knew more about baseball than

any coach in our league—maybe even in the whole town. He taught us the fundamentals and made sure we executed them properly in practice and in games. If we didn't execute to his satisfaction, he let us know about it with his words and his eyes. Like Coach Wooden, his eyes delivered his message, even if you missed his words.

Coach Kaiser had the respect of every player on our team, partly because he had been a great high school athlete in Ohio—a basketball and baseball letterman, and captain of his football team. After graduating, Ohio State offered him a scholarship to play football, but World War II broke out and he joined the navy instead. Much of our respect came from his service in that war. We looked past the fact that he coached us from his wheelchair—he was a paraplegic as a result of the Japanese air and submarine attacks on his aircraft carrier, the USS *Hornet*.

I think my teammates were afraid of Coach Kaiser, and I probably would have been just as afraid if I had not known him or seen him in a different light. Sitting on Uncle Dick's couch in his living room and listening to him tell funny stories and hearing him laugh put me at ease. I felt comfortable and relaxed around him, but I knew there was a limit.

Uncle Dick showed me his limits one morning when my brother and I stayed overnight at his house. When Aunt Lorraine placed a plate of over easy eggs in front of us, we told her and Uncle Dick, "We don't eat eggs."

Dick turned and gave us a look. "Oh, yes, you will."

We learned to eat eggs that day and like them.

I knew, if I didn't listen carefully to Coach Kaiser on the ball field, that I would risk seeing that same penetrating look.

I saw it in Coach Wooden's eyes for the first time one morning in our office. After a casual conversation, he got up from our swivel chair in front of the desk, stepped toward the door, and prepared to leave. I left my seat in the chair next to the wall and sat down in the swivel chair he had just vacated. We were about to say goodbye when I leaned back in my chair, raised my feet off the floor, and set them on top of our desk.

When I looked up at Coach, I thought I was seeing my Uncle Dick all over again. His eyes said, "We don't do that here, Gary."

Yes, Coach Wooden and Coach Kaiser were two similar coaches in many ways, but especially in the way they taught their lessons—just by the way they looked at you.

I always felt welcome around Coach Wooden, but I knew there was a limit—an invisible boundary that I didn't care to trespass because of my respect for the man. When I was with Coach Wooden, I believe I felt much like his players must have felt when they played for him—and like my teammates and I felt many years earlier, when we were playing for Coach Kaiser.

OUR HEROES

There were times, in our office, when Coach Wooden and I just sat back in our uncomfortable chairs and talked about anything and everything. Topics ran from world events to UCLA campus events (mainly sports), but we both particularly enjoyed discussing our favorite heroes.

One of America's most famous cowboys, Will Rogers, once said, "We can't all be heroes, because somebody has to sit on the curb and clap as they go by."

What he said is true, but Coach Wooden put a more positive spin on the subject. "Without heroes," he said, "we are just plain people, and would not know where we could go." I never knew if that was his original idea or if he was quoting someone else, but I knew that he truly believed it.

Abraham Lincoln's name came from Coach's lips at almost every discussion we had about heroes. I believe John knew as much about Lincoln as any historian did. As John said, "I have many books about Lincoln—probably as many books about him as any American." John often quoted from memory much of what Lincoln had written and said. He hardly made a speech without some reference to Lincoln.

Coach also admired Martin Luther King Jr. Although Coach

didn't say so, I assumed that part of his admiration for King came from the fact that he was a devout Christian. King, being a Southern Baptist minister, of course, was more obvious about his belief in Jesus. Coach did not wear his religion on his sleeve, and regular acquaintances would never have known he was a Christian unless they asked . . . or got to know him well enough to figure it out.

One day, when we were talking about character, Coach said, "It is easy to be nice and polite after a win and when all is going well for you, but you must learn to have the same quality of character even when you lose and things are not going well."

Then he quoted Martin Luther King Jr.: "The measure of a man is *not* where he stands at times of comfort or convenience, but the ultimate measure of a man is where he stands at times of *challenge*."

Coach then said to me, "Don't be reluctant to use King's quote when your team is going through rough times, Gary."

I never forgot it. I used it often, as my players would attest—during rough times and almost always on the holiday honoring Martin Luther King Jr. I wondered if Coach's players ever heard John use King's quote. His teams rarely experienced hard times, although every NCAA playoff game was a challenge.

John considered Mother Teresa to be a heroine. Coach respected her very much, because, as he said, "her life was spent helping others."

Besides discussing our heroes of all genres, we also spent hours talking about our sports heroes. Coach recalled with some nostalgia his Yankees idol, first baseman Lou Gehrig. "When I was a youngster playing baseball, 'Iron Man' Gehrig was the player I pretended to be every time I came to bat—even though he hit from the left side, and I hit from the right.

"When I became a coach, my heroes were other coaches, such as my basketball coach at Purdue, Ward 'Piggy' Lambert. Amos Alonzo Stagg and Frank Leahy were my favorite football coaches, and I admired the Brooklyn Dodgers manager, Walter

'Smokey' Alston."

Listening to Coach, I learned a great deal about these men. The way he respected and honored them was evident by the tone in which he spoke. I'm sure he felt that each one of his heroes, in some way or another, had helped mold him into the coach and the man he had become.

John's greatest hero—and his best mentor—was his dad. He would always, but briefly, remind me of this fact whenever we talked about our heroes, yet he talked less about his dad than he did about Lincoln and the others.

I'll never forget Coach's reaction when I told him who my hero had been in my youth. "Nuxhall?" he asked, his nose wrinkled and eyebrows furrowed. "You mean the boy who pitched for the Reds?"

"Yep," I answered. "That's the one. Joe Nuxhall lived in my hometown, Hamilton, Ohio. He was ten years older than me, but all of us youngsters had heard stories about the 'wonder boy' who played on the same ball fields and basketball courts that we played on. He was a hero for all of us who played sports."

Coach said, "Well, I don't have to tell you that he holds the record for being the youngest player ever to play in the major leagues."

"Yes," I said. "Joe was only fifteen years old."

Coach shook his head. "I rarely use the word 'never,' but I do believe that is a record that will never be broken."

I told John how I followed Joe ten years later to the same junior high school that he attended. Joe was a giant for his age, at six feet three inches and 195 pounds, and the star of the ninth grade basketball team. Most folks in Hamilton believed he would be a better basketball player than a baseball player. In fact, Joe's junior high team was so good that their coach, Louis "Bud" Dubois, scheduled games with high school teams—and beat them.

When I made the Wilson Junior High basketball team and it came time for Coach Dubois to hand out uniform jerseys, everyone on the team wanted to wear Joe's jersey. I wanted number fifty-nine so badly that I tussled with some players for it until I finally put it on. I wore it at every game, even though it hung below my knees and I had to roll it up and tuck it inside my trunks. Half of the "59" disappeared inside my pants, making it look like I was wearing "–0" instead.

Coach grinned at this, and asked, "Did your team play the high schools, also?"

"No, Coach," I said. "We had no boy wonders on our team. We were undersized and had trouble beating the other junior high teams."

Yes, Coach and I enjoyed talking about our heroes, but there was one particular day when John asked me a question that sparked even greater interest in the subject.

Coach slowly leaned forward in his chair, pointed a finger in my direction, and asked, "Of all the great athletes we've had at UCLA, who would be most qualified as an American hero?"

I asked, "You mean who was not only great in sports at UCLA, but also did great things outside of sports?"

"Yes, Gary, who served our country and spent their lives helping others as much as they honored UCLA in athletics?"

I hesitated. I had never considered the question before. Finally, I said, "Probably Jackie Robinson would be one." Coach nodded in agreement.

The two of us talked at length about the exploits of Jackie Robinson at UCLA and his amazing life afterward, but eventually John said, "Certainly Jackie is one great American hero. Now, anyone else from UCLA you would call an American hero?"

My mind went blank as John patiently waited for another name. By the look on his face I knew he had a name in mind, maybe more than one. Still, I sat silently, scratching my head.

John offered a hint. "You should know this great man . . . after all, you went to school with him."

The first person I thought of was Billy Kilmer, but knowing how John felt about Kilmer's lack of athleticism, I ruled him

out. Suddenly, I pulled the chain on the light bulb hanging over my head, and I bolted out the answer. "Rafer Johnson!"

Coach smiled broadly and, with a wink, said, "Those two— Robinson and Johnson—are slam-dunk UCLA-American heroes." He was teasing me a bit, because he knew I was aware of his dislike of slam dunks.

Coach suggested a couple more candidates for our prized list. "How about Ralph Bunche, Gary? He played basketball here. In fact, he played on UCLA's first-ever basketball team, and was the valedictorian of his class in 1927."

This was the first I had ever heard of Ralph Bunche ever playing basketball at UCLA. I only knew that he had attended UCLA and eventually won the Nobel Peace Prize, and that there was a building on campus named after him.

Thinking only of that building, I told Coach, "That building they built in his name is the darned awfulest ugly thing on our campus. Looks like a giant waffle iron, if you ask me."

Coach snapped a quick grin, but stuck to the topic at hand. "He is a solid candidate, don't you think?"

How could I disagree? "Yes, of course, John."

Then Coach added with a frown, "But, if I do recall, he wasn't a front-line player on the basketball team—that might exclude him."

Then he mentioned UCLA's Arthur Ashe, a great tennis player. Coach enlightened me on Ashe's career. "You know Gary, our basketball team was not the only UCLA national championship team in 1965. Arthur won the NCAA men's single title and led our tennis team to the championship. Besides, he's the only black man to win the Wimbledon Tournament. In my opinion, he's doing the most to make tennis a popular sport in America."

At that time (1981), neither of us knew what Ashe would accomplish outside of tennis, and how he would become a huge voice in the battle against AIDS after contracting HIV from a blood transfusion during his second heart surgery that ultimately led to his death in 1993. We also didn't know that he would be active in civil rights causes, especially the fight against apartheid in South Africa. Had we known then what we learned subsequent to 1981, Coach and I would have placed him near the "slam-dunk-two."

Coach became slightly agitated when he brought up the name of Kenneth Washington. The veins in his neck were more evident as he said, "Our nation honors Jackie Robinson for breaking the color barrier in baseball—and rightfully so—but it is a disgrace that our Kenneth is not honored also for being the first black man to play in the National Football League. The NFL was just as segregated as Major League Baseball, until Kenneth came along."

I told Coach that I was aware of Washington playing football and baseball at UCLA, but I admitted that I didn't know whether he was a good player or not.

Again, Coach enlightened me. "I don't know about his baseball-playing days at UCLA, either, but I have heard from some former UCLA football players that claim he was the best college football player in the nation."

I checked on Washington's career at UCLA and learned that he had led the nation in total yards in 1939—the year I was born. UCLA honored Washington as a charter member of the UCLA Athletic Hall of Fame in 1984. He was also inducted into the UCLA Baseball Hall of Fame as a charter member in 1988.

After John and I discussed Kenneth Washington, he asked me, "Gary, are there any other UCLA baseball players that might make our list of American heroes?"

"Yes, there's one who was a star baseball player, who also, as you said before, served others: Dr. Bobby Brown."

Coach's eyes grew brighter, "Of course, Bobby Brown, he played third base for my Yankees. I didn't know he went to UCLA."

"Yes, he started out attending Stanford, but eventually played baseball for UCLA and graduated from here. I know that he led the Bruins to their first-ever league championship. I be-

lieve it was sometime in the mid-1940s."

John knew Brown's record as a Yankee. "Well, Gary, he also played on some of the best Yankees teams when they won some World Series championships. As I recall, he played his best in those World Series games."

"I don't know about that, John, but I do know that he studied to become a doctor while he was with the Yankees. That's why I think he makes our list of American heroes . . . he became a doctor, and that in itself says how much he helped others."

Several weeks after we discussed Dr. Bobby Brown, I learned that Coach's memory was, once again, right on—Brown certainly rose to the occasion when he played in the World Series. His batting average was .439 in seventeen games. Also, Brown's teams won the World Series in four of the eight years he was with the Yankees. Dr. Brown also became Major League Baseball's president of the American League for ten years (1984–1994).

One of Brown's closest friends, and his roommate when the Yankees went on the road, was Yogi Berra. There's a story about the time the two of them were in their hotel room. Yogi was reading a comic book, and Brown was reading *Boyd's Pathology*. When Yogi finished his comic, he turned to Brown and said, "So, how's yours turning out?"

When Bobby was inducted into our UCLA Baseball Hall of Fame, he told me another funny story regarding his good friend, Yogi. He said, "My wife and I were in a New York hotel on a hot summer day for an event I had to attend as the president of the American League. I was in my coat and tie, my wife was all dressed up, and we were on the elevator when it stopped at another floor. The door opened, and there was Yogi standing there, looking quite dapper in his coat and tie. My wife said, 'Gee, Yogi, you certainly look cool this evening.' To which Yogi replied, 'Thanks, Mrs. Brown, you're not looking so hot yourself.'"

One of John's stars on his last NCAA championship team in 1975, Dave Meyers, had a younger sister who played women's basketball at UCLA. Ann Meyers's name had recently been in the news because she was the first and only female to sign a National Basketball Association contract. In 1980, she reportedly signed for $50,000 to play for the Indiana Pacers.

Coach was a big fan of Ann's, saying, "I enjoyed going to the UCLA ladies games and watching Annie play. She dominated the game, not just because of her offense, but also because of her defense. It was amazing how she anticipated where the ball was going. She stole a bunch of passes every game I attended."

Ann was most instrumental in putting women's basketball on the map—both in collegiate sports and professionally. John and I didn't know in 1981 that Ann would choose to marry one of our Dodgers heroes, Don Drysdale, five years later. We were delighted when it happened, although their marriage didn't influence our decision to include her in our honored list of UCLA's and America's heroes.

I had the privilege of talking with Ann about Coach Wooden, and she confirmed how much Coach loved baseball. Ann affectionately called Coach "Papa" as she described the time he came to her home to celebrate Don's birthday. "I watched Gene Mauch, Vin Scully, Don, and Papa sit down and talk about baseball for a long time. Papa was in seventh heaven."

Coach reminded me of two other ladies who deserved our attention. "Gary, don't forget about our softball team," he said. "Sharron Backus has done quite well coaching our ladies to national championships, and that young girl, Sue Enquist, was quite a player."*

Talking about our UCLA heroes was one of our greatest pleasures when we shared that tiny office in the athletic department. Although I can't remember everyone we discussed,

---

* Coach Wooden mentioned these two coaches before we knew just how successful they would become. Sue Enquist assisted Sharron Backus for nine years and eventually became the head coach. Between the two of them, they led UCLA's softball team to eleven national championships—one more than Coach Wooden. I coached alongside Sharron and Sue for thirty years. I was amazed at their ability to teach and lead their players, and how much they cared about them. In turn, their players respected and loved their coaches dearly.

names surfaced that most UCLA fans would know instantly, like Lewis Alcindor (Kareem Abdul-Jabbar), Gary Beban, Paul Cameron, Bob Davenport, Gail Goodrich, Walt Hazzard, Kirk Kilgour, Donn Moomaw, George Stanich, Bill Walton, Bob Waterfield, and coaches Jim Bush, Glenn Bassett, Bob Horn, Billie Moore, Red Sanders, "Ducky" Drake, Al Scates, and a football coach who was just beginning to make a name for himself, Terry Donahue.

Time and again, when John and I happened to meet on or off campus, he would ask, "Do you have any new candidates for our list of UCLA-American heroes?" Sometimes I would beat him to it, and ask him the same question.

We had no doubt that the top two on our list were Jackie Robinson and Rafer Johnson, but we were always looking for that third slam-dunk hero to come along. We finally discovered him several years later. He isn't even in the UCLA Athletic Hall of Fame. That's a story for the middle innings.

THE MIDDLE INNINGS
1983-2002

A TOUGH FOURTH INNING

Coach Wooden told me more than once that the middle innings of a ball game are the toughest ones to play. "The first three innings, everyone is excited," he explained. "The adrenalin is flowing after the national anthem, and the coach's pep talk is fresh in mind." John said this, even though he seldom gave pep talks before games, and certainly not elaborate ones.

"Most people think the *last* three innings are the toughest," John continued. "They are tough for the coaches because they are the ones who need to do the cerebral work, big decisions such as pulling the pitcher or leaving him in, pinch hitting for a weak hitter to spark a rally or keep the original hitter at the plate because his defense is superior.

"Yes, the last innings can be tough on the coaches and managers. But I believe they are the easiest on the players. Young people have a tendency to save their energy and enthusiasm until the end—that's when their foot presses harder on the accelerator. They have a natural tendency to coast during the middle innings. Frankly, I believe players should keep their foot pressed firmly on the accelerator in *every* inning, being especially careful to maintain it in the middle innings.

"I always told my players that a free throw made in the middle of the game is just as important as the one made late in the game. It takes a real competitor to compete as hard in the middle of the game as he does at the beginning and the end of the game."

John had a habit of checking major league line scores of ball games. He would look to see who scored the most runs in the fourth, fifth, and sixth innings. "Gary," he said, "you'd be surprised how many games are won or lost in the middle innings."

After listening to John, I began looking at the line scores, giving particular attention to the middle innings. I looked again at the photo sitting on my shelf at home—the one of my friend, Chris Krug, facing Koufax in the top of the ninth. That photo shows the stadium scoreboard behind Koufax. Underneath every inning, except one, there are zeroes. The Dodgers won it with a single run in the fifth inning—right smack in the middle of the game. I never kept a *written* record of my findings, but Coach's theory rang true as I scanned the line scores.

I always reminded my players that the middle innings were just as important, or more important, than the early and late innings. I told them many times when those middle innings came up, "Let's keep our foot on the gas pedal and beat them in the middle innings." I think it helped motivate them.

In the summer of 1982, Coach suddenly stopped coming to our office and seldom visited UCLA. His priority now was Nell, his wife of fifty-one years. She went to the hospital for a hip replacement, but her heart stopped beating in the middle of the surgery. The doctors were able to restart her heart again and finished the surgery, but immediately afterward, she suffered another heart attack. She lapsed into a coma and didn't come out of it for ninety-three days.

John's life changed. His entire schedule depended upon Nell's condition. For two and a half years, Nell was in and out of ill health until she finally died on March 21, 1985. It was a devastating blow to Coach. He was hit, surprisingly, by a pitch thrown from God—a thousand times harder than any pitch had ever slammed into a batter. John had watched Nell suffer for a long time. He couldn't understand why a good and understanding God would allow this to happen. His only solace was that he believed she was in a better place. Still, he felt unrelenting sadness because his beloved Nell had left him behind.

He told me, years later, "When my Nellie died, depression overcame me. I wanted to die so I could be with her. But I never thought of suicide."

Those years from 1982 to 1985 were the beginning of the middle innings of our friendship, yet they were much tougher than any fourth inning a ball game could ever muster. Coach battled hard to overcome the adversity that befell him.

He tried everything to snap out of it. It helped to write letters to Nell, which he did every twenty-first day of each month. He would seal the letter, kiss it, and lay it on the pillow on her side of the bed. He never let anyone read those letters. "They were just between Nell and me," he said.

His good friend, Tony Spino, told me that he thought the birth of Coach's first great-grandchild, in September of 1985, had a way of revitalizing John. "When Cori came into Coach's life, it was something like a miracle," he said. "I think Coach thought of Cori as a gift from God, to fill the void left by Nell." Tony might be right, because after a tough fourth inning, Coach began living again . . . but he never stopped writing his letters to Nell.

When we talked about the middle innings, I was reminded of how tough Coach was in his own personal battle. He walked the walk, living up to his own words: "It takes a real competitor to compete as hard in the middle of the game as he does in the beginning and end of the game."*

---

* In the 2012 MLB Playoffs and World Series, the teams that prevented their opponents from scoring more runs than their own team scored in the *middle innings* won thirty-two of the thirty-three games played. In the final World Series game, the Giants beat the Tigers 4–3 in ten innings, outscoring the Tigers 2–1 in the middle innings.

THREE
SLAM-DUNK HEROES

Coach and I regularly discussed the greatness of Jackie Robinson and Rafer Johnson as true "UCLA-American heroes," and consistently researched who our third "slam-dunk" hero should be.

We had scores of UCLA athletes to choose from, which is why UCLA has won more NCAA championship titles (108, as of March 2012) than any college in America. UCLA has supplied the USA Olympic teams with more Olympians and won more Olympic Gold Medals from 1984 to 2012 than any other institution. In fact, if UCLA was a country, it would stand in fifth place behind the USA, China, Russia, and Germany for most gold medals won since 1984. UCLA's all-time medal count, as of 2012, is 250 medals won—half of them gold.

UCLA is also among the top universities in producing professional athletes. In baseball, for example, in the 1991 season, twenty former Bruins were playing in the major leagues, and another Bruin, Dr. Bobby Brown, was the American League president at the time—a record for the most major league players in one season coming from the same college.

Most UCLA alumni will be able to answer this two-part trivia question: What college in America is the only one to have had the Most Valuable Player in the NFL's Super Bowl, the NBA's Championship Series, and the MLB's World Series?

The easy answer is "UCLA." However, not all alums can name the athletes who won those three MVP awards. The answers are: Troy Aikman in the 1993 Super Bowl; Kareem Abdul-Jabbar in the 1985 NBA championships; and Troy Glaus in the 2002 World Series.

During all of our discussions about that third slam-dunk hero, Coach Wooden's name never came up. He did not qualify. He did not play any sport at UCLA, though I am positive that, had he even played on the tiddlywink team, he would have easily been our third. I doubt he would have appreciated the title, though—"*slam-dunk* hero."

Nevertheless, Coach sincerely enjoyed playing our little game of hero-naming.

I once wrote something on a scratch pad that pretty much explained my reasons why Coach was an American hero:

> *John is more than just a coach, more than just a legend, because of the championships and number of games he won. John Wooden is a man whose life, after he finished coaching, had just as great an impact on America as his life during his coaching. He was not only our greatest coach in American history; he was our greatest ex-coach. A mentor, role model, and teacher for thousands of young and old Americans, John became a national hero because of the wisdom of his words, the way he lived, and the way he helped others.*

It was hard to hide my excitement when I told John that I had another outstanding candidate for our third slam-dunk hero. He seemed anxious to hear how I had made my discovery "so late in our game."

In 1988, when I was looking for a way to inform the UCLA

alumni and its fans of the tradition and history of UCLA baseball, I decided to inaugurate a special Baseball Hall of Fame. I also
did it to educate, inspire, and motivate the current UCLA teams.

I asked the baseball alumni to nominate the players for
induction and to include information about each one. In that
first year, there were twelve charter members selected. Jackie Robinson was the most familiar name, but others were certainly recognizable, such as Dr. Bobby Brown, Chris Chambliss,
Kenny Washington, Art Reichle, and Eric Karros.

But one unfamiliar name captured everyone's attention the
night of the inaugural Baseball Hall of Fame induction ceremony. The audience was in awe of his heroics in World War II and
more. When I told Coach Wooden about this man, "flabbergasted" is the best word to use for describing his reaction.

LYNN "BUCK" COMPTON

Lynn "Buck" Compton played football and baseball at UCLA.
His 1942 football team was the best team in UCLA history
up to that time, and had earned a bid to the Rose Bowl. Buck
played both ways for the Bruins, a guard on defense and offense, blocking for his great quarterback, Bob Waterfield. In
baseball, he was a sure-handed All-Conference catcher and line-
drive hitter for three years, batting "about .340" his final season, when his teammates voted him captain.

That is a brief synopsis of his UCLA sports history. What
happened *after* he finished at UCLA helped shape American
history. When I told Coach Wooden the story of Buck Compton, he emphatically concurred that Buck belonged in the slam-
dunk category with Jackie and Rafer.

John remembered Buck. "He was one of the first people I
met in California," he said. "It was at Art's home. I think Buck
was president or director of the American Legion outfit near
Westwood. I spoke at their luncheon during my early years at
UCLA. Buck didn't say anything about his heroics in the war."

Lieutenant Buck Compton's heroism in World War II won him the Silver Star, the third highest military decoration for heroism in combat and for valor in the face of the enemy. He also received a Purple Heart for the injuries he sustained in combat.

Tom Hanks and Steven Spielberg produced and directed an HBO series called *Band of Brothers*, and Buck's character played a large part in that production. The series centered on Buck's Company E paratroopers and their military missions in Europe. Their first mission was on June 6, 1944, the night prior to the famous invasion of Normandy. Company E parachuted in the dark to meet the enemy head-on for the purpose of softening the beach landing for 23,000 troops the next day.

No doubt about it, the allied troops landing in Utah Beach in Normandy had an easier time of it because of what Buck's 2d Platoon of Easy Company accomplished. Buck, with a few others, knocked out four 105 mms guns that were firing on the troops landing on the beach. Buck and his men saved many boys' lives on D-Day, which was the start of the allied effort to free Europe from Nazi occupation.

On the afternoon of July 19, 2010, I called Buck at his home to get more details of his role in that invasion. We had last talked at his Baseball Hall of Fame induction in 1988. I told Buck that I sometimes related his story of bravery to my teams, but most of my information came from some of the older UCLA alumni. This is the version of Buck's heroics as I learned it.

Buck's troops were stalled by some Nazi gunners that were located inside a waist-high trench. Buck and another volunteer were sent to take out the Germans. He crawled on his belly, bullets blazing over his head. Finally, he came to the trench, where he spotted two Germans firing their car-size Howitzer from the far end of the trench. Buck surprised them when he jumped into the trench with the intent of taking them out. He pulled the trigger of his submachine gun, but it did not fire. It had jammed.

This is the place in the story where Buck had to correct

me when I told him the UCLA alumni version. That version claimed that the quick-thinking lieutenant had grabbed the hand grenade at his side and, with no thought of his own welfare, threw it at the Germans. I had been told that Buck knew it would probably be the end for him, as the exploding grenade's shrapnel would kill him also. As the story was told, Buck was wounded severely and received the Purple Heart and Silver Star for his bravery.

I believed this version of the story was true, so I told it to some of my teams. They were amazed at the courage displayed by the former Bruins catcher. It also accomplished one of my goals of expounding the tradition of UCLA baseball. The story provoked tremendous pride. I also wanted my players to see how a Bruin was willing to sacrifice his life for his country. No man can do more. They knew my message was about making sacrifices for the good of our team. If Buck had made the ultimate sacrifice to win a war, the least they could do was make smaller ones required for winning baseball games.

When I finished telling Buck my story, he corrected me. "I don't know where anyone got that version of the story, Gary, but that's not the way it happened."

"But, Buck," I said, "Wasn't that when you were injured and why you received the Silver Star and the Purple Heart?"

"No, Gary, not in that trench . . . I got injured later on and received the Purple Heart." He didn't say why he received the Silver Star.

Then he proceeded to tell me what really happened. When he finished, he said, "You know, Gary, you can read about it in my book, *Call of Duty*. The whole story is in that book."

So I sent away for Buck's book, and with that as one source of information and Buck's words as another, I got the true story, starting at the point where Buck's gun jammed.

In our phone conversation, Buck said, "I looked at the Germans, and they looked at me. They looked as scared as I was—but both of 'em were armed to the hilt. I wasn't. Then I heard a machine gun fire behind me. It was Bill Guarnere, who had crawled with me, but we had gotten separated earlier. Now he was in the trench, firing away at the two Germans. He knocked off one of them quickly, but the other one jumped out of the trench and took off, running across a field. That's when I took the grenade off of my belt and hurled it at the fleeing Nazi."

In his book, Buck describes his throw this way: "The grenade was right on the money. It detonated in the air right above the German's head, killing him instantly. That was my first kill."

Buck's description of the German's death, when he described it to me over the phone, was a bit more gruesome. "Gary, that Nazi was about from home plate to second base. I was used to throwing at that distance since my catching days. The throw was perfect. I saw my grenade explode and it blew that German's head right off. I don't want you to think I'm not a compassionate man, Gary. But we were trained to kill the enemy, and that's what we did."

He went on to tell me a short story that showed he was a compassionate man. "This occurred shortly after the trench event," he said. "We had just captured us a German prisoner. I think he was afraid we were going to kill him. He never did offer any resistance, just stood there, holding his hands up high in the air. He was just a kid, cryin' like a baby. Actually, I felt a little sorry for him. Three of us were watching him and waiting for him to settle down a bit before we could ask him some questions, when one of the guys ran out of patience. He grabbed his knife, which had brass knuckles on its handle and slugged the poor German square in the mouth. Blood sprayed out of that kid's mouth, and some of his teeth came with it. I think his jaw was broken, too. I couldn't believe what I had just seen. It was a crazy, senseless act, because our prisoner wasn't offering any resistance. I couldn't hold back as I grabbed our guy and shook the daylights out of him. I yelled in his face, 'Get your crazy ass out of here! We don't need your crap!'"

Buck said the fighting in Normandy was bloody, but they

had expected it. He did *not* expect to be battling the Germans for thirty-three days, because they were assured it would only take three days to control the small amount of territory. On June 6, Easy Company had parachuted with 139 men. When they pulled off the line thirty-three days later, Buck was one of seventy-four remaining.

Buck described how he obtained that injury for which he was awarded the Purple Heart: "About three months after the trench event, our E Company parachuted into Holland. Our purpose was to establish a corridor across the Rhine River and into Germany. I was leading my men up a road that was too quiet. All of a sudden, we were surprised by a German Panzer unit, and bullets ripped over and into us like hail. All I could do was yell to my guys, 'Get down! Get down!'

"I was so intent at getting the message to my platoon that I failed to follow my own orders. I got hit in the butt with something—I didn't see it comin'. I felt like I'd been hit with a fastball. It knocked me clear off my feet.

"I just kept lying on the ground, while bullets rained over my head. A medic came runnin' up to me, while bullets were still blazing all around us. He poured some sulfa powder on my butt. I don't remember much after that.

"In the movie *Band of Brothers*, they showed my buddies coming out and crouching next to me, but I sure don't remember it. They wanted to carry me off, but I told them all to get out of there, 'cause I was too heavy. I supposedly said, 'Just leave me for the Germans.'

"A little later, when all the gunfire had stopped, a jeep came for me. They cut a seat out of my pants and stuck a bandage on my butt. Then they threw me over the hood of the jeep—like a deer across the hood of a car."

In Buck's book, he wrote about how embarrassing it was as they traveled to the hospital, giving the GIs "a prime look at my backside." But, as Buck told me, "I preferred getting hit in the butt than an inch higher. It would have shattered my spine."

Buck's Easy Company was supposed to be in Holland for only a brief mission, but with troops numbering 154 men, they were there for eighty days. When they left, a third of the company was either dead or wounded.

After being treated for his wound, Buck rejoined his troops about a month later, in France. His last battle was the worst—the Battle of Bastogne. In dead winter, with snow on the ground, bullets were blazing, bombs were blasting, shrapnel was flying, and even large trees were falling, like victims of the war storm. It was slaughter alley, with soldiers lying on the ground, bloody. "Death was everywhere," Buck said in his book. "I had seen men die before. I had seen men get wounded before. But this was different. This was unprecedented gore."

In Bastogne, he was only a few feet away when he saw one of his men get shot that blew a hole in his back the size of a grapefruit.

This was also the battle where Buck's best buddies were seriously wounded. "Two of the toughest guys in the platoon," he said. When there was a lull in the fighting, Buck hopped out of his foxhole. Everywhere he looked in the red and white snow, he saw death and injury. When he found "Wild Bill" Guarnere, the man who had saved him in the trench that day in Normandy, lying in the bloody snow with his other friend, Joe Toye, he yelled for the medic. He watched as a medic tied a bandage around what was left of Toye's leg and gave him a large hit of morphine. Then the medic did the same for Guarnere. Both were missing their right legs, but both survived.

Guarnere was quoted in the introduction of Buck's book: "Second platoon was indeed 'blessed' to have Buck Compton as our leader. He was a quiet and strong officer who, above all, listened and talked to all men under his command. I could never say enough to express my thanks and admiration for Buck Compton."

For a month, Easy Company fought on the front line at Bastogne. They had arrived with 120 men; when they left, Easy

Company had about 60. Buck was sent to the hospital, where both of his feet were treated for severe frostbite.

Buck's reflections on war struck home with me (and if Coach Wooden had read what Buck wrote in his book, I am sure it would have resonated greatly with him). "There is a sense of guilt that will always be part of the war for me," he wrote. "It's the guilt I feel because I survived. . . . Why does one man live through a chaotic situation when another man doesn't? . . . Out of all the horror of war, the guilt of survival is one of the things that haunts me most to this day. I will never know why I survived when so many others did not. When it comes to understanding any of this, I have long since given up trying."

When I talked to Buck about all he experienced in the war, I told him, "You were a hero to all of our UCLA players and coaches. Maybe that one story that was passed along from our alumni was not completely accurate, but it accurately portrayed your character. I'm glad I told them how brave you truly were."

Buck seemed embarrassed by my comment. He was a humble man, just like Coach Wooden. Why is it that most great men are so humble? Maybe it's because they don't need to say much about themselves; the way they lead their lives says it all.

As a testament to his humility, Buck wrote these words in *Call of Duty*: "I don't think what I personally did in the war was any big deal. The men who didn't come back again, so that we can enjoy the freedoms we hold today—the men who gave life and limb for us—they are the real heroes. I don't want anybody venerating me for my military service. Venerate those who live with injuries today, and those who didn't come back."

I'm grateful to Buck for allowing me to do a little venerating of his heroics in World War II.

Like Coach Wooden had remembered, Buck confirmed that he was one of the first "UCLA-ans" to meet John Wooden. "I met him at Art Reichle's home the summer of 1948," he said. Art invited me to be there because I played for him in 1941 and 1946, after I returned from the war, and we established a close friendship. Art and his wife hosted the dinner party for the Woodens to welcome them to Los Angeles."

Buck admitted to me that he didn't remember much about that evening. 'There were only three, maybe four, couples at the dinner. As for Coach Wooden, he seemed like a nice guy . . . rather quiet, I thought."

Buck laughed. "I'd never heard of the guy before," he said. "All I knew was that he coached at some small school in Indiana."

The two of them never met again, until Buck invited John to speak at his Los Angeles American Legion Luncheon Club. Buck, being the president of the club then, called John on the phone and was surprised at how willing he was to accept his invitation. Buck couldn't remember the exact year of John's speech but he knew it was between 1949 and 1952. "I do know it was before John had ever won a national championship," he said. "But he had winning teams then." In fact, John's teams had won a Southern Division or Pacific Coast Conference championship in three of those years.

Buck described John's speech that day. "John just spoke to our club about his basketball team and the prospects of the upcoming season. I don't remember him talking about anything else besides basketball. But I do remember that he was very friendly, stayed to answer questions, and was not a standoffish guy—really a reachable guy."

"What do you mean by 'reachable?'" I asked.

"Well, I had to call him a lot to make the arrangements and give him directions and other details. He was always accessible. He answered the phone every time I called."

After Buck's military tour of duty was over, he returned to UCLA in 1946 and played his final year of baseball. After graduating with a law degree from Loyola University and passing the bar exam in 1949, he worked his way up the ladder from detective to the chief deputy district attorney for the city of Los Angeles. This led to his notoriety in one of the biggest cases in U.S. history.

An event that shocked America occurred just after midnight on June 5, 1968 in Los Angeles—the assassination of Senator Robert F. Kennedy. Named the leading prosecuting attorney in the case against Sirhan Sirhan, Buck Compton was placed in the public eye.

It is with bitter irony that two of the three "UCLA-American heroes" recognized in this book played major roles in the tragic death of Bobby Kennedy. Rafer Johnson was a witness in the Sirhan trial, because he was standing next to Kennedy when Sirhan gunned him down.

The official trial began January 7, 1969, with Sirhan pleading not guilty. No television cameras were permitted in the courtroom, but court artists and reporters were everywhere. The spotlight was on Buck. It was he who cross-examined Sirhan.

Fifteen weeks after the trial started, the jury reached a first-degree murder verdict of guilty. Although Sirhan was sentenced to the death penalty, California subsequently changed the law and had abolished capital punishment. He has been in prison ever since. Buck had won the case, but was disappointed that Sirhan had not been sent to the gas chamber to receive the justice he deserved. As Buck stated in his book, "This country does not change its government with guns."

Not long after the trial, Buck became an appellate court judge for the state of California, serving twenty years until he retired.

Just like John, Buck has always *loved* baseball. His favorite team growing up was the old "farm team" of the Chicago Cubs and the Los Angeles Angels, in the Pacific Coast League.

"I used to ride my bike to the corner of Forty-Second and Avalon to watch my Angels at Wrigley Field. In high school, I even took the boat over to Catalina Island to see the Cubs play during spring training. Gaby Hartnett, their catcher, was my favorite player. That's why I wanted to be a catcher."

"How did baseball affect your life?" I asked Buck. I was quite surprised at how quickly and firmly he answered me.

"A lot!" his voice thundered through the phone. "Baseball changed the direction I was headed." He explained to me that it was about a year after the U.S. officially entered the war that he went to Officers' Candidate School at Fort Benning, Georgia. When his commanding officers heard that Buck was a baseball player from UCLA, they assigned him to play on their Fort Benning team. He played the outfield, because they already had another catcher. Many good players, including some famous pros like Joe DiMaggio, Hank Greenberg, and Ted Williams, played ball for the armed forces. The purpose was to boost the morale of the other soldiers, sailors, and pilots. It was rare that anyone playing ball was sent to combat duty, even though most of them requested to serve. Ted Williams and Bob Feller were two that did. They both won medals for their bravery in WWII.

Buck was not content to just play ball. He wanted to head overseas and *fight* for the USA, not *play* for the USA. He knew his commanding officer would block any transfer by a ballplayer . . . unless he applied to be a paratrooper. So, Buck signed up for jump school in the dead of summer in 1943, and by the dead of winter he was with Easy Company in faraway England.

In *Call of Duty*, Buck described his decision to join the paratroopers: "Truthfully, when I signed up for the paratroopers, I had no idea what I was getting myself into. My biggest goal was to get transferred out of playing baseball. . . . What would my life have been like if I hadn't made that decision? I probably could have spent the rest of the war stateside, getting up whenever I wanted, eating long meals, swimming at the officers' club, and being a morale booster in the outfield."

Instead, Buck Compton became an American hero.

John's surprised reaction to Compton's story was no surprise to me, because it was the same kind of reaction I had had when I first learned of Buck's amazing life.

"Gary," Coach said, "I had no idea that Buck was a war hero, and that he was involved in the Sirhan case. Goodness gracious,

I didn't even know he played football at UCLA."

"Same here, John. Until our Baseball Hall of Fame event, I was ignorant of most of Buck's accomplishments, too."

"Is he in our UCLA *Athletic* Hall of Fame?"

"Not yet, John, but I'm sure the athletic department will honor Buck someday."

John said, "I certainly hope so."*

RAFER JOHNSON

The spring of 1959 was my first semester at UCLA, and Rafer Johnson's last semester. The first time I saw him, he stood between me and my twin brother Gene in the small, crowded shower room in the UCLA men's gym. We had finished baseball practice and Rafer had just concluded his workouts on the track and field.

Gene described his feelings to me upon seeing Rafer. "Before I stood next to Rafer showering, I always felt I could have competed and held my own with anyone in any sport. But seeing this superman physique looming over me, I realized I would have no chance of competing against him. I was relieved that I chose to play baseball . . . and he didn't."

Like his UCLA basketball coach, Rafer had played baseball at an early age, on an open baseball field behind his church in an all-black neighborhood in Dallas, Texas. He could not recall ever playing football or basketball in Texas.

When his dad moved his family from the cotton fields in Texas to the fertile fields of the San Joaquin Valley in California, Rafer began playing other sports. He played two years of baseball for Kingsburg High School and hit over .500 in one

---

* As of this writing, Lynn "Buck" Compton has not been honored in the UCLA Athletic Hall of Fame. I talked to Buck again on the phone in early February 2012. His voice was slightly gravelly, but he was cheerful. If he had not mentioned at the end of our conversation that he had just returned from the hospital because he had suffered a heart attack, I would never have guessed he was any worse off than the healthiest of us. Unfortunately, on February 25, 2012, Buck passed. He was ninety years old. America will miss him.

season. But his experience with baseball had its share of bad breaks, which included a ripped-off big toenail from a hard grounder, a lot of broken bats (at first, until he stopped batting cross-handed), and a broken finger that occurred later, when he was playing church softball. I never asked Rafer, but I doubt he would have ever expected to appear in a book that was mostly about a coach's love for baseball.

I asked Rafer about his high school baseball-playing days. "I seldom struck out," he said. "With two strikes on me, I just tried to put the bat on the ball, because I knew I could beat out most ground balls to the infielders."

He sounded a bit like Gail Goodrich when he said, "I had trouble hitting the curve ball. I was determined to get better at it. I always wanted to take batting practice off of guys who knew how to throw a curve."

He was a star on his basketball and football teams. He made All-League three straight years in basketball, leading his team to three league titles. In football, it was a similar success story—his teams won two consecutive championships, and he made the All-State team his senior year.

Despite his success in those three popular high school sports—baseball, basketball, and football—track and field was his favorite. During Rafer's first couple of years in high school, he strictly entered the sprint events at meets, but his coach, Murl Dodson, convinced him to use his athletic ability to become a multi-event competitor. It proved to be a wise decision. Rafer added the high jump and long jump, the high and low hurdles, the shot put, and the discus to his repertoire. Later, he added the javelin and the pole vault and, finally, the events he disliked the most, the grueling long races—the 400 and 1,500 meters. Rafer had made a commitment to the decathlon event by the time he finished high school, and with that commitment came an obsession to become the Olympic decathlon champion.

Because of his triumphs in football, basketball, baseball, and track, Rafer was often compared to the great Jackie Rob-

inson. Robinson is still the only athlete in UCLA history who lettered in all four sports—and he did it all in the same year. Many UCLA boosters had hoped Rafer would attend their university and become another Jackie Robinson. Rafer had always envied Robinson, and being compared to his hero was the ultimate compliment. As it turned out, Rafer lettered in two sports at UCLA—basketball and track.

When Rafer chose to attend UCLA over the offers from USC and Cal, he never imagined that, by his senior year, he would be sitting down to dinner with Jackie Robinson and his wife, Rachel. The dinner was hosted by Nobel Peace Prize winner Ralph Bunche and his wife, with the Robinsons and Rafer as their guests.

Something Rafer said about that dinner reminded me of the way I had felt the first day Coach Wooden and I had a long talk in our office. In his autobiography, *The Best That I Can Be*, Rafer wrote: "I was so awestruck that I forgot to ask most of the questions I had in mind. . . . What I found remarkable about them . . . was their ability to just be ordinary, and to make me feel perfectly at ease. That, in itself, was a valuable lesson."

It was not just the size and strength of Rafer's muscles that made him the greatest athlete in the world—it was the size of his heart. Coach Wooden once said to me, "Rafer's heart gave him the spirit to always give his best effort, whether it was on the basketball court or on the track field."

I asked John what kind of a basketball player Rafer had been when he had played for him in the late fifties.

"Obviously, he was very athletic on the court—a great rebounder because of his jumping ability and his aggressiveness on the boards," Coach said. "He had outstanding one-way speed. Some other players may have been a little quicker at changing directions, but none could beat Rafer to the other end of the court straight away."

"Do you think Rafer could have played pro basketball?"

"Yes," Coach replied. "If Rafer had concentrated on basketball, he might have even been an All-American in college and become good enough to play in the NBA. But Rafer's passion was not with basketball—it was with track and field. That's where his heart truly belonged."

Coach Wooden did not call Rafer an American hero simply because of his success in the Olympics. "It was through track and field that Rafer made a name for himself," Coach told me, "but it was his humbleness in victory and graciousness in defeat that made him such a wonderful ambassador for the United States. I don't know of any athlete who spread more good will for our country than Rafer did."

Coach Wooden was right. Rafer embodied the true spirit of the Olympics, which had more to do with improving friendships among nations than winning. Yet Rafer also realized that he should always give his best effort when competing.

Rafer felt that politics had no place in the Olympic Games. He turned down invitations by other black athletes to boycott the Olympics in protest of racial conditions in America. It wasn't an easy decision for him, because he knew that blacks were not permitted to eat at some lunch counters, and were forbidden to attend certain colleges.

For his refusal to boycott the Olympics, Rafer was accused by some African-Americans as not being "black enough." Some even called him an "Uncle Tom" for not standing up with them for equal rights. But Rafer held firm in his belief that he could do more good for the black cause by participating and giving his best effort to win with dignity.

At the 1960 opening ceremonies in Rome, Rafer, as captain, led his USA team in the parade of world athletes. He said afterward, in his autobiography, that the picture of him, a black man carrying the American flag in the world's newspapers and magazines, "probably did more good than a boycott would have."

Rafer Johnson was destined to be an American hero from a very early age, when he saved his brother's life. One hot summer day, Rafer and his younger brother, Jimmy, went swimming in

an irrigation ditch near their home in Kingsburg, California. Swimming was forbidden in the ditch, because the water hole was dangerous—it had a drop-off that, with a single misstep, could take the water over the heads of most youngsters.

Jimmy ventured too far and fell into the deeper pool of water, knocking his head on the concrete walkway as he fell. Rafer didn't see Jimmy fall, but he did notice shortly afterward that his brother was nowhere in sight. Finally, he spotted Jimmy bobbing in the water, and jumped in after him. He grabbed his brother and, with the help of some friends, pulled him out of the water.

When they got Jimmy on land, he wasn't moving. Rafer started pressing on Jimmy's chest, all the while praying that he was doing the artificial respiration correctly. Finally, his brother threw up water and recovered. Years after that episode, Jimmy told everyone that, as a boy, he had always looked up to Rafer, but after Rafer saved him, his brother became his hero.

Rafer never looked at himself as a hero. In the 1960 Olympic Trials, after he broke the world record for the most points ever scored in the decathlon, people called him a hero. Rafer would have none of it, saying in his autobiography, "Everyone treats me like a hero for winning a sporting event, but Ernest is a *real* hero."

Rafer was referring to Ernest Green, one of the black students who had integrated Central High School in Little Rock, Arkansas, in 1959. Ernest had been teased, taunted, and threatened with his life on a daily basis, yet he managed to complete his high school education. Rafer knew the difference between being a success in the sports world and being a hero in real life.

There are many examples of Rafer's courage, humility, and dignity while competing in the decathlon. As a testimony to those qualities, I have chosen to tell the story of his journey to winning the 1960 Olympic gold medal.

In the very first event of the decathlon, he ran the 100 meters in a disappointing 10.9 seconds—three-tenths of a second slower than he had run in the trials, and a whopping 132-point difference behind his toughest competitors, C.K. Yang of Taiwan and Vasily Kuznetsov of Russia.

Rafer's sub-par performance in the 100 meters was not entirely of his own doing. At the start of the 100 meters, an opponent jumped the gun, and all the runners had to start again. Then it happened not only a second time, but also a third and a fourth time! On one of those false starts by his opponents, Rafer ran full throttle for forty meters before he heard the recall gun. The four false starts affected Rafer's performance. C.K. Yang and Kuznetsov, on the other hand, had the good fortune of running in different heats, without wasting energy on someone's false starts.

Some athletes may have taken this opening disaster as a bad omen. Not Rafer. He threw it out, tried not to think about it, and concentrated on doing his best in the next events.

In the tenth and final event, the grueling 1,500 meters, Rafer fought his way back to take the decathlon lead. Although he led C.K. by sixty-seven points, his work was cut out for him—this was one of C.K.'s best events, and he had already beaten Rafer by twenty-three seconds in a previous 1,500 run. Rafer needed to come within ten seconds of C.K.'s finishing time in order for him to win the gold medal.

One sports writer called this race between C.K. and Rafer "the most dramatic head-and-head competition in the history of track and field." That writer probably called it "dramatic" not only because the gold medal was riding on this race, but because Rafer and C.K. were the best of friends. They had trained together at UCLA under the watchful and experienced eyes of one of the greatest track and field coaches of all time, Elvin C. "Ducky" Drake. They had taught each other and learned from each other. They had the utmost mutual respect, but they both wanted to win.

Rafer's strategy, as advised by Coach Drake, was to stick close to C.K. during the entire race. Ironically, Ducky's advice

to C.K. was to try and distance himself from Rafer. The UCLA coach, true to his principles, showed no partiality.

Rafer stuck close to C.K. from the beginning and, although C.K. tried hard to shake him off at the halfway point, Rafer stayed right behind him. On the third and next-to-last lap, C.K. turned on the accelerator in a sprint that surprised Rafer, but he reached deep down with his last bit of strength and sprinted after C.K. He stuck with his opponent until C.K. crossed the finish line, only 1.2 seconds ahead of him.

Both runners had run their fastest times ever in the 1,500 meters, and Rafer had fulfilled his high school dream. He did not have to settle for a silver medal as he had in the 1956 Olympics; this time, he had won the gold medal, in a decathlon record of 8,392 points. C.K. also broke the old record, with 8,334 points. Rafer wrote in his autobiography, "As good as I felt about winning, I felt equally bad that my friend had lost; as bad as he felt about losing, he felt equally good that his friend had won." That is the type of attitude that made Rafer a special athlete.

Eight years after Rafer had won the gold medal, he happened to observe the California Angels players going through their spring training drills in Palm Springs. He was near the batting cages as my good friend, Chris Krug, an Angel at the time, was taking his turn hitting off the pitching machine.

"After I finished and was leaving the cage, Rafer asked us if he could take some swings," Chris told me. "We all said sure— who were we to say no to Rafer Johnson. None of us mentioned it, but I think we were all curious to see if an Olympic decathlon champion could hit a baseball.

"Well, I handed my bat to Rafer, and he stepped into the cage. It didn't take long for a crowd of players to gather around and watch this great athlete's attempt at executing what sports experts claim is the toughest thing to do in sports.

"Rafer's first few swings looked like a girl's who had only played Church League softball. All of us were a little embarrassed for him. But when he got the timing of the machine down—wow! His swing looked as good as a major leaguer's. All of us were in awe. We talked about it for a long time afterwards."

Yes, Rafer was a special athlete, but his life outside of the sports world was equally special. His principles were challenged six years after his gold medal win in the Olympics, while working as a sports reporter for the Los Angeles television station KNBC. It was a different and difficult adjustment for him to make, and filled with the stress of deadlines, memorizing scripts that changed from minute to minute, and demands his superiors made of him. They asked him to do some things that, in his opinion, overstepped the bounds of privacy. Once, when Sandy Koufax and Don Drysdale were negotiating with the Dodgers over their contracts, Rafer was asked to do something that crossed the line. They wanted him to either camp outside Drysdale's house or knock on his door and shove a microphone in front of him. Rafer refused his boss's orders, and quit. Just like his refusal to boycott the Olympics, he stood firm on his principles.

Coach Wooden told me that Rafer was one of the most gracious players he ever coached. "I didn't have to remind him to be a *team* player," he said. "When Rafer was thrown the ball from a teammate as he raced down the court for an easy lay-up, he always gave his passer a sign or a look of thanks—I didn't have to teach him that. He came to me already as one, perhaps because of his parents or the coaches he had in the small town he came from."

When Mike Wallace interviewed Rafer on television a year after he won the Olympic gold medal, Wallace said that the town of Kingsburg was "just another truck stop on Highway 99, until Rafer Johnson put it on the map." But Rafer put it differently, saying, "It was Kingsburg that put Rafer Johnson on the map."

I attended a banquet honoring Rafer a couple of years ago. He told a story of how the people of Kingsburg—an almost

hundred-percent Swedish community—had first heard of Rafer Johnson's exploits on the sports fields. "They assumed," he said, "that with a name like 'Johnson,' I was a little Swedish athlete—until they saw me."

He was grateful that the townspeople accepted him and his family as equals and that he was given the opportunity to play sports, go to school, and attend church just like the rest of them. Rafer has always returned to Kingsburg to show and tell them of his everlasting appreciation.

The assassination of Senator Robert Kennedy was a moment in Rafer's life that tested his courage more than anything that had ever happened to him on any athletic field. Bobby Kennedy was one of Rafer's closest and dearest friends.

Rafer and Bobby were literally so physically close during the democratic primary elections in 1968, that many people believed Rafer was one of Bobby's bodyguards. There were times, in fact, when Rafer did help keep Bobby and his wife, Ethel, from being physically bothered by pushy fans.

Just after midnight on June 5, immediately following Senator Kennedy's win in the California primary election, Kennedy delivered a memorable speech at L.A.'s Ambassador Hotel that ended with these five words: " . . . and now, on to Chicago." Only moments after those words were spoken, the presidential candidate was making his way through a crowded pantry room when Sirhan Sirhan shot him.

I had watched the news on television in despair, and heard the voice of a man yelling, "Get his gun, Rafer! Get his gun!" Most reporters said it was Roosevelt Grier, the former great lineman of the Los Angeles Rams, who yelled those words. But forty-three years later, Rafer corrected me. "No, Gary, that was a newsman standing on a table overlooking Bobby," he said. "He was filming everything that happened."

With Rafer's family members sitting around the table in a crowded and noisy banquet hall, and only a few minutes before Rafer would be delivering his speech, he obliged me by telling his story of one of the most horrific events in his life.

I had heard that Rafer didn't like reliving this tragedy, especially in the years immediately following, but he didn't seem reluctant to talk about it. Rafer told me that, when he heard the shots, he turned in that direction, and saw smoke from a gun that was close to Bobby's head. He pushed Ethel out of harm's way and then grabbed the hand holding the gun. "Everyone was screaming and yelling," he said. "The crowd that was once surrounding Bobby was running for cover. But once I grabbed the gun and took Sirhan to the floor, Rosey dove down on top of me, and Sirhan couldn't move. The people who had at first run away at the gunshots started coming back. They were angry—really angry. They wanted to kill Sirhan. Some were kicking him in the head when he was down, but Rosey and I kept them from killing him."

I asked Rafer what it was like when he took the witness stand at Sirhan's trial. "My part didn't take long," he said. "The prosecutor [Buck Compton] showed me a gun and asked, 'Is this the gun you saw that killed Kennedy?' I simply answered, 'Yes.' That's all they asked me, and all I said."

Rafer then looked away for a brief moment. I could see that this was a part of the story he would like to forget. "Gary," he said, "there were no bullets left in that gun. Sirhan emptied it on Bobby. I wish I had gotten to the gun *before* it was fired."

I felt guilty about putting Rafer through this all over again. I still regret my intrusion on his privacy and on a night that he deserved to enjoy his celebration.

"Some people tried to say there was more than one assassin, but I saw everything," Rafer continued. "I'm telling you, no one else was involved in the killing. I know there was only one—Sirhan. I know it."

I heard U.S. Marine Corps lieutenant colonel Oliver North once say, "A hero is a person who puts himself at risk to save others." Rafer did that for his friend, Bobby Kennedy, and for Bobby's wife, Ethel.

Rafer has given most of his life to serving and helping others. I recognized this trait in Rafer shortly after I graduated from UCLA. He called me on the phone one day and asked if I would be interested in volunteering for the Peace Corps. He was helping to recruit volunteers for his good friend and Peace Corps director Sargent Shriver. Rafer specifically asked me to go to Thailand as a volunteer. I was honored that he even thought to consider me for President John Kennedy's new peace and goodwill program. I was tempted to accept the offer, but I told Rafer that I had already committed to a graduate assistant coaching job with UCLA's baseball team. Rafer understood and was his usual polite and courteous self while wishing me good luck.

Rafer's pride and joy project became the Special Olympics, because he believed that athletics could help disabled and neglected young people realize their potential, gain self-confidence, and, in Rafer's words (also Coach Wooden's), "be the best that they can be."

The first Special Olympics were held in Chicago in 1968, a month after Bobby's assassination. Rafer was still grieving, but the Special Olympics became the best medicine he could have taken to relieve his pain. He wrote in his book: "Here were children and young adults who all their lives had been made to feel unworthy and incompetent. . . . Now they had a chance to know the thrill of accomplishment . . . and their faces lit up with joy. They competed with one another but every participant was made to feel like a winner. It was impossible to come away from that without feeling better about the world. I made a commitment to help Special Olympics."

Rafer became one of the founding members of the Special Olympics in Southern California, serving as the national head coach and chairman of the board of governors. After over forty years of service in the Special Olympics, he had been the engine that kept the wheels rolling—and the youthful legs walking and running.

Rafer has won many awards, but one of the most cherished honors he received was the George Washington Carver Memorial Award for Meritorious Service. He called it one of his proudest moments, because Jackie Robinson was the only other athlete to have won it.

In 1984, the president of the Los Angeles Olympic Committee, Peter Ueberroth, asked Rafer to be the final runner and torchbearer in the countrywide relay ending at the L.A. Coliseum. This meant that Rafer would need to run 100 yards on the track straightaway, then jog ninety-nine steep stair steps to the top of the coliseum, holding the torch all the while. Once at the top, Rafer would then light the flame of the giant Olympic torch.

It was a great honor for Rafer, one that he had earned and truly deserved. Rafer humbly accepted Ueberroth's offer, but at forty-nine years of age, he knew he had better start training. He had only ten days to go before the opening ceremony. In addition, his nemesis—baseball—had struck again when he broke his finger playing in a game only a month earlier.

Rafer trained for this event as if he was training for the decathlon, running up any staircase that would help get his legs and lungs back in shape. As for the broken finger, he would let his other four fingers carry the torch.

Rafer completed his task without any problems. "Standing at the pinnacle of the Coliseum," he said, "having been afforded this singular honor, with my face being beamed to a billion homes around the world as ABC's Jim McKay called me "a great American"—well, it was a long way from the cotton fields of Hillsboro, Texas. It was all I could do to keep from weeping."

Although Rafer was emotionally drained from that memorable moment, he still enjoyed the pride he saw in his wife's face and the joyful hugs of his two children, Jenny and Josh. Jenny let her dad read what she had written in her diary that night: "Today at the 1984 Olympics, my father Rafer Johnson lit the torch. I was so proud of him when he did it that I cried.

Seeing him go up those stairs made me proud to be Rafer and Betsy Johnson's daughter. Wow! When my dad told me about it, I thought that it was great. But I didn't realize how great it was until I saw him do it."

In the last sentence of Rafer's autobiography, he wrote, "I'll be happy to be remembered as someone who was of service to his family and community, and tried to be the best that he could be." These words are so familiar to one of Rafer's favorite mentors, Coach Wooden, who beamed with pride and joy every time we talked about Rafer Johnson.

JACKIE ROBINSON

Coach Wooden missed out on coaching Jackie Robinson by seven years—or should I say Jackie Robinson missed out on playing for Coach Wooden? When I reminded John of his unfortunate timing, he said jokingly, "You know, Gary, he only played two years of basketball at UCLA. I was hoping he would come back in the off-season of baseball to finish his eligibility with me." John was aware of Jackie's prowess in basketball, as Jackie twice led the conference in scoring.

What can one add that has not already been written about Jackie Robinson? I will try, starting with a few conversations I had with Buck Compton, who played football and baseball with Jackie at UCLA. Besides being teammates, Buck and Jackie had something else in common. They both had lost their fathers— Jackie's abandoned him and his family less than a year after birth, and Buck's dad committed suicide the summer Buck was accepted to UCLA.

When I spoke to Buck, I was impressed with his sharp mind and memory at age 87. He made it clear that he was impressed with Jackie Robinson, both as a man and as a football player. He used terms like "amazing," "awesome," and "spectacular," and remembered that Jackie had led the nation in punt return average in 1940 and was UCLA's first consensus All-American in football.

He was not impressed, however, with Jackie as a UCLA baseball player back then. "Baseball was Jackie's worst sport," he said. "I don't think he even hit his weight. He was strictly a singles hitter, and most of those were drag bunts and infield hits that he legged out. Never . . . never in a million years would I have thought he would play in the major leagues! I guess when he went to the pros, they taught him how to hit doubles and home runs."

At first, Buck's words may seem demeaning toward Jackie, but he was only praising Jackie's determination to become a better player. "I admire him greatly for coming so far in his development as a baseball player," Buck said.

Buck was positive when he talked about Jackie's defense. "Boy, he was quick! His feet were as quick as any cat's. Wooden would have loved him. He could move almost as fast sideways as he could forward. In two steps, he was already at full speed, in any direction. Even when he went after pop-ups that were hit over his head, he was at high gear in two steps and making spectacular catches in front of our outfielders. He was our shortstop, but he didn't have a shortstop's arm. His range was amazing—he got everything that was hit to the left side of our infield, except straight at our third baseman.

"His hands were even quicker than his feet, and whenever he got his hands on the ball, it stayed in his glove. He had the quickest and surest hands I've ever seen on a ball player. Jackie was just awesome on defense, and that's why he started most of our games. It sure wasn't because of his bat."

"What was Jackie like as a teammate?" I asked Buck.

"Oh, he pretty much kept to himself. He certainly wasn't a loudmouth. The players all liked him. He was a team player—never complained, and he worked hard. We only had three black players on the team, but that was a lot in those days."

Buck then told me a story about Jackie that he said he wasn't proud of. This incident happened when the UCLA foot-

ball team traveled by train to play Cal Berkeley. Buck was playing cards with Jackie when a player came up to them and said, "Hey, they got a girl up in one of the berths, and she'll do anybody!"

Buck said that the girl had a bad reputation. He said he had given Jackie a wink and asked him if he wanted to go.

"Jackie looked at me as seriously as I ever saw him," Buck said. "No smile—just a real stern look, and said, 'Hell, if I did, they'd lynch me.' We just kept on playing cards."

Jackie's best baseball game for the Bruins came in his first game, just after he came out from basketball. He went four for four and stole four bases, including home twice.

In 1963, when I was assisting Art Reichle on the UCLA baseball team, we were standing on Joe E. Brown Field and I asked him, "What was it like coaching Jackie Robinson?" Art had been the assistant coach when Jackie played in 1941.

"It was fun, Gary," Coach Reichle said, "especially on our game days, when our track and field team held their meets."

By my expression, Reichle knew I didn't get the connection between track and baseball. He pointed over to our left field chain-link fence, "The track being close to our field made it easier for Jackie to take his turn at the broad [long] jump."

"How did he do that, Coach? The track is close, but when would he have had time to do the broad jump while he was playing in your ball game?"

"That's the funny part," Coach said, smiling. "Jackie waited patiently for the opportunity to race over to the track. When he knew he probably wouldn't be coming to bat in an inning, he would quickly take his baseball spikes off, put on his track spikes, and bolt out of our dugout, heading for the track. I can still see him leaving our dugout with all of his teammates and coaches hollering, 'Good luck, Jackie!'

"It was a race against time. He would have to go over there, take his jump, and then be back to take his position at shortstop before the opponent's first hitter came to the plate. Sometimes our hitters tried to stall, especially when there were two outs and Jackie hadn't shown up yet. I made our hitters step out of the box and grab some dirt and rub their hands with it. I even made them take pitches until they had two strikes. There were a couple of times when Jackie barely made it back in time. He would come racing down the left field line, carrying his baseball pants and jersey with only his socks and shorts on. We'd toss his spikes out to him at shortstop, and he'd sit down and quickly put everything on. Like I said, it was a lot of fun coaching Jackie."

Perhaps the most amazing thing about this story is the fact that Jackie only needed one jump to win the broad jump event. He not only became the conference champion in the broad jump that year, but he also won the NCAA title with a jump of twenty-four feet and ten inches.

In 1990, I was asked to take part in a TNT movie production called *The Court-Martial of Jackie Robinson*. The director of the movie wanted me to teach Andre Braugher, who played Jackie's part in the movie, how to swing the bat similarly to Jackie Robinson's swing. I knew the story of Jackie's refusal to sit at the rear of the military bus, which was the reason for his court-martial trial. It was an excellent example of Jackie's fight against segregation at the time, and his determination to do what he thought was right, despite the consequences. He won in his fight and was given an honorable discharge.

I spent two summer days throwing batting practice to Andre in the batting cages at UCLA, trying to mold his swing into a legitimate reproduction of Jackie's. After those two days, the director asked me how Andre was doing. I told him that Andre had no trouble hitting the ball, but it would take some time to get his swing to look respectable.

"We don't have time, Gary," he said. "We're shooting the action shots tomorrow."

The next day, I remained in the background as I watched them film Andre hitting the ball, which he did every time. After

a couple of takes, the director came looking for me. "Well, Gary, what do you think?" he asked.

My first thought was, *Jackie would be embarrassed.*

Out loud, I said, "I think it would be best to take your shots of Andre from either close-up, say at the top of his shoulders and on his face, or take shots from a distance. Otherwise, it's just not authentic-looking. It doesn't look like Jackie's swing."

We never had the chance to polish up Andre's swing, although Andre would have liked to do it because he was a hard worker and enjoyed taking batting practice. I admired his desire to get better, and always thought that, because of his determination, he was perfect to play the part of Jackie.

When the movie came out on television, I was anxious to see how the director had shot the scenes of Andre at bat. I was pleased to see that he disguised Andre's swing quite well by showing the beginning and end of the swing, leaving out the middle. It looked authentic—neither Andre nor Jackie would be embarrassed.

Jackie, like Coach Wooden, impacted many lives. Both, in fact, agreed that caring for others was a principle they lived by. John always said that he wanted to be remembered as a man who cared about others. Jackie was famous for saying, "A life is not important except in the impact it has on other lives."

I told John that I learned how Jackie could make an impact on a person when I was only eight years old, growing up near Cincinnati, Ohio.

Early in 1947, my mom took my brother and I to see our favorite team, the Reds, play the St. Louis Cardinals. All I remember about that game was Stan "the Man" Musial hitting a home run in the ninth inning to beat my heroes after our mom yelled at the top of her lungs to Stan, "You can't hit!" We never let her forget it.

A little later that year, mom took us back to Cincy's Crosley Field to see the Reds play the Brooklyn Dodgers. I remember more about what went on in the grandstands that day than what happened on the field.

Hundreds of African Americans ("Negroes" was the politically correct term in those days) were sitting together, high in the bleachers on the Dodgers' dugout side of the field. I don't know if the Reds segregated the seating or not. Maybe they just wanted to sit together so they could be a greater force rooting for their hero, Jackie. I *do* know that it had not been that way when we went to the Cardinals game earlier that year. I don't remember seeing any African Americans at that game.

All day long I watched them from the other side of the stands as they cheered for the Dodgers, while my side rooted for the Reds and against the Dodgers—especially against Jackie. There were insults and jeers thrown at number forty-two all day long.

One of Jackie's teammates, Ralph Branca, recalled how the fans had thrown black cats and watermelons out on the field. He had heard opposing players yell from their dugout, "Hey boy, come pick my cotton!" From my seat in Crosley Field, I hadn't heard anyone rooting for Jackie. I don't think any whites wanted Jackie to do well that day. I didn't know it then, but I did learn later that in 1950, Cincinnati was the city where someone had sent a note to Jackie saying that, if he showed up to play on Crosley Field, "we will kill you."

Jackie's teammates had tried to ease the tension prior to the game, joking that they would all wear a number forty-two on their jerseys to confuse the gunman. Before that game, Pee Wee Reese, the Dodgers captain and shortstop who hailed from the Southern state of Kentucky, had put his arm around Jackie for everyone in the stands and the opposing players to see. That act had the long-ranging effect of changing some attitudes among whites—especially Southern whites. Who knows . . . that single act of compassion may have saved Jackie's life. Pee Wee reputedly said he did it because he felt sorry for Jackie and all the abuse he was taking.

I have played a lot of baseball in my day, and I know that the

game is tough enough to play without the abuse Jackie endured every day he stepped out on the field. But Pee Wee was right. Jackie endured the barrage of insults and bigotry silently and with dignity, and performed like a Hall of Famer on the field.

In 1981, I had a chance to meet Jackie's wife, Rachel. On that day, we dedicated our UCLA baseball stadium in Jackie's name. I couldn't help but recall how things had changed since 1947, Jackie's first year in the major leagues. I remember what he once said about how brave Rachel was in those days. "She went to all my games," he said, "because it was the only friendly face I could see."

Today, Jackie's life-size bronze statue overlooks our playing field. When I coached at UCLA, sometimes I would tell my players to look up at his statue so they would be reminded of what Jackie stood for: *courage and determination.*

In 1997—the fiftieth anniversary of Jackie's introduction to Major League Baseball—I asked the Reebok Company, who supplied our UCLA baseball team with uniforms, to inscribe Jackie's number, "42" on all of the sleeves. I can't speak for my players, but I know that every time I looked at that number on my players' sleeves, I was reminded to remain determined to give my best effort. Maybe it was just a coincidence, but we qualified for the NCAA College World Series that year.

Although sports were once one of the worst parts of our segregated society, today they are the most colorblind aspect of our society, mostly thanks to Jackie Roosevelt Robinson.

*   *   *

Why would John regard these three great UCLA athletes— Buck Compton, Rafer Johnson, and Jackie Robinson—as American heroes? It was *not* just for the bravery and courage each displayed on the battlefields or the athletic fields. It was much more than that. It had to do with their demonstration of honesty, sincerity, and humility, and their absence of vanity.

Above all, it would be their eagerness to serve others.

Coach is a mold of all three of these men. Although he never participated as an athlete at UCLA, he stands with these men as one of UCLA's all-time American heroes. But what is truly remarkable about John Wooden is that he believed it was within easy reach for all of us to be heroes.

BREAKING THE RULES

Walking across the UCLA campus on a warm summer morning, an unusual quietness surrounded me. Unlike the regular school days, when students crowded the busy walkways, on this day, only an occasional summer school student passed me by. I was heading for the J. D. Morgan Center to pick up my mail.

As I approached the building, Coach Wooden exited through the doors and walked toward me with a noticeable limp. We greeted each other warmly; it had been some time since we had seen each other. John had visited UCLA infrequently since the passing of Nell in the spring of 1985. It was now the summer of 1986.

When I mentioned his obvious limp, he shrugged it off. "Oh, it's just my knees," he said. "Some days, they give me more trouble than others."

In keeping with his sense of humor, Coach smiled and added, "Well, Gary, as old Satchel Paige once said, how old would we be if we didn't know how old we were? On days like this, I'd rather not know I was seventy-five. That's three-quarters of a century."

He spied a bench along the walkway and, knowing we could

be talking awhile, asked if I'd mind sitting a spell. After we sat down, he asked me how my summer baseball camp was going.

"Great, John," I said. "I have a lot of fun coaching the little guys." I hesitated to tell him that this particular day would be different, because I had to deal with a troubling matter that concerned the NCAA and the Major League Baseball Players Association.

Despite my reluctance, I told John about my troubles. "Today I have to meet with the associate general counsel of the MLB Players Association to defend my relationship with an agent, Dennis Gilbert, who has signed several of my players. The Players Association probably wants to know if Dennis is paying me off for leading my players to him. He's signed a couple of our guys, like Tim Leary and Todd Zeile, for some big bonuses."

It had been eleven years since John had coached, and in those days, he didn't have to deal with the coach-agent relationship, so I explained further. "It is against MLB PA policy for agents to pay finder's fees, and it's also a violation of NCAA rules for a coach to receive payments or extra benefits from an agent."

John's next question was a direct one. "What's your defense, Gary?"

"I guess the truth is my best defense, because I have never taken a dime from Dennis. He is a member of our booster club, but his membership fees have always gone to the UCLA Athletic Fund, which is allowed per NCAA rules. Besides, Dennis and I were friends before he ever became an agent, and before I ever became a head coach."

John's response was blunt. "Don't worry about it, Gary. The NCAA and the Players Association can't make you halt a friendship that started way before he became an agent. I think they call it a 'pre-existing relationship.'"

When John put it that way, my shoulders felt lighter. What he said next, however, did the most to relieve my fears.

"You know, Gary," Coach said, "I violated an NCAA rule— and I did it almost every year I coached."

Like a third baseman snagging a lightning bolt line drive, his words quickly caught my attention. "As you probably know," he continued, "it is against the NCAA rules to have players eat meals at their coach's home. Nell and I hosted our out-of-state players regularly during the holidays. Nell would fix a home-cooked Thanksgiving or Christmas dinner for the boys who lived clear across the country—like Lewis [Alcindor], Lucias [Allen], Walter [Hazzard], and others. The boys wouldn't have to eat by themselves at some hamburger place in Westwood. We were their home away from home, and a substitute mother and father.

"I knew it was against the rules, but the NCAA wants us to play basketball during those holidays, and we must practice to prepare for those games. Our players can't go home like the rest of the student body does, and most of them could not afford the airfare anyway. Nell and I always believed we were doing the right thing."

I asked John if the NCAA had ever questioned him about it.

"No, they didn't," he said. "But even if they would have forbidden it, I wouldn't have changed. I would have told them they should change their bad rule, instead of me having to change a good one."

With John's words fresh in my mind, I met Gene Orza of the MLB Players Association that same afternoon, at our Jackie Robinson Stadium clubhouse. Mr. Orza gave me a friendly presentation of his duties, which included handling player grievances, salary arbitrations, and agent relations. Then he proceeded to interview me about my relationship with Dennis Gilbert. He asked me questions like, "Have you ever had lunch or dinner with Dennis?" I answered affirmatively. He asked me if Dennis came to many of our games, and again, I answered affirmatively. He even asked me if Dennis ever sat in our dugout during ball games, to which I answered, "Yes and no. Yes because he did so with our old-timers alumni team once, and no because he never sat in our dugout during regular games or practices."

After about fifteen minutes, he finally asked me, "How long have you known Dennis?"

"I've known Dennis for over twenty years," I replied, "when I was an assistant coach at the University of California, Riverside and he was coaching a summer baseball team. I scouted his team for recruits, and we became friends. This was years before he became a sports agent."

When I told Mr. Orza this, he responded with an answer almost identical to what Coach Wooden had told me earlier. "Well, Gary," he said, "we can't tell you who your friends should be." With that, he closed his folder and thanked me for answering his questions.*

A few weeks later, I thanked Coach for his wise words, which had helped relieve my tension that morning. He was pleased that everything had turned out okay, but he revealed a secret that he had kept from me at that time. With a twinkle in his eyes and that sly grin of his, he said, "Gary, I didn't even tell you about another NCAA rule I broke when I bailed a player out of jail. I won't go into detail, but I did it for the same reason I broke the 'dinner rule'—it was the right thing to do at the time."

---

* I never heard from the Major League Baseball Player's Association again, but I did follow Gene Orza's career and noticed that he became the MLBPA's chief operating officer in 2004. He announced his retirement in 2010. When I heard that he was retiring, I called his office to ask him one last question: "Whatever came of your investigation?"

Gene said, "Nothing came of it, Gary. There never was any evidence to support the allegations against you or Dennis." I always believed those allegations came from other agents who were jealous of Dennis signing the highly talented players from UCLA.

Years after the investigation, Dennis endowed a $100,000 baseball scholarship to the UCLA Athletic Fund. No complaints were made.

CHALLENGING DECISIONS

In 1986, I had to make a difficult decision, and if it were not for Coach Wooden, I doubt my decision would have been the right one. He had told me a story that occurred when he was coaching at Indiana State. I remember it well; I always hoped I would never have to face the same kind of situation.

He had caught one of his star players coming back to the hotel several minutes past curfew the night before a conference game. Coach shook his head and said, "I didn't know what I should do. This was one of the toughest challenges I'd had to face up until that time, and I struggled with my decision."

Coach never mentioned his real name to me. "I'll just call him Jimmy," he said. "Besides missing curfew, I was suspicious that he had also been drinking alcohol. When I asked him if he'd been drinking, he said he hadn't. Still, I believed he was lying to me because of his bloodshot eyes, the way he talked, and the way he was swaying back and forth.

"I didn't tell my assistants, or anybody else. I just went to bed that night and didn't get much sleep, wondering what I should do. I thought that there should be consequences for Jimmy's actions; I just didn't know what they should be. At worst, I could suspend him for one or two games. At the least,

I could ignore the situation and do nothing, and no one would ever know. No one, that is, but me and him."

The next morning, Coach decided that he would not allow Jimmy to suit up for the game that day. He wouldn't even let him sit on the team's bench.

"I knew Jimmy and I would be asked questions about why he didn't suit up," Coach said. "But I figured we both could take the consequences of our decisions. Well, Coach Gary, I was right about that—we both got bombarded with questions, first by the players on the team and then by the news media. I was pleased with Jimmy's answer to the questions, which was similar to mine: 'Coach has his reasons, and they are good ones.'"

"Did you win or lose the game?" I asked.

He smiled. "We won, which was a good thing because I believe we would have gotten even more questions if we had lost."

With that, Coach ended his story. "The main question you need to ask yourself about discipline is, 'Will the player learn from it?'" he said.

At the time Coach told me that story, I remember thinking, *Hope I never have to face a decision like that. Would I have the courage to do the same thing if I thought we wouldn't win without my star player?*

I wasn't that lucky. In 1986, our Bruins traveled to Fresno by bus to play the always tough Fresno State Bulldogs in a three-game series. It was still early in the season and we were off to a disappointing start. We had won seven and lost four, but I felt that, with the talent we had, we should have been no worse than ten and one.

The Bulldogs fans packed the stadium for that first game on Friday night, and we disappointed them by winning 6–0. I believed we had finally put everything together in that game— great pitching, superb defense, and timely hitting.

After the game, I told the players that they should be proud of the way they played, but I warned them not to be satisfied. "Get plenty of rest and be prepared for two tough games

tomorrow," I said, adding that I would be conducting room checks that night and curfew was eleven o'clock. I didn't always have room checks on road trips, but this being our first trip of the year, I wanted them to know that I was serious about them getting a good night's sleep.

After a late meal, I watched television for a while. At eleven o'clock, I stepped out of my room and began knocking on my players' doors.

About halfway through the room check, things were going well. Everyone was in their rooms. Then I knocked gently on a door where no one answered. After a few more mild knocks, I banged on the door loudly. Still, no answer. This was the room of two of our best players. I decided I would come back to that room later, after finishing up with the rest of the team's rooms.

Several minutes later, I returned to the room. Still, no one answered. Disappointed, I decided to park myself on the carpeted floor in the hallway with my back leaning against their door. About a half an hour later, I heard the elevator stop. Loud laughter and yapping came bursting from the inside. The two players stepped out of the elevator and continued their noisy stroll down the hallway. I'll call them David and Sammy.

When they saw me, I expected them to quiet down. But they kept walking and gabbing, as if I wasn't there. I stood at the door and said, "You guys know you are way past curfew?"

"Yeah, we're a little late, Coach." When they spoke, the smell of alcohol made me feel like I was standing in a Westwood pub.

"Have you been drinking?"

They looked at each other, and then lied to me. "No, Coach."

It's amazing how certain memories come shooting back so quickly at times, but when I asked that question and listened to their denial, I couldn't help but think of Coach Wooden's story. I did not want to return to my room and trouble myself about how I should discipline them. Instead of losing sleep like Coach said he did, I dealt out my justice right there in the hallway.

Without raising my voice, I said, "Neither one of you will

suit up for tomorrow's double-header. You can watch from the stands."

"You won't win without us!" David yelled back at me, slobbering all over himself. It was something he never would have said if he had been sober. There was no doubt now that he was intoxicated. Sammy, with bloodshot eyes, looked just as inebriated as he slurred, "Yeah . . . you won't win without us."

"Well, you can watch us try," I replied, trying to speak confidently.

Despite my swift reprimand, I didn't sleep much that night. Like Coach Wooden, I was deeply concerned about how I would answer questions about my decision. It wasn't the press's questions I was troubled about; the press didn't follow UCLA baseball the way it followed UCLA basketball, or even Indiana State basketball. I was more concerned with David and Sammy's parents. I knew they had traveled to see the games. They would want to know why their sons were not playing—why they were not even suiting up. In fact, their sons would probably be sitting next to them in the stands.

I decided to handle it the same way Coach Wooden had, by letting the boys answer to their parents and teammates. I would tell them, "I had my reasons, and they were good ones."

I know David did not tell his parents the *whole* story—the drinking part—because he did have an alcohol problem that he and I talked about afterwards. I told him to see Dr. Parham, a psychologist at UCLA who had experience handling this kind of problem. "As long as you continue to see Dr. Parham and deal with it, I won't tell your parents. You have my word. If you don't do this, I *will* tell them."

I have never regretted making that challenging decision that night in Fresno—and not just because we won the double-header the next day. I was pleased and relieved because David found the courage to face his drinking problem. Both young men helped us win the PAC-Six championship that year, and both played professional baseball. They turned out to be solid

citizens and good family men, who continue to contribute positively to society.

I have often wondered if I would have made the same disciplinary decision if I hadn't known how Coach Wooden had handled *his* situation. I thank Coach for helping me see the whole picture and for doing the right thing for our team, including those two young men.

WHAT DO YOU CALL A MAN LIKE COACH WOODEN?

When J. D. Morgan introduced me to Coach Wooden, I was so awestruck that I found myself saying, "Nice to meet you, Mr. Wooden." That was in the top of the first inning of our relationship, and the last time I ever called him "*Mr. Wooden.*" Mostly, I called him "Coach," even though he eventually told me, "I'm no longer a coach, but if my former players or other coaches want to call me 'Coach,' that is fine with me." He preferred for his friends to call him John, saying that he was "still a teacher and always will be, but I know most people will call me 'Coach.'" As our friendship grew in the middle innings, I was consistent in my inconsistency—sometimes calling him "Coach" and sometimes "John." In the late innings, I mostly called him John.

The media often referred to John as "the Wizard of Westwood," a label that he disliked. Unfortunately, the nickname caught on with the public, and he was forced to live with it—sort of. Before a UCLA basketball game, John and I were holding a conversation on the sidelines of Nell and John Wooden Court, when a middle-aged man holding a basketball asked Coach, "Would you please sign 'the Wizard of Westwood' on my ball?"

John smiled. "I am not a wizard," he replied, calmly and politely. "I don't know a single magical trick. If you don't mind, I would be pleased to sign my real name."

The man nodded. "Of course. Thank you, Mr. Wooden."

Another time, at a restaurant, a man passing by pointed at John and said to his son, "There's the Wizard of Westwood."

"Did you hear that, Gary?" Coach asked.

I played dumb. "Hear what, John?"

"He called me a wizard. Goodness gracious! I'm not a wizard. I don't do sorcery or magic tricks, and I'm not wearing one of those cone-shaped hats!" The veins in John's neck puffed, but as those veins returned to regular size, he explained, "You know, Gary, people are mistaken when they call me that. Now, I can understand why they would call Walt Hazzard "the Wizard of Westwood," because he appeared to handle the basketball like a magician. It was Walter who I first heard referred to by that name."

I nodded, knowing that Walt had arrived from Philadelphia with a style of play that had never been seen before on the West Coast.

"Walter had large hands that made it possible for him to handle the basketball as if it were the size of a baseball," John continued. "The opponents never knew what he was going to do with it—shoot, pass, dribble—until it was too late to stop him. Even his teammates had to keep a close eye on Walt. If they didn't, he'd conk them on the back of the head with one of his patented 'no-look' passes. Yes, Walt was the *first* Wizard of Westwood."

John paused, then offered another figure often referred to as the Wizard of Westwood by the media and the public—Al Scates, UCLA's volleyball coach for almost fifty years. "Al has won more national championships than I have," Coach said. "They call him a wizard, as if his wins came about because he's a magician or has done something on the sly. If he doesn't mind being called a wizard, fine. That's up to him. But I won't ever call him a wizard. He doesn't win because he is a wizard—he wins because he is a great coach, and a very good teacher."

Whenever John left me notes on the desk we shared, he called himself "JW." Once he admitted to me, almost in a whisper, that Nell sometimes called him "John-Bob."

"You mean, almost like John-Boy on *The Waltons*?" I asked.

"Yes," he said sheepishly. "But most of the time she called me 'John' or 'Johnny,' and sometimes 'Honey.'"

John's mother, father, and brothers called him "Johnny." "But they were family, and that fit for them," he explained. I never even thought of doing so. To me, "Johnny" just doesn't fit the size of John Wooden.

COMPETITIVE GREATNESS

When Torey Lovullo graduated from UCLA in 1987, in addition to picking up his diploma, he also picked up the lead in the Bruins' all-time career batting statistics:

1. Most at bats (856)
2. Most hits (266)
3. Most runs scored (211)
4. Most home runs (51)
5. Most RBI (188)
6. Most bases on balls (180)

On top of all this, Lovullo's 45 doubles was second only to Lindsay Meggs (49).

This slick-fielding second baseman was named First Team All-American in 1987, and he is the only Bruin ever to be named Pac-10 Player of the Year two times in a row. These statistics alone are enough to qualify him for placement at the top block of Coach Wooden's Pyramid of Success—*competitive greatness*.

Torey's character *off* the field was equal to his accomplishments on it. His quiet, humble, and polite manner made him a friend to his teammates and everyone who met him (sounds a little bit like the man who constructed the Pyramid of Success).

Shortly after our 1987 season, which ended with a loss to

Arizona State University in the final game of the NCAA West Regional Playoffs, I ran into Coach Wooden in the Morgan Center.

"Gary," he said, "I see that my hometown boy was Pac-10 Player of the Year once again."

"Hometown boy?"

"Yes—Torey Lovullo. We both live in Encino."

This was news to me. "Well, Coach, your neighbor certainly had another great year. We're going to miss him next season."

"Did you think he was going to be that good when you recruited him?" he asked.

"No, I didn't. I just hoped he'd become good enough to be a utility player for us—he can play anywhere in the infield, you know."

"How did you convince him to come here?"

"I stole a page from your recruiting book—spent as little time recruiting him as I could without losing him."

Coach smiled. "Are you saying that I didn't spend much time recruiting?"

"I think you know the answer to that, Coach. Like you, I never made a home visit to the Lovullo's. I don't remember ever having called him on the phone, and I saw him play only once."

Coach chuckled. "It does sound familiar," he admitted. "You know how much I disliked that part of the job."

I decided to tell Coach my Torey Lovullo recruiting story. "I had heard from Torey's coaches that he was a good high school player who worked hard, was a good student, and was a fine young man," I began. "I decided to watch him play an American Legion game early that summer, at Jackie Robinson Stadium.

"I sat in the stands and watched his actions in pregame infield. He had quick but sure hands. I thought his feet were a little heavy for a middle infielder, but when I saw him swing the bat in the game from both sides of the plate, I figured his hitting would outweigh his feet. His bat speed was surprisingly quick for such a skinny kid.

"I had planned to stick around after the game to talk to him

. . . that is, until he finished his last at bat. I didn't mind the fact that he struck out on a curveball in the dirt, but I didn't like how he reacted to it. He threw his bat on the ground in disgust, and it spun its way to the backstop. When I saw that, I thought, *That outweighs everything else.* I decided not to recruit him, and I went home thinking that was the end of that."

Coach nodded and said, "Can't blame you. But how did he end up here? Did he just come on his own?"

"Not exactly. His dad, Sam, called me on the phone shortly after that game. He probably heard that I was in the stands, watching his son play. He asked me if I'd meet with him and Torey at UCLA. He sounded like a good guy, and he wasn't pushy at all. I didn't know at the time that he was the producer of the popular *Hee-Haw* show on television. I said, 'Okay, I'll meet you at Jackie Robinson Stadium.' I had to go to the ball field anyway, because of my summer baseball camp."

"You really did use your time wisely," John interrupted.

"Yes, Coach. Like you, I put in just enough effort to land him."

"At first, when they came to visit, I was pretty much going through the motions, but the more I talked to Sam and Torey, the more I liked the thought of recruiting him. I found myself thinking, *Torey threw his bat, but he did it only because he was disgusted with himself—he didn't throw it because he was angry with the umpire or mad at his teammates.* I knew this kind of thing could be overcome with maturity and coaching. Although I didn't bring up the bat-throwing incident at the time, I decided to give him a second chance. It was my gut feeling that I had witnessed a rare event—and a teachable one—for Torey."

Coach nodded. "At times, I've taken risks recruiting some players with questionable behavior," he said. "Sidney Wicks was one who became a wonderful team player . . . but, in my opinion, he wasn't one to begin with. I just believed he would become one."

"That's how I felt about Torey," I said. "I was glad he and his dad visited and talked to me, although they also revealed that they were planning to pay a visit to Arizona State and meet with Coach Jim Brock. Knowing of Coach Brock's reputation as a great recruiter, I stepped on the accelerator in my recruiting efforts—something you did with Lewis Alcindor, when you flew back to New York to see him."

"That's right," Coach replied. "I didn't routinely make home visits, but I wanted to show Lewis that I was serious about wanting him to come to UCLA."

"Well, I didn't have any scholarship money to give to Torey—it was all promised to others," I said. "You'll never guess what I offered Torey to persuade him to come to UCLA, without him ever going to visit ASU."

"Free tickets to UCLA basketball games?" Coach quipped.

I laughed. "No, much better than that. I remembered Sam saying that Torey's favorite number was three. We were standing outside our antique clubhouse, and I excused myself. I quickly ran through the open door, hopped up the thirteen wooden steps, and sped to my desk, where a current roster was lying. I scanned it to see if any of our returning players would be wearing number three next year, then hurried back down the stairs and gave them the news: 'Number three is available—it's yours if you want it.' Sam looked at his son, and Torey nodded his head. He turned to me and said, 'I'm coming here.'"

"Thank goodness for superstitious baseball players, Gary!" John said, grinning from ear to ear.

Torey became a great player, wearing his number three for the next four years. As it turned out, the bat-throwing incident proved to be a false indicator of the real Torey Lovullo, one of the most gracious, considerate team players I have ever coached.

I thought that my crafty recruiting move of offering him the number three was the key to Torey choosing UCLA. Years later, I learned the real reason from Torey himself. He wanted to attend UCLA because Coach Wooden had laid the foundation

for his recruitment when Torey was only eleven years old.

Torey said he had met Coach Wooden during a basketball camp at Pepperdine University in 1976. "I'll never forget the day I was playing in a scrimmage game, and Coach Wooden saw me stop the game so I could re-tie my shoes," he said. "He pulled me off the court and said, 'Young man, never ever tie your shoes during a game. Make sure you double-tie them so you don't give your opponent an advantage by resting and catching up.'"

I asked Torey if he ever saw Coach again, after his days at the camp. "Yes, in 1985," he said. "My sophomore year at UCLA, we met at the Pioneer Chicken restaurant. I was in my UCLA uniform, and I heard an elderly gentleman behind me ask, 'Did you win your game today?' I turned and recognized Coach Wooden immediately. I answered, 'Yes, we beat USC.' He looked pleased to hear the news. Then he said, 'Don't ever forget that those four letters across your chest should mean something to you. You beat those Trojans every chance you get.' I wish I had seen him again so I could tell him we beat USC thirteen straight times, starting with that game."

Torey gave credit to his dad for putting the idea of attending UCLA in his head, but he credited Coach Wooden for cinching it. "When I was growing up," he said, "my dad, who went to UCLA, always talked about how great the school was, so I was definitely leaning that way. But when I met Coach Wooden, it just fortified my ambition to be a Bruin."

I now realized how little I'd had to do with Torey choosing UCLA. It had really been the magic of John Wooden. I have often wondered if John knew that this great UCLA baseball player was the same youngster he pulled off the court at his basketball camp and talked to at Pioneer Chicken. Maybe he did remember, and that is why he took such a personal interest in Torey's career. I do know that he was proud of his hometown hero.*

---

* Torey played in the major leagues with the Tigers, Yankees, and Angels. He became a big league coach with the Toronto Blue Jays and, in 2012, was named the number-one assistant—the bench coach—for the Boston Red Sox. It would not surprise me if someday he became a big league manager. He'd make a good one.

DADS, WIVES, AND CHILDREN

Coach and I had conversations about our dads, which also led to talking about our wives and children. His dad, Joshua, never played a basketball game in his life, and mine never played a baseball game—not even for fun. When John was very young, Joshua had worked in the barn and fields on his farm, but knowing that his sons loved to play basketball, he had made a basket by knocking a hole in the bottom of a tomato basket and nailing it to the wall inside their barn.

John's dad spent his free time reading books to John. Mine spent his taking me and my brother fishing, but knowing that we loved baseball, he allowed us to throw rocks across the creek when we got bored—which was most of the time. While John's dad worked in the fresh air on the farm, my dad worked amidst the smoke and fumes of a steel factory. There was no mistaking that both John and I felt the love of our dads—and they felt ours for them—despite the fact that they missed most of the games we played in our youth. We knew that they had a good excuse for missing the games, though. They needed to put meat and potatoes on our dinner table.

Whenever John spoke to groups, which was often, he liked quoting his dad's "two-sets-of threes"—rules which, along with the teachings in the Bible, were standards for his dad's sons to live by. One day in our office, I handed John my interpretation of those rules as they would apply to baseball players. He wasn't too amused at first, but several weeks later he told me that he might use my interpretations in a speech to "baseball people" to add some humor.

His dad's list—with my exceptions—looked like this:

First Set of Threes

1. Never lie . . . *except when you trap a fly ball.*
2. Never cheat . . . *except when using the hidden ball trick.*
3. Never steal . . . *except second, third, or home.*

Second Set of Threes

1. Don't whine . . . *except to the umpire.*
2. Don't complain . . . *except to your coach.*
3. Don't make excuses . . . *except when the sun gets in your eyes.*

I doubt that John ever used these—at least, he never admitted it to me.

Coach once said to me, "It is not the *quantity* of time that is most important for your children, it is the *quality* of time—although your children should know that Dad is thinking of them in his absence."

I know John thought of his two teenage children when UCLA hired him. He *made* time for his children. He moved into a place less than fifteen minutes from campus, so he could stay home longer and get home sooner. He limited his practices to a mere two hours so he could spend more time with his family. Most college coaches dragged their practices on for three or four hours.

Coach also spent little time away from his children to recruit players. He told me that he never made more than eight visits to recruits' homes in his entire career. Most basketball coaches make that many in one year, and so do college baseball coaches today. I know I did. It isn't healthy for the child-dad relationship. Thinking back on it, I wish I had only made eight home visits to recruits in my career. Sometimes coaches lose track of their priorities. On practice days, I always tried to get home in time to read bedtime stories to my five daughters, but when we had night games, I never got home before their bedtime. Most road games on weekends meant at least three, sometimes four nights away—no Dad, no bedtime stories.

About a dozen years after he retired, Coach Wooden gave me a wise suggestion for when I went on long trips. He said, "When you go on a road trip, you might want to bring a book home for your daughters. Try to get them a book about the area that you just visited."

I wish he had suggested it in time for my first three daughters, but his idea was religiously followed for my last two. My daughters loved to read—especially about the areas I had been to. When our UCLA teams played at Arizona State and Arizona University, I brought home storybooks about desert animals. When we played our annual series with the University of Hawaii schools, I brought home books about whales or rainbows or mermaids. It was a great way to share with them the world their daddy had just visited, and it was proof, as John said, "that dad was thinking of them in his absence." Reading those stories to them was also a good way to spend quality time with them. Every time they picked up one of those books, it would be a way of staying in touch with dad.

Not long after John suggested the book idea, he really hit a home run when he told me, "The best gift a father can give his children is to love their mother."

I thought it was one of the wisest sayings I had ever heard, and I told him so.

"Not my saying, Gary," he said. "It was my dad's favorite Abraham Lincoln quote. But Dad also told me that if you don't go further, it is useless."

"What did he mean by that?"

"It's more than just feeling your love for her or telling her you love her. It is even more than telling her in front of your children. You have to *show* her and *show* your children that you love their mother."

"That isn't always easy for me to do," I said.

It surprised me when I heard Coach say, "Me, too."

This conversation was being held on a bench outside the Morgan Center, as students rushed by us with books in hand, on their way to class. We paid them little attention as I kept my eyes trained on this man, who was willing to share some of his most private thoughts. Coach's arms were folded in that familiar pose I saw so often in our tiny office.

"It was also difficult for my father to show affection," I said. "At least, I didn't see much hugging and kissing. But somehow, I knew by the way he talked and showed kindness toward her that he clearly loved her."

"I don't know why it is so difficult for men to show affection to their loved ones," John said. "I mean, how hard is it to open the car door for the lady you love? Or hold her hand when going for a short walk? Your wife and your children can *see* your love when you do those things, and that gives more meaning to the words, 'I love you.'"

John smiled, not so much to me, but more to himself, as he fondly recalled a memory of long ago. "One way I learned to show my affection for Nell happened when I played my first high school basketball game," he said. "The game, in those days, always started with a center jump. Just as I prepared myself to retrieve the tip around the half-court circle. I looked at where Nellie was sitting in the stands, and I gave her a wink. She acknowledged with the 'okay' sign"—John formed an "O" with his thumb and forefinger to demonstrate Nell's signal. "It was her way of wishing me good luck. When she did that, I waved back to her, with barely enough time to see the referee make his toss for the jump ball.

"Gary, ever since that game, I looked up to the stands before every game—often, she had to stand up and wave her arms so I could find her. I waved my rolled-up program in her direction, and she gave me the 'okay' sign. That good luck sign became our special way of saying, 'I am thinking of you, and I love you.' It meant a lot to me, and I know it meant a lot to her, knowing that I was thinking of her even before coaching a basketball game—be it a big game or a less crucial one."

Coach and Nell's tradition had a big impact on me. What a wonderful way to show my loved one that I truly cared about her. I decided to tell my wife about the idea. "Sandy," I said, "when I'm coaching, whenever you see me touch the Bruin patch on my sleeve, you will know I am thinking of you and that I love you." I didn't tell her I got the idea from Coach Wooden.

Unfortunately, unlike Coach Wooden and Nell, there was no set time for "the touch," and sometimes, especially at games played on the road, I didn't know where she was sitting. Sometimes, I touched the patch without looking up to the stands, like after the *Star Spangled Banner,* or on my way to the third base coaching box. Once, I even touched the patch right after the umpire threw me out of a ball game—it helped calm me down.

Another good thing resulted from this tradition. Our children knew about my touch signal. Sitting next to their mommy, they could *see* that their daddy loved their mommy, even when he was working. As they grew older, they knew that my signal was also meant for them.

Some years later, I told Coach about "the touch" and thanked him for the idea he and Nell had originated.

"Did you find it easier to touch your shoulder than to say you loved her in person?" he asked.

I nodded.

His eyes drifted away for a second before returning to mine. He then repeated almost the same thing he had said years before. "Why is it so difficult for men to say, 'I love you' to our loved ones, even when we know we do? And why is it almost

Coach Art Reichle (right) with twins Gene and Gary Adams, 1959.

Gary Adams batting for UCLA, 1962.

**Signed photo from Coach Wooden to Gary Adams, 1975.
Wooden wrote: "For Coach Gary Adams, who teaches my favorite
sport, with best wishes always. John Wooden."**

Top: Ed Cowan pitching for UCLA, 1976.

Bottom: UCLA second baseman Bobby Dallas scoring the winning run in the championship game versus USC, 1976.

Top: Personal note from Coach Wooden to Gary Adams after UCLA beat USC to win the 1976 California Intercollegiate Baseball Association championship.

Bottom: Signed photo from Coach Wooden to eleven-year-old Torey Lovullo, 1976. Wooden wrote:
"For Torey with best wishes. John Wooden."

Top: Tim Leary pitching for UCLA, 1979.
Bottom: UCLA athletic director J. D. Morgan, 1980.

Top: Note from Coach Wooden to Gary Adams, accompanying clippings from the 1980 *Collegiate Baseball* article in which Coach Wooden stated: "Baseball's my favorite game—always has been."

Bottom: UCLA's Rich Amaral turning a double play against Stanford, 1983.

Gary Adams and Coach Wooden, 1985.

Jack Gifford in his UCLA uniform, 1986.

Torey Lovullo fielding for UCLA, 1987.

Gary Adams congratulating Eric Karros as he rounds third base after hitting a home run against USC, 1988.

Top: Coach Adams arguing with an umpire, 1990s.

Bottom: Gary Adams with daughters Audrey and Jessica, 1992.

David Roberts batting for UCLA, 1993.

Troy Glaus playing for UCLA, 1995.

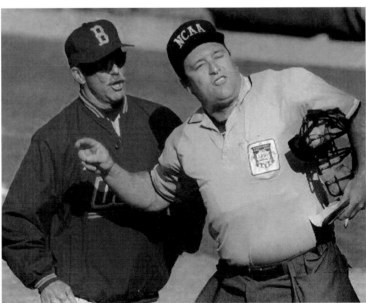

Top: Pete Zamora delivering the pitch that would hit Arizona State University's lead-off batter, Mikel Moreno, 1996.

Bottom: Coach Adams being ejected after ordering Pete Zamora to intentionally hit the lead-off batter for ASU, 1996.

Eric Byrnes playing for UCLA, 1997.

UCLA's Chase Utley turning a double play against
Arizona State University, 2000.

Top: The Valley Inn Gang, 2003.

Bottom: Coach Adams with Rafer Johnson at
the UCLA Hall of Fame Banquet, 2003.

John Wooden
11-20-04

Dear Gary -
        Congratulations
on your thirty years at the
helm of the UCLA baseball
teams and best wishes in all
your future endeavors.
        You outlasted me by
three years, but of course, I
was forced to do my teaching
indoors with seventeen of
my twenty-seven years confined
in the poorly ventilated "B.O. Barn".
Quite naturally this brought about
a pre-mature retirement!
        May true joy be with you
and yours in the coming years.
                Sincerely, John Wooden

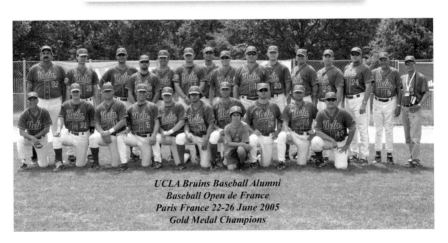

UCLA Bruins Baseball Alumni
Baseball Open de France
Paris France 22-26 June 2005
Gold Medal Champions

Top: Personal note from Coach Wooden to Gary Adams
upon Adams's retirement in 2004.

Bottom: The UCLA Alumni Team at
the Paris International Tournament, 2005.

Top: Coach Wooden and Tony Spino, circa 2007.
Bottom: Gary Adams and Eric Byrnes with Coach Wooden, 2008.

Top: Baseball party thrown in Coach Wooden's honor, 2010. Clockwise from left: Mike Scioscia, Joe Torre, Zev Yaroslavsky, Dan Guerrero, Jeff Moorad, Coach Wooden, and Gary Adams.

Bottom: Guests at Coach Wooden's baseball party, 2010. Left to right: Dan Guerrero, Gary Adams, Mike Scioscia, Angelo Mazzone, Zev Yaroslavsky, Coach Wooden, Jeff Moorad, Nan Wooden Muelhausen, Vin Scully, and Joe Torre.

Top: The Jackie Robinson statue overlooking the
UCLA baseball stadium.

Bottom: A replica of Coach Wooden's den at
the UCLA Athletics Hall of Fame.

COACH WOODEN'S PYRAMID OF SUCCESS

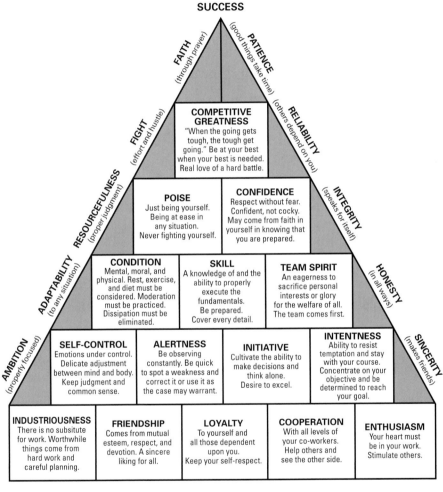

SUCCESS

FAITH (through prayer)

PATIENCE (good things take time)

FIGHT (effort and hustle)

RELIABILITY (others depend on you)

COMPETITIVE GREATNESS
"When the going gets tough, the tough get going." Be at your best when your best is needed. Real love of a hard battle.

RESOURCEFULNESS (proper judgment)

INTEGRITY (speaks for itself)

POISE
Just being yourself. Being at ease in any situation. Never fighting yourself.

CONFIDENCE
Respect without fear. Confident, not cocky. May come from faith in yourself in knowing that you are prepared.

ADAPTABILITY (to any situation)

HONESTY (in all ways)

CONDITION
Mental, moral, and physical. Rest, exercise, and diet must be considered. Moderation must be practiced. Dissipation must be eliminated.

SKILL
A knowledge of and the ability to properly execute the fundamentals. Be prepared. Cover every detail.

TEAM SPIRIT
An eagerness to sacrifice personal interests or glory for the welfare of all. The team comes first.

AMBITION (properly focused)

SINCERITY (makes friends)

SELF-CONTROL
Emotions under control. Delicate adjustment between mind and body. Keep judgment and common sense.

ALERTNESS
Be observing constantly. Be quick to spot a weakness and correct it or use it as the case may warrant.

INITIATIVE
Cultivate the ability to make decisions and think alone. Desire to excel.

INTENTNESS
Ability to resist temptation and stay with your course. Concentrate on your objective and be determined to reach your goal.

INDUSTRIOUSNESS
There is no subsitute for work. Worthwhile things come from hard work and careful planning.

FRIENDSHIP
Comes from mutual esteem, respect, and devotion. A sincere liking for all.

LOYALTY
To yourself and all those dependent upon you. Keep your self-respect.

COOPERATION
With all levels of your co-workers. Help others and see the other side.

ENTHUSIASM
Your heart must be in your work. Stimulate others.

"Success is peace of mind, which is a direct result of self-satisfaction in knowing you made the effort to become the best you are capable of becoming."
—John Wooden

COACH ADAMS'S SPHERE OF COMMITMENT

as difficult for us to say, 'thank you' to our wives? Those might be the most underrated terms in the dictionary."

I listened to this wise man searching for answers. I couldn't help him one bit.

John gave me a puzzled look that I doubt few of his players ever saw. "And how difficult is it," he continued, "to say to your love, right in front of your children and after you have eaten a home-cooked meal, 'Honey, that was delicious. Thank you.' Those two words, 'thank you,' are almost as necessary in a loving relationship as the three words, 'I love you.'"

John shook his head. "Goodness gracious, I wish I had used them more often."

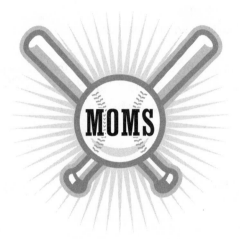

MOMS

John Wooden's mother, Roxie Anna, married twenty-year-old Joshua Wooden when she was just sixteen. Once married, she quietly went about her business inside the home—cooking meals, canning fruits and vegetables, washing clothes, and performing other household chores. Like her husband, she was clearly aware of John's and his three brothers' fondness for baseball and basketball. John said she surprised them all when she sewed some old rags together and stuffed them into a pair of her black cotton stockings, then handed them a home-made basketball.

"It was a wobbly ball that got a bit lopsided over time and it didn't help me learn much about dribbling," he said. "But it was helpful with my passing and shooting."

When John told me this story, and about how quietly his mother went about her daily life, I was reminded of my mom. Bernice also cared about me and my brother and our favorite sports. But she was not quiet, like John's Roxie Anna.

Mom was the most avid and outspoken baseball fan we twins ever knew. She claimed that the reason we loved baseball so much was that, when she was pregnant with us, most of her time was spent listening to every Cincinnati Reds game on the radio. The Reds cinched the National League pennant in September 1939—the same month and year Gene and I were born.

One of my first memories of playing ball came when we were about eight years old. Most of the boys in our neighborhood were two or three years older. In the summer, these boys would play ball in the middle of the street in front of our house. A manhole cover was home plate, someone's glove was thrown down for second base, a patch of worn out grass between the curb and sidewalk was first base, and a tree on the opposite side of the street, which you had to tag with your hand, was third. The older boys would choose sides, and Gene and I would sit on the curb and watch.

One day, I heard a sharp voice coming from behind me. I recognized it immediately.

"You boys let my boys play!" Mom yelled at the top of her lungs, standing behind the porch rails of our home. That was all she needed to say; her authoritarian tone and the scolding look on her face were enough to scare the older boys. Thanks to Mom, from that point on, we played. That's where we first learned the game.

John never once heard his mother complain about anything—although, he said, she had every reason to. "Mom lost a daughter at birth," John told me. "She never even had a chance to name her. That same year, she lost Cordelia, my two-year-old sister, to diphtheria after a long time of suffering. I don't know how Mom got through it and still managed to care for the rest of us."

I told John, "Your mom never complained, but my mom always complained—she was a glass-half-empty kind of lady."

Mom complained about her own cooking, and she complained about Dad always being warm when she was "freezing to death." But mostly—even though she loved it—Mom complained about the game of baseball.

Mom always sat next to our UCLA dugout, where the players could overhear her complain when our pitchers put a runner on base in the first inning. We all laughed when we heard her say to those sitting next to her, "Well, there goes the ol' ball game!"

The umpires were her favorite targets. They could distinguish Mom's high-pitched voice clear through a roaring crowd. She rarely agreed with their decisions, from the time I began playing organized Knothole ball when I was ten, to the day I finished coaching at age sixty-five.

"The umpires knew her," I told John. "Not that they had ever met her—but they knew her voice. Sometimes, when I went to home plate before the games to hand the umpires my lineup card, one of them would ask, 'Gary, is your mom here today?' John, you would've laughed if you'd seen their faces drop every time I told 'em, 'Oh, yeah, she's here. So you'd better be on your toes.'"

John told me that his mother kept her faith throughout her fifty years, dedicating herself to raising her four sons with love and devotion. "Mom always praised my brothers when I won, and she always found a way to make me feel equally loved when my brothers won," he said. "She never showed favoritism toward any of us."

With a half-smile, I told John, "My brother was born before me, and being the only child for ten minutes, he was the spoiled one. But I never once thought my mom favored my brother over me, and I know he never thought she favored me over him."

"I believe our mothers were like most mothers," Coach said, "who, for some unknown reason, have the ability to divide their love among all their children, and yet each child still feel all of their mother's love."

I nodded and thought of my Mom's words whenever I left the house to play or coach a ball game: "Good luck, Gary, and remember—I'm behind you, win or tie."

WHAT IS SUCCESS?

John and I didn't always agree on the definition of success, but we did agree that it was *not* about winning and losing.

One evening in 1992, my five-year-old daughter, Audrey, helped me realize that losing should not be as devastating as we sometimes make it. Sitting in our living room, I heard Audrey ask her mother, "Mommy, why is Dad sad tonight?"

"Because he lost his game today."

Audrey turned and looked at me. I could tell she was puzzled. I asked her, "Audrey, have you ever lost a game?"

"No, daddy," she answered, "but I've lost some pieces to a game."

Her reply made me smile. Without knowing it, she had reminded me that the game I lost that day was only one piece of the greater game of life.

I have heard John recite his definition of success many times. His definition is the basis of his famous Pyramid of Success:

"Success is peace of mind, which is a direct result of self-satisfaction in knowing you made the effort to become the best you are capable of becoming." He never changed his definition since he coined it in 1934, and he spent the next fourteen years formulating his Pyramid of Success.

One day, in the early 1990s, I told John that I had heard another definition of success he might like that was attributed to one of his favorite ball players. This piqued his interest. "I'd like to hear it," he said.

"Success is making the most of what you've got."

"That's pretty good, Gary. But I have a couple questions. How does one know whether he has made the most of what he's got? Don't you think he should have peace of mind and be satisfied with himself that he gave his best effort?"

While I thought over his questions, John asked, "Who was this favorite player of mine who made this quote?"

"Pete Rose," I answered with a smile.

He returned my smile. "Used to be my favorite player," he said, "until he was caught betting on baseball."

Later on, in the summer of 1994, John and I were discussing success again. I had just finished one of the worst seasons I had ever had, in terms of wins and losses.

"Gary, I didn't need to win ten national championships to feel successful," John said. "I would have been just as satisfied with my coaching if our teams had not won any of those trophies."

I stared at him. I saw a sea of blue before me: his favorite powder-blue button-down sweater, and his penetrating, deep blue eyes.

"It's true," he said. "Every year I coached, I gave it the same effort. Sometimes that effort resulted in a championship . . . sometimes it didn't. But I always believed that I was just as successful in those years absent a championship as those years we won a championship."

Then he recited a familiar quote, with one change. This time, he applied his quote to the coaching profession.

"A coach is no different than his players, when it pertains to 'success.' At the end of the season, the tally that should matter most to a coach is not the one that measures his wins or losses,

but the one that measures his effort . . . and only *he* knows if he's given his best effort."

I struggled to look him in the eyes. "That's the problem I have, Coach. I've had a few years when I felt like I didn't give my best effort. I thought I could have done more."

"Gary, that is only natural. At least you aren't blaming someone else—that's being a failure, for sure."

Both of us were silent for a while. I didn't know what else to say. In fact, I felt embarrassed, and began to regret having admitted this to John.

Finally, he asked, "Were those years mostly the ones where you lost more games than you won?"

"Mostly."

"Did you bounce back and give it your best effort the years after your losing years?"

"I think so."

"I admire coaches who haven't won." He paused and saw my surprised reaction. "People complain all the time about coaches who have losing years or don't win enough championships. Coaches should ignore all of that. Goodness gracious! How many coaches who have had a losing season can come back and coach as hard as those coaches who have won? To me, those are the coaches who are special and to be admired by all. Despite the disappointing results in their minds and in the minds of others, they continue to give their best effort. That's being successful."

John always had a knack for making people feel better, and that day, that's what he did for me.

Ann Meyers Drysdale told me once, "I don't want to look back on my life and say, 'What if?' Don't worry about failure. Try it, and if it doesn't work out, that's okay, because at least you tried." Annie was a great example of her own words; she was not afraid to compete against the best players in the NBA, many of them a foot taller than she was.

UCLA's director of athletics, Dan Guerrero, successful as both a college baseball player and administrator, quoted an anonymous source when trying to explain the secret to success. He said, "I can't tell you the secret to success, but I can tell you the secret to failure—trying to appease everyone." Not a bad quote to remember when you have to make controversial and tough decisions for a large university athletic program. UCLA is fortunate to have a man with the courage to make those decisions, whether they end good or bad.

Coach told me once that he had probably heard more versions of what success is than any man, alive or dead. There is one version I doubt he ever heard that I never had a chance to tell him. It was written by my favorite American author, John Steinbeck, in one of his least popular books, *The Log from the Sea of Cortez*. I imagine Coach would say it is a *unique* description of success:

> Ed [a biologist] held that one couldn't tell from a quick look how successful a species is. "Consider now," he would say, "if you look superficially, you would say that the local banker or the owner of a cannery or even the mayor of Monterey is the successful and surviving individual. But consider their ulcers, consider the heart trouble, the blood pressure in that group. And then consider the bums over there—cirrhosis of the liver I will grant will have its toll, but not the other things."

Ask any ten successful people, "What does success mean to you?" and they will give you ten different answers. Reba McEntire, one of country music's most successful singers, had a unique formula for success. She said, "To succeed in life, you need three things: a wishbone, a backbone, and a funny bone." Johnny Cash once said, "Success is having to worry about every damn thing in the world, except money."

Coach's formula for success—his Pyramid—may also be the best way to achieve it, though he may get an argument

from Arthur Rubinstein, the great pianist who received the Presidential Medal of Freedom twenty-seven years before Coach Wooden did. Rubinstein said, "There is no formula for success, except perhaps an unconditional acceptance of life and what it brings."

Then again, maybe Rubinstein's philosophy was not too far from Coach's, since "an unconditional acceptance of life and what it brings" is another way of achieving the "peace of mind" in John's definition.

Coach Wooden's Pyramid of Success formula has withstood the test of time. There are thousands of people who believe that Coach has discovered the best formula for them.

As I mentioned at the beginning, John and I didn't always agree upon our definition of success, but it was mainly a matter of semantics, not content. I told him that I thought his definition hit the mark, but was a bit long, slightly confusing, and difficult to remember.

He smiled. "Well, how would you write your definition of success?" he asked.

I was prepared for his question, and replied, "Success is being satisfied that you made the most of what you've got." Coach knew that I held no resentment for Pete Rose, being a loyal fan of those players who wore a Cincinnati Reds uniform.

John tilted his head slightly and gave me a wry grin. "I think I'll stick to my original definition," he said.

Even with all his success, Coach remained a man of unquestionable humility in his attitude, behavior, and spirit. I never heard John utter a boastful word about his success in all the years I knew him, but I did hear him say this: "I don't want to be like the guy who coughs as he's putting his offering in the church plate."

COMMITMENT

The dictionary says that "commitment" means one is bound—intellectually and emotionally—to someone or something.

Coach Wooden demanded that his players be committed to, not just involved in, his brand of basketball. I sometimes told my players that the difference between being involved with something and being committed to it was like the bacon and eggs breakfast you have in the morning—the chicken was involved, but the pig was committed. Like Coach, I wanted my players to be committed.

Although Coach Wooden could not control what his players did before or after they spent two hours a day with him at practice, he certainly hoped that they were just as committed off the court as they were on it. His Pyramid of Success came in mighty handy, helping ease Coach's mind when he was not with his players. Although he did not originally design his pyramid for this reason, he felt it was a good reminder for his players about how to behave in their everyday lives. This included being committed to their academics.

Coach got the idea for his Pyramid of Success from his high school teacher and basketball coach, Glenn Curtis. Coach

Curtis taught his students and players to follow his "Ladder of Achievement," using an illustration of a five-rung ladder. Years later, in 1948, his first year at UCLA, Coach Wooden unveiled his Pyramid of Success. It was not a fly-by-night invention. He had given it a tremendous amount of thought over many years prior to its final form.

One of the first questions I ever asked Coach was, "Why the illustration of a pyramid?"

His answer was a simple one. "I wanted a visual image that my players could look at and immediately understand—and re-member," he replied.

John told me that he thought every coach should find a way to get his philosophy across to his players. This can be done verbally, if he is good with words and doesn't mind repeating his philosophy often.

"Written hand-outs are useful, too, if you don't give your players too much information at once," he said.

John even used poetry as a way to communicate his philos-ophy to his players. He loved poetry and wrote many poems, frequently reciting them to his players. "Boys remember things better when the words rhyme," he said. He quickly added, "Al-though, I'm not a poet, Gary. I'm a rhymer."

Coach believed that the old saying, "A picture is worth a thousand words," was one of the best ways for a coach to get his message across to his players. But he was careful to add, "The best picture you can show your players is the picture of yourself. They see their coach almost every day. You must paint a picture—set an example—of your philosophy and be true to it."

After considerable thought, and with only ten more years to go in my coaching career, I finally formulated a visual image of my philosophy. Why I didn't see it before, I don't know—it had been in front of me almost all of my life. It was the image of a baseball.

I called it the "Sphere of Commitment." It is not my

intention to discuss it here, but I will say that, without Coach Wooden, I would never have thought of offering my philosophy in the form of a visual image, and it would never have come into being.

I have included a picture of my Sphere in this book to show the similarity of ideas and the influence Coach had on my own philosophy—although I did not fully absorb it until late in my career. There will never be a better visual image and teaching tool than John's Pyramid of Success.

"Commitment" was a strong and meaningful word in John's mind. In one of the last books he ever wrote, *A Game Plan for Life*, which he said may have been his "most important work," he wrote: "You have the potential—no, you have the responsibility—to be a mentor and to be mentored. And so I write this book for you, too. Thank you for making this commitment."

John strongly believed that it was essential to be committed to whatever one's task might be. He demonstrated this in his own life when he announced his retirement after winning a tough, hard-fought NCAA semifinal game in 1975 against Louisville. His announcement caught everyone by surprise—especially his players.

Almost a year after that memorable day, when he and I were talking privately in our little office, I asked him why he had decided to quit coaching. He told me that, when he won that semifinal game, he should have been filled with elation, but instead, he felt "sort of empty." He knew that he should not be coaching with that kind of feeling. "A coach needs to be *fully* committed," he said. "There is no such thing as being partially committed." I understood his answer, and I never forgot it.

I thought about how Coach might have felt at the time of his retirement. Maybe he just didn't see himself staying exactly the same, watching the busy, changing lives of his players and putting more unappreciated trophies on his and UCLA's shelves. Most likely, he wasn't tired of teaching his *players* how to tie their laces on their shoes, but maybe he was tired of tying

up his own, walking into the gym, and coaching—the same thing he had been doing almost every day of his life. He didn't want to do it the *rest* of his life. He needed change, too. He was committed to it.

RESPECT VS. FEAR

oach Wooden once told me, "It is important to teach your teams to *respect* all of their opponents, but to *fear* none of them."

I tried my best to adhere to that philosophy when I showed my players my Sphere of Commitment. I told them, "It does not say 'the *Fear* of Commitment.'"

A good example of applying Coach's "respect versus fear" philosophy occurred in 1985, when I took a UCLA team to Stanford to play a three-game series. At the time, Stanford was ranked number one in the nation. Unfortunately, we were not ranked anywhere in the polls.

In the first game, we lost, 4–3. I watched as we made some critical errors at critical times. It was obvious to me that our players were uptight and playing scared. I honestly believed that we could have won that game, had our players not been so fearful of the *number-one* team in the nation.

I blamed myself. It is the coach's responsibility to prepare his players mentally for competition. I had failed them. That night, I tossed and turned in my hotel room, trying to think of a good way to eliminate any fears our players might have. I didn't think Coach Wooden's words alone would be enough.

I needed to find a way to paint a picture of his words. Despite spending most of the night in deep thought, I arose the next morning without any idea how to fix the fear situation.

When we arrived at Stanford's Sunken Diamond, I took a solitary walk behind an old set of wooden bleachers. I noticed that a bleacher plank had fallen and was lying on the ground in front of me. Just for fun, I walked along the top of the plank. Before I got to the end of the plank, an idea struck me.

I called my team over and asked them to line up in single file at the other end of the plank, and walk on the plank toward me. After I said this, I never saw so many eyebrows raised at the same time. They stared back at me as if I had gone a little wacky.

After they had all walked the plank with nary a misstep, I asked them if they had been scared that they might fall off the plank. Of course, they all shook their heads and said, "No."

I then pointed at Stanford's Hoover Tower in the distance, which overlooked the campus. I knew it was almost as tall as a football field is long. As the players turned to look at it, I asked them, "What if there was another tower standing alongside it, and this same plank was connecting the two at the top of the towers? Would you walk with the same confidence as when the plank was lying on the ground?"

I waited, but no one said a word.

"Yesterday, you played as if this plank was as high as that tower," I continued. "It was not your best effort, because you were afraid of falling. Today, I expect you to play the game the same way you walked the plank just now—*without* fear and *with* confidence."

I turned my back on them and walked to the field to prepare for the game. My players followed silently.

Well, this story has the kind of ending I had hoped for on that day. We beat Stanford, 9–6. What I remember most about that game was how the players encouraged each other to stay confident, with three simple words: "Walk the plank!" Those words still ring in my ears when I think of that 1985 team.

This would be a *better* story if we had had another victory on the third day we played . . . but it was not so. Stanford won, 9–8, but unlike the first game, we did not play scared. And we did not beat ourselves. Our players played with the same confidence as the day before, and they gave it their best effort. I was as proud of them as if they had won.

Yes, Stanford won the series, and we *respectfully* shook their hands when it was all over. But, to this day, I thank Coach Wooden for teaching me the difference between respecting your opponent and being fearful of them.

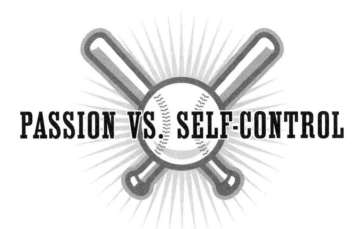

PASSION VS. SELF-CONTROL

One morning in 1993, I literally bumped into Coach Wooden in the J. D. Morgan Center's diminutive mail room. After cheerful greetings, he asked, "How's Mick doing, Gary?"

Coach Mickens had been retired for a couple of years, after serving as my assistant for fifteen years at UCLA. He and John had become good friends when Mick was Art Reichle's assistant, ten years prior to my term as head coach. I told John that Mick was enjoying the retired life on the beaches of Hawaii, and that I talked to him frequently.

"Say hello to him for me," he said, smiling. "I always enjoyed talking to Coach Mickens."

"And I know why," I replied. "He loves talking about baseball."

"Yes, Gary, he was passionate about the game. I can still hear Mick cheering the players on from your dugout. Sometimes he'd yell something at the umpires, but nothing insulting. I never saw or heard of Mick getting thrown out of any ball games. He was passionate without losing control."

I thought about what Coach had said, and he was absolutely right in his characterization of Coach Mickens. Although Mick was filled with a passionate love for baseball, he always maintained his self-control.

Self-control. That term appears in John's Pyramid of Success, in the first block on the second row. Underneath it, Coach wrote these words: "Control emotion, or emotion will control you." In his children's book, *Inch and Miles,* he wrote, "Control yourself so others won't have to."

John said that he liked for his players and assistant coaches to be passionate about basketball, but not to the point of "losing it."

When I thought of John's choices for assistant coaches, "passionate" did not resonate as loudly as "self-control." One of his first assistant coaches at UCLA was the rather reserved Bill Putnam. My first sighting of Coach Putnam came when he was pushing a floor mop alongside Coach in the old gymnasium. I saw him again when I played on the baseball team because he was a friend of Coach Reichle's, and Coach would occasionally invite him to accompany us on a few road trips. I cannot recall Coach Putnam ever uttering a word above a whisper at any of our games. Even on Coach Wooden's bench, Coach Putnam sat rather stoically. In my eyes, he was much more self-controlled than passionate.

In John's book, *They Call Me Coach,* he gave Putnam the ultimate form of praise: "Bill was one of the most loyal, hard-working coaches who ever worked with me." I noticed that John wrote, "*with* me," not "*for* me."

Gary Cunningham was a valuable assistant during most of John's NCAA championship years. Gary played for Coach in the 1960s, and John once described him to me as being "a very intense player and coach."

I wondered if he was talking about the same Gary Cunningham I knew. Gary had never seemed passionate or intense from where I viewed him. I got to know Gary quite well when we were both attending UCLA. During both of our senior years, we were practically roommates. He lived across the hall from me at our apartment complex at 501 Gayley Avenue. He was

roommates with my twin brother and Noel Trout, and all three of them were captains of their respective teams that year: Gary in basketball, Noel in track and cross country, and my brother, Gene, in baseball. Noel became my first-ever assistant when I coached the UCLA freshman baseball team in 1964.

I asked Noel if he ever saw any sign of intensity or passion emanate from Cunningham.

"Once," Noel answered. "We were studying together, and he was working on a report about fats in the diet. We got to talking about it, and I saw a glimpse of some passion as he explained his report to me. The more he talked, the more he got all fired up about it."

Gene and Noel did admit that Gary could have possessed the same type of personality that each of them had when it came to competing on the field, the track, or the court. Both admitted that competition in sports brought out a passion and intensity in them that may not be obvious to others.

When I told John that Gary seemed far from passionate, Coach was quick to respond. "Don't be misled by what you see off the court," he said. "Gary was one of the two best free throw shooters I ever had—Henry Bibby being the other. I think Gary made about thirty-five in a row at one juncture. That takes some intense concentration, and a lot of passion for doing the little things correctly. Of course, it also takes self-control, which he had."

Coach wasn't finished. I believe he wanted to make sure that my impression was a false one. He stuck with the facts.

"Gary, did you know that Coach Cunningham has the best winning percentage of any basketball coach in UCLA history?" he asked. "Better than mine. Maybe he didn't win any national championships in his two years as head coach, but his teams were ranked second in the nation at the end of both seasons. I know a lot of coaches who would take that. Cunningham was *quietly* intense and *quietly* passionate. He didn't wear his passion on his sleeve, like some athletes do and some coaches—like

Bobby Knight, for example. He kept his passion hidden inside."

I decided to ask Cunningham about John's remarks. "I think I was passionate, or else I wouldn't have been able to achieve all the things I did in basketball and life," Gary said. "However, there might be better words than 'passionate' to describe me—like 'driven' or 'determined.' I will admit that, when I was a UCLA student, I was very shy and quiet. But internally, I was intense, determined, and driven."

Sometime after my conversation with John, I thought of how those two words, "passion" and "self-control," were contradictory. John was able to link those words together in a positive way. Who else would have the wisdom to teach his players to be passionate, and at the same time, be able to maintain their self-control? Who else could teach it so well? Coach accomplished this difficult task by his own strong example, which rubbed off on his players—and on his coaches, like Gary Cunningham.

There were times when my passion got the best of me, and I lost my self-control enough to be ejected from games over two dozen times in my coaching career. Compared to Coach Wooden's two technical fouls in his long career, my ejection statistic doesn't look too good.

I am amazed at how Coach kept his composure with the referees. I know there were times when his passion for basketball brought him *close* to losing his temper with the men in stripes, but he was able to keep his self-control because of his greater determination to set a good example for his players. Just as important to him was his desire to show the officials that they had his utmost respect.

As a spectator at baseball games, Coach razzed the umpires much more than he ever heckled the basketball referees. I believe he razzed the men in blue more for the fun of it, not because he was angry with their missed calls.

A COMEBACK PLAYER

Not long after the Dodgers defeated the Oakland A's in the 1988 World Series, I saw Coach Wooden at UCLA. He greeted me with a big smile and a question.

"Did you see that our Tim Leary was named the National League's Comeback Player of the Year?" he asked.

When he said "our" Tim Leary, I wasn't sure whether he was referring to his Dodgers or his Bruins, but I answered, "Yes, I did, Coach. Tim deserved it. The Dodgers wouldn't have made it to the World Series without him." Leary had won seventeen games, posted a 2.91 Earned Run Average, pitched nine complete games, and led his pitching staff in strikeouts. He also led all National League pitchers in batting average, winning the coveted Silver Bat Award for being the best hitting pitcher in the league.

Coach and I spent a little time talking about the amazing improvement Tim had made after a mediocre performance the previous season when, as a spot starter, he won only three games and lost eleven, and had a 4.76 ERA.

Coach remembered that Tim was an All-American pitcher at UCLA, and was a first round draft choice by the Mets. I added, "Tim was also an *academic* All-American, majoring in economics."

Coach was already impressed, but I went a step further. "Despite all of Tim's accomplishments and honors, in all the years I've known him, I never heard him boast about his laurels. He is a humble young man who always gives credit to others for what he has accomplished. You're going to like this, Coach—you know how you taught your players to always acknowledge their teammates whenever they received a pass that led to them making a basket?"

"Oh yes," he replied. "I insisted upon it—whether it was a finger pointed in his teammate's direction, or just a look or a nod."

"Well, Coach, when Tim pitched for UCLA, he did it on the baseball field. Whenever a player made a nice defensive play behind him, he would turn and point a finger at him in a gesture of thanks. I remember a sensational play our second baseman, Mike Gallego, made—diving for a grounder on the grass behind second base, throwing the batter out, and preventing a runner from scoring from second. I watched Tim rush over the top of the mound with his fist in the air, pointing at Mike. I thought he was going to run all the way out to shallow center field and give Mike a big hug."

Coach grinned. "You're right, Gary," he said. "I do like that. How did you recruit Tim?" John always liked hearing about how players came to choose UCLA.

"Tim didn't get much attention from the pro scouts while he pitched in high school—he wasn't even drafted," I said. "But I had watched him several times, since Santa Monica High School was near UCLA and on my way home. Of all the pitchers I had scouted that year, I believed he was the best I'd seen. Coach Mickens, who saw Tim also, agreed.

"I was afraid some other college coach would see the same thing I saw in Tim. I was sure there were more than a few coaches who had already made offers. So, I asked him to come visit me at UCLA. I personally showed him around the campus, took him to lunch, and gave him the royal treatment. Not having an

on-campus ball field to show him, I purposely ended the day in a spot where I was certain he would be impressed—your place, Coach. Pauley Pavilion."

I told Coach that when we had walked into the pavilion and stood on the concourse that circled the basketball court below, I could see that Tim was impressed. "I gave Tim some time to soak it all in," I said. "Then I prepared to make an offer that would at least be equal to all other offers Tim had received. I said, 'Tim, I'm offering you a *full* baseball scholarship to UCLA. What do ya think of that?' I leaned back from the railing overlooking the basketball court, and waited for his answer. It didn't take him long. He said, 'Gee, Coach, you don't have to do that—nobody else has offered me anything.'"

Coach Wooden's jaw dropped—just like mine had when Tim told me this a dozen years ago.

"Well, I was stunned to say the least," I continued. "I remember thinking, *Should I tell Tim that is a splendid idea?* But, instead, I found myself saying, 'Tim, I believe you will be worth every penny of it. My offer stands.' And Tim said, 'I'm coming here.' I knew he would be true to his word."

Shaking his head, Coach said, "In all my years of coaching college basketball, I never had a player refuse a scholarship—and still attend my school."

In 1991, I saw Coach again, shortly after Tim had made a sizeable donation to the UCLA baseball scholarship fund. Tim was still pitching in the big leagues. I told John that it was another "comeback" from Tim, who became the first professional ball player from UCLA to endow a baseball scholarship.* (Others, like Eric Karros, Shane Mack, Todd Zeile, Chase Utley, and the Torey Lovullo family, followed with sizeable donations.)

---

* Tim Leary came back again when I asked him to be our pitching coach in 1997. He coached for pay that year, but he chose to coach with no pay the next three years because he wanted our volunteer coaches in those years—Brian Criss and Robert Hinds—to be paid instead, "So they don't have to live off of meal money alone." It was no coincidence that, in Tim's five years as pitching coach, our UCLA teams went to the World Series once and to the NCAA Playoffs in four of those years.

"Coach, I didn't ask him for the donation," I said. "He did it on his own, because, as Tim said, 'It was the right thing to do, to pay back for what UCLA did for me.'"

"That must have been a wonderful feeling, right Gary?"

"Yes, Coach, it's always a nice feeling when you are thanked for helping someone."

"No, Gary, I don't mean the feeling that you and UCLA felt for *receiving* the gift from Tim. I'm talking about the wonderful feeling Tim had in *giving* it."

REFEREES AND UMPIRES

One day, after John had listened to me complain about an umpire's missed call that went against our Bruins, he told me about a call against him that he had never been able to put out of his mind. His tale was new to me then, but in later years, I heard him tell it often at his speaking engagements.

"One of the nicest and truly most honest referees in the game of basketball—but also, one who routinely made inexact calls—called a foul on one of our players that I felt was an obvious incorrect call," John began. "I didn't want to yell across the court at him, so I just waited for him to come close to our bench while our opponent was preparing to shoot his free throw. I quietly told him that he had missed that call. He looked straight at me and said with a wry grin, 'They liked it at the other end, John.'"

Coach and I agreed that the ideal official is the one who notices everything on the field or court, but is seldom noticed himself.

"No one comes to a basketball game because so-and-so is refereeing," Coach would say, "but there are a few refs who believe *they* are the show."

Despite these unflattering words, John, unlike many of his

coaching peers, respected and trusted the officials as a whole. "There's no use fretting over the officials, because that's like fretting over the weather. You have no control. In general, I trust the officials."

Coach elaborated by quoting one of his favorite men, Abraham Lincoln: "It is better to trust and occasionally be disappointed than to mistrust and be miserable all the time."

John refrained from battling the referees, because he didn't want to show his players that the officials controlled the outcome of the game. He felt that those coaches who constantly waged war with the officials were, by their behavior, just giving their players an excuse to lose. Besides, it would not be setting the kind of example he wanted his players to follow.

When John told me that he had only had two technical fouls in his long career, I asked him, "Is that because you never used profanity?"

A wrinkle of a grin appeared, and then vanished as quickly as it came. "That probably had something to do with it, Gary," he said. "I can thank my dad for that . . . he set a good example. I never heard my dad ever use a cuss word. Of course, the whipping he gave me out in the barn helped with that, too."

Coach and I spent more time talking about umpires than we did referees. He told me that he was aware that managers argued incessantly with umpires, even if they knew the umpire wouldn't change his decision. "I believe part of their reason for arguing is just to let the umpire know that he can't be careless in making calls, especially on the close plays," Coach said. "By arguing with him, they're ensuring that the umpire will bear down and think twice about making a call against the team whose manager will make the biggest fuss."

I agreed with Coach, but he was quite puzzled as to how a manager could be ejected from games as often as Bobby Cox. (We didn't know then that Cox would eventually retire with a major league record of 158 ejections.) I gave John my explanation.

"In baseball, the umpire has a call on every pitch—whether

it's a strike or a ball, a fair or a foul ball, or a safe or an out," I said. "In basketball, as you know, the referee has to decide if he should make a call or ignore making a call—which is a 'no call.' Since the umpire makes more calls in a game than a basketball referee does in his games, there's going to be a greater chance for controversy.

"It's a baseball tradition for managers to argue and get ejected when those controversies occur. Besides, John, I think you'll agree that most fans enjoy watching managers feud with the umpire." I thought I saw John give a reluctant nod.

"In baseball," I continued, "the confrontations with umpires are expected by the manager's players. Sometimes the players feel let down when their managers don't stick up for them on close calls." In defense of Cox, I said, "I'm sure that many of his ejections were done on purpose, just to prevent his own players from being thrown out. I've seen Bobby shove his own player away from the umpire, before the umpire had a chance to eject him. Bobby's no dummy—he knows managers are expendable, and players are not. I told him that I had been ejected about two dozen times in my forty-one years of coaching college baseball, and most of those times, I *wanted* to be thrown out."

"So you're saying you were under control, even though you were thrown out?" Coach asked.

I knew how he felt about coaches losing their composure. "Yes, John," I admitted. "But one time, I really lost it."

"Tell me about it."

"Well, it's a long story, John."

"I have time," he said, with that easy grin he was so well-known for.

"It happened up at Stanford," I began. "Top of the ninth and we're losing, 7–6. We have a runner on second base and our best hitter, Shane Mack, up at the plate with two outs. He hits a line drive over the third baseman's head that ended up in the left field corner. I'm coaching third base and waving the tying run into home. Shane pulls up at second base with a double, and now we have the go-ahead run in scoring position.

"All of a sudden, I see the third base umpire, Charlie,* running into the middle of the field, waving his arms and yelling, 'Foul ball! Foul ball!' I couldn't believe what I was seeing and hearing. From my view in the coaching box, it looked like it was fair by at least a foot. At this stage of the event, I kept my cool and requested that Charlie ask the plate umpire for help with the call.

"Charlie said, 'No, Gary, it's not his call. It's solely mine.'

"It was then that I went into stage two of irritability. I began pleading for him to reconsider, saying that I had a better view of where the ball landed than he did. I also held my hands up about a foot apart, right in front of his face, to show him just how fair the ball had been. But Charlie was stubborn. Despite my pleading and yelling, I knew there was no changing his mind—just like all the other times I had argued with umpires. That's when stage three kicked in . . . and I lost it. I kicked some dirt on his shoes."

"Is that when he threw you out?" Coach asked.

"Yep, but I wasn't finished. I stomped over to the third base bag and straddled it. I looked at him and said—rather coolly, I thought—'Charlie, you're not using this base to call balls fair or foul anyway, so I'm going to get rid of it.' I thought his eyes might pop out of his head when I pulled the bag out of its anchor and raised it over my head. I proceeded to walk to the garbage can sitting next to our third base dugout, and slam-dunked the base into the can.

"They didn't resume the game until Charlie had retrieved the base and he saw me sitting on the bank of the hill overlooking the field. Shane Mack had to come to the plate a second time, and the game ended when he hit a deep fly to center field. We lost, 7–6."

---

* Name has been changed.

John shook his head. "Goodness gracious, Gary, that doesn't sound like you."

"Maybe not, John, but you always say to stick up for what you believe in . . . and I believed the ball was fair."

A moment of silence passed. "There's more to the story," I said finally.

John cocked his head questioningly. "I have time," he said again.

"The next day," I said, "while we were taking batting practice prior to our game, I kept hearing a voice from the Stanford seats yelling, 'Coach Adams, I need to talk to you!' He was persistent, and since the tone of his voice sounded friendly, when we finished batting practice, I walked over to where he was seated across the barrier in the first row. From my spot on the field I asked, 'Yes, what is it?'

"Although I knew he was a Stanford fan—he was wearing a bright red shirt and a red cap with an 'S' on it—he was very friendly. He said, 'You know that argument you had with the umpire yesterday?' I nodded, wondering in what direction this conversation was heading.

"'Well, Coach,' he continued, 'I have my camera here, and I watched that play on video last night. I must say, you were mistaken about that ball being fair by a foot.'

"I could hardly believe what I was hearing. The man repeated, in a serious tone, 'Yes, you were mistaken.' He then smiled and spread his arms far apart. 'It was fair by *this* much,' he said.

"His words made me happy and, at the same time, I felt some irritability creeping inside. I thanked him for the information and, knowing that I would be meeting with the umpires at home plate in a short while, wondered what Charlie would say to me. Mostly I wondered what I should say to him.

"The meeting was pleasant enough. Charlie didn't mention the previous day's events, and neither did I . . . until the meeting ended. Charlie was the plate umpire that day, so after the other two umpires and Coach Marquess of Stanford left, I was alone with him.

"I said, 'Charlie, despite what happened yesterday, I still consider you the second-best umpire in the conference.' He thanked me, but as I began to walk away, his curiosity got the best of him—just as I had predicted, since curious Charlie often asked me where I ranked him as an umpire.

"'Oh, Gary!' he said. 'By the way, who ranks first?' It was the question that I had been hoping for. I stopped and turned around to face him. 'All the rest are tied for first, Charlie.'"

John chuckled. Before he could say anything, I added, "No, John, he didn't throw me out of the game. I didn't cuss, and I didn't *sound* insulting."

"Did he ever umpire in any more of your games?" Coach asked.

"Yes, and I actually thought he became one of the best. He did start wearing eyeglasses after that. He told me, 'It sure makes a difference.'"

John and I laughed together.

"A few years later, when Charlie told me he was retiring from umpiring, I told him once more that I thought he was the second-best umpire in the conference. But this time, no one was tied for first. We both laughed about it."

"I never wanted to be ejected," John said. "That is why I tried not to show up the referees in front of the fans. I used my rolled-up program as sort of a megaphone when I yelled at a referee—that way, he could hear me, but the fans couldn't. Referees don't like to be embarrassed in front of the fans."

With a hint of a grin, he added, "I did talk to them when they came close to our bench, just loud enough for only them to hear me. I believe that showed more respect for them than if I had yelled and made a big demonstration in front of the fans after a bad call."

I told John that there were times when umpires were reluctant to throw me out, partly because I rarely cussed at them. "Many of them refused after I pleaded with them to eject me so

I could fire up my players. 'Gary, why would I throw you out?' they would say. 'You're angry and I understand that, but you haven't called me any names or used foul language.' Sometimes, I was frustrated enough that I reluctantly resorted to a foul word or two, and that usually sealed the deal for my ejection."

I told John that there was one time when I intended to get thrown out, but the umpire changed my mind with just a few words.

John gave me a puzzled look and asked, "Did he threaten to forfeit the game to the other team?"

"No, John. Not even close."

I explained that I was so intent on getting thrown out of the game that, before I went out to argue, I pointed to one of my assistant coaches to take my place as manager, saying, 'I will *not* be returning to the bench.' My whole team heard me make that bold statement.

"I rushed out to the field, where the umpire was waiting for me after calling our runner out for stealing—his third missed call of the game that went against our team. I got as close to his face as I could—even turning my cap around backwards, so the bill of it would not prevent me from going nose to nose with him.

"I must have given him one full minute of a scorching tirade before I let him say anything. I waited for his rebuttal, which had always come from umpires in the past. Instead, he looked at me sorrowfully and said, 'I'm sorry, Gary, I'm having a real bad day. I know I've missed some calls. I'm so sorry.' He looked completely humiliated. I thought he might even start to cry. I backed a step away from him and found myself placing my hand on his shoulder. 'That's okay. Don't worry about it. I understand.' Then I sheepishly returned to our dugout, where all my players sat stunned.

"My assistant asked me what had happened. The only thing I could say was, 'He admitted that he missed some calls. I didn't have the heart to say anything bad.'

"From listening to experienced managers, however, I

learned an *almost* sure-fire trick for getting ejected. If you want to be thrown out, don't tell the umpire he made a 'horses——t call.' Just tell him he's a 'horses——t umpire.'"

John liked my next umpire story, which involved one of his favorite managers, Gene Mauch. I told John, "You've probably heard that Mauch was an expert at arguing with umpires without being tossed from the game. Well Coach, there was one time when he thought he could outsmart the umpire with an insult and not get ejected.

"Mauch, though furious about a bad call, calmly approached the plate umpire, Shag Crawford, and politely said, 'Mr. Crawford, would you throw me out of the game for what I'm *thinking* of that call?'

"'No, Gene, not for what you're thinking.'

"'Well then . . . I think that was a horses——t call!' With that, Crawford threw him out."

Coach chuckled. "Did you ever use Mauch's technique?" he asked.

"Well, sort of, John. I tried it once, but before I could finish, the umpire said, 'Gary, I've heard that story before, so don't even go there.' He said it with a smile, and it dampened my anger enough that I didn't say anything afterwards to warrant ejection."

John admitted that he wasn't always a saint when an official made a bad call, but he never resorted to profanity—unless "Goodness gracious, sakes alive!" could be interpreted as such.

The more Coach and I talked about referees and umpires, the more it sparked old memories. I could tell by the twinkle in John's eyes that this topic was a special one for him.

Coach told me about the time he was playing on a summer league semi-pro team, and one of his teammates was criticizing the umpire. The umpire tried to appease his critic, saying, "I just call 'em the way I see 'em."

John couldn't conceal a smile as he said, "My teammate yelled back at him, 'Why not call them the way they are?'"

Coach enjoyed watching the UCLA games when the ball field was on campus and close to his office. He admitted that he would, on occasion, make comments to the umpire from his seat, as close to the umpire as he could get.

Gail Goodrich, who played on the freshman baseball team, remembers John sitting close to home plate at his games. "Sometimes Coach was the only one watching our frosh games, and he jabbered at the plate umpire regularly. He wasn't loud, but I certainly heard him—and so did the umpires."

Coach Mickens, who coached with Art Reichle when baseball was played on Joe E. Brown Field, echoed Goodrich. "John sat near home plate," he said. "I never saw him show any animation and never heard him cuss, but he always said enough to remind the umpires that he was watching them. I never heard any of the umpires ever say anything back to John."

"Gary," Coach said, "do fans and players still yell out to umpires, 'Hey, ump! I've seen better eyes on a potato!'"

"Yes, Coach . . . except there's a modern version."

I told him that a fan had used this in one of our home games, and his timing couldn't have been better. After the umpire called a strike on our batter that was another obvious missed call, the fan stood up and held out his cell phone to the umpire. He yelled, "Hey, ump! Is this your cell phone? Because it has three missed calls on it!"

Coach liked this new version. It reminded him of another story about a major league umpire, George Moriarty.

"When asked to spell his last name," Coach said, "George would always say, 'Moriarty . . . that's Moriarty with one "i."'" Ball players were known to yell from the dugout, whenever he made a questionable call, 'Hey, Moriarty with one "i" . . . that's one more than you've got in your head!'"

It's ironic that one of Coach Wooden's all-time favorite poems was written by none other than that same umpire, George Moriarty. Coach could recite the entire poem by heart, but on this day, he only recited the last two stanzas of "The Road

Ahead or the Road Behind":

> *For who can ask more of a man*
> *Than giving all within his span*
> *Giving all it seems to me*
> *Is not so far from victory.*
> *And so the fates are seldom wrong*
> *No matter how they twist and wind*
> *It's you and I who make our fates*
> *We open up or close the gates*
> *On the road ahead or the road behind.*

Coach was keenly aware that the coach-official relationship was too often one of misunderstanding and mistrust. He recognized this early in his career, and discussed the topic in the first textbook he ever wrote, *Practical Modern Basketball*. He wrote that no official would admit that he could ever be affected by a partisan crowd, or that he had "rabbit ears," or carried a grudge that might consciously or subconsciously affect his officiating. The standard reply was, "I call them as I see them."

On the other side, the coaches, too, refused to admit that they had any weaknesses, but John wrote that they "seemed to feel that the officials were out 'to take the bread right out of our mouths."

Many officials hear the uncomplimentary names being yelled in their direction by the coaches who question their integrity. They see the coach jump off the bench, gesturing frantically to arouse their fans against the officials. These referees and umpires cannot understand why coaches question their calls, when these coaches mistakenly believe that they are in a better position to see things from where they are.

John served on the Officials Committee of the National Association of Basketball Coaches for several years. In 1966, after listening to the coaches' complaints and the officials' complaints, John wrote that "both groups seemed to feel that

the main problem was a mutual lack of trust and faith in each group for the other. . . . In the final analysis, perhaps the most important thing we need in all walks of life is more mutual trust, faith, and understanding of the problems of others. If we could acquire and keep that, the coach-official relationship would cease to be a problem."

It's no wonder that John remembered and so often quoted Abe Lincoln's wise words: "Better to trust and occasionally be disappointed, than to mistrust and be miserable all the time."

BEANBALL WAR: PART I

While most of the nation's attention was focused on the semi-finals of the 1996 NCAA Basketball Tournament, our UCLA Bruins baseball team was quietly playing at the home of the Arizona State Sun Devils.

On this particular Saturday, the Final Four was being played in Rutherford, New Jersey. Rick Pitino's number-one seeded Kentucky squad was well on its way to defeating John Calipari's number-two seeded University of Massachusetts team. Kentucky would go on to defeat Jim Boheim's Syracuse team on the following Monday for the NCAA championship.

March Madness erupted with thousands of crazed fans cheering wildly in front of their television sets, in sports bars, and at friends' homes. I pictured the eighty-five-year-old John Wooden sitting in his comfortable easy chair, watching the games on his own small-screen television set, perhaps with his daughter, Nan, and son, Jim, with their families surrounding him. Coach hadn't attended many Final Fours since his beloved Nell passed away. "It's just not the same without Nellie," he once told me.

Meanwhile, our own quietly played game in Tempe, Arizona, was turning into a March Madness of its own—a game that

would eventually garner national attention, because of a bean-ball war.

The war between the eleventh nationally ranked Bruins and the fourteenth ranked Sun Devils began in the Arizona desert, during the second game of a three-game series. It didn't end until twenty-three days later, in the sixth and final game in Los Angeles.

A few weeks after the sixth game and shortly after all the publicity in the radio, television, and newspapers, John wanted to know the details. "How did it start, Gary?" he asked.

I described the events from beginning to end, starting with the first game. "The first game at ASU went rather peacefully. Both teams were battling hard, but ASU led 4–2, going into the seventh. We scored eight runs in the last three innings, with four of those runs coming off their ace closer, Ryan Bradley. We won 10–6."

Knowing what John was probably thinking, I added, "No players were hit by pitches in *that* game.

"Game two, on Saturday, was a different story. Going into the top of the eighth, we were leading, 8–7. Once again, they brought in Bradley to hold us down. And once again, we scored an insurance run against him to go up, 9–7. The top of the ninth was when the war began."

Although I explained to John what happened next, for a more objective view, it's best to quote the words from a man who had the best seat in the house—home plate umpire Kevin Gilmore. This is what he reported to Lou Pavlovitch Jr., the editor of *Collegiate Baseball* newspaper:

> The previous batter for UCLA in the top of the ninth grounded a ball to first base. . . . The first baseman tossed the ball to Bradley, who applied the tag to the runner at first base a little harder than he normally would. The UCLA bench said something to him, and I ran down the line to put a stop to it.

Bradley was back on the mound, and began shouting profanities at the UCLA bench and he said: 'You want me, come and get me,' among other stuff.

The next batter up [Troy Glaus] saw the first pitch being low and inside at the knees. Bradley's second pitch was six inches inside by the numbers of Glaus's jersey. The third pitch hit him square in the head, and he went right down.

I immediately threw the pitcher out because it was obvious Bradley was going right up the ladder with this batter. It was not pretty. It was sickening to see. The batter was unconscious for some time.

I have been umpiring for fifteen years and have never seen a kid go down so hard. He was hit by a ninety-mph-plus fastball.

Kevin described it pretty much the way we Bruins saw it. The ball struck Troy's helmet next to his ear; another inch closer to his eye would have been disastrous. Still, he lay unconscious at home plate for at least five minutes. I raced to Troy's aid, along with our trainer. I felt helpless as I knelt down beside him.

"I was scared for Troy," I told John.

"I can understand why, Gary," Coach replied. "Remember Tony Conigliaro?"

I nodded. "I only know he was beaned, and he played for the Red Sox."

"Tony C. was beaned by a pitch right out here in Anaheim's Angel Stadium," Coach said. "The ball smashed into his face near his left eye. He was a right-handed batter, too—like Troy. Tony was a young player for the Red Sox with a bright future, maybe even a Hall of Famer, had it not been for that beaning. I believe he was the youngest player to ever lead the American League in home runs—only twenty years old."

I leaned closer to John to hear him better, since his soft voice often trailed off toward the end of his sentences. I realized that he knew the Tony Conigliaro story much better than I.

"Yes, that beaning took Tony C. out of playing for the rest of that season, and all of the next," he said. "He played a few years after that—even won the Comeback Player of the Year once. But his vision was permanently damaged—a torn retina—and he was never the same. I think Tony retired at the age of twenty-six, right when most players are starting to reach their prime."

"Whatever happened to him?" I asked.

"That's sad, too. He had a heart attack, and then a stroke, which caused him to be in a coma for almost eight years. I remember when he died—around the time my Nell passed. He was only thirty-seven."

Getting back to our game against ASU, I told Coach that, when Troy was down and I was kneeling next to him, I had hoped that this wouldn't be the end of his career. "I thought that, even if he's physically capable, you never know how he might react mentally. You know, Coach—the fear factor."

John nodded, and I continued the story.

"Our Bruin players surrounded the home plate area, jabbering at the ASU players, who remained in the dugout because they didn't want another brawl. They were on probation for a fight they'd had with USC two weeks earlier. That donnybrook resulted in a suspension for three ASU players, including Bradley and the pitching coach, Bob Welch.

"ASU's head coach, Pat Murphy, stood close to home plate, denying to the umpires that Bradley had hit Troy on purpose. He kept saying, 'We were just trying to pitch him inside.'

"I had heard enough. I yelled back at him, 'If that's what you're tryin', then teach your pitchers how to do it without hitting batters!' I believed that Bradley had tried to hit Troy on purpose.

"Troy was taken by ambulance to the hospital, where he

was diagnosed with a concussion and ordered not to play again for at least six or seven days.

"Murphy later told the press, 'Why would Ryan purposely hit Glaus? Even though he is a fine player, he had not hurt us the entire series.'

"My answer to that was a simple one: If anyone asked any coach in our conference who the most dangerous hitter was for the Bruins, they would say, 'Their number-three hitter in the order, Troy Glaus.'"

With a hint of sarcasm, I told John, "I think Troy's performance may have hurt the Devils a little bit. In the two games up to that point, Troy had gone to bat five times, had two hits, and they walked him once. He scored two runs for us. Besides, pitchers use up so much energy trying to get Troy out, that our hitters who follow him have an easier time of it with their at bats."

"How close did Troy stand to the plate?" John asked

When he asked that question, my first thought was, *Why didn't I think of that when I yelled back at Murphy?*

"Troy is six feet five inches tall," I told John. "He has long arms, so he stands farther from the plate than any hitter on our team. For a pitcher to hit him, it would take a pitch almost two feet inside to even come close to him."

I continued the story. "The game ended with Bradley ejected, and a 9–7 victory for our side," I said. "The most meaningful stat of that game appeared near the bottom of the box score, where the three letters, 'HBP'—'hit by pitch'—had ASU hitting two of ours. We hit one of theirs.

"The third and final game's only controversy came when Coach Murphy placed Bradley in the lineup to play first base. Knowing that the NCAA rules required a four-game suspension for any pitcher purposely throwing at a batter, I protested. The umpires removed Bradley from the lineup. *Los Angeles Times* reporter George Dohrmann wrote, 'Murphy claimed he forgot about the NCAA rule.'

"Without Glaus in our lineup, our team played hard but lost, 12–9, in a relatively uneventful game. We left Arizona winning two of three games, losing Troy for an indefinite time, and ASU leading us one-to-nothing in purposely hit batters. Our biggest concern was for Troy and what effect his beaning would have on his future performance."

Although March Madness was over, nineteen days later, ASU visited Jackie Robinson Stadium for another three-game series. The controversy over batters being hit by pitches had not yet grown to the extent of national awareness, but it certainly was on the minds of the locals. I tried to squash the rumors that more brouhahas with the Devils might come into play in the upcoming series.

The *Daily Bruin* newspaper quoted me saying, "We're not going to try to beat them in a fight, we're going to try to beat them at the game of baseball. . . . I don't think that either team is interested in fighting. We plan to root for our team, and that is it."

Little had I known what loomed ahead.

I briefly described the first game to Coach. "It was played without incident—no hit-by-pitches, and no confrontations—but our hitters didn't treat Ryan Bradley with much kindness. We won, 12–9, on Jon Heinrichs's grand slam home run in the bottom of the eighth, off of the big closer. Troy Glaus, fully recovered from his beaning, drove in four runs with a single, two doubles, and a home run in his five at bats.

"The next day, the Devils won, 8–4, but this game was reminiscent of the second game at ASU. Once again, Troy reached base in four out of his five appearances at the plate. But it was *how* he reached base that mattered most to our fans, players, coaches, and, especially, me.

"ASU's pitchers hit Troy *twice,* making it three HBPs in the last three games he played. The first HBP came early in the game, when their starting pitcher hit Troy in the elbow. Troy could hardly feel his glove on his left hand in the next inning. In

Troy's last at bat, Bradley drilled him in the middle of the back with one out in the bottom of the ninth, a runner on second, and the Devils with a four-run lead.

"Troy was the only player hit by a pitch in the game. I was livid. So was Troy, who took a few steps toward the mound before Gus Rodriguez, the home plate umpire, stopped him. We found it hard to believe that Bradley was not ejected—he wasn't even given a warning—especially since the umpires were aware of the recent history between the two ball clubs."

I didn't witness what had occurred immediately after ASU had beaten us in the second game, but later I read about it in *Collegiate Baseball*:

> According to Pacheco, who was umpiring along the first base line, and several other eyewitnesses, Bradley then turned to the UCLA fans and shouted, "F——k you all." The incident was immediately reported to the Pac-10 Conference. After a review of the situation, the Pac-10 suspended Bradley for the final game of the series because of his obscene language aimed at the pro-UCLA crowd, according to Jim Muldoon of the Pac-10.
>
> It marked the third major incident of the year for Bradley. He was involved in a brawl against Southern California earlier in the season, which resulted in a three-game suspension.

That night, I went to bed thinking of three things:
1. How best to beat ASU on Sunday
2. How best to send ASU a message that we had had enough of their purposely thrown HBPs
3. How best to control our players

That third thought troubled me as much as anything else,

because I knew our players were angry. I knew they wanted revenge. I felt the anger, too, but for a different reason. I wasn't
interested in revenge. I was intent upon delivering the message
to ASU that they couldn't target my players with beanballs. My
players were my family. I was old enough to be their grandpa,
and I wasn't just going to stand by and watch my grandsons
continue to be drilled with ninety-plus-miles-per-hour fastballs. My intent was simply to *protect* my players, by delivering
a strong message to ASU.

How could I do that without instigating a full-fledged brawl
between fifty ball players, in plain sight of all the fans? I knew
the Bruins fans were hot, too, and a brawl on the field could
start a bigger brawl in the stands between the loyal Bruins and
Sun Devils fans.

On the other hand, I was afraid that, if I did nothing, our
players might take out their frustration and anger with their
fists, which could lead to a near riot at Jackie Robinson Stadium. Ugly things can happen in baseball brawls. Players can
get seriously injured, and a whole season of hard work and sacrifice by a team can be wiped out by a senseless melee. I was
the "skipper" of this ship, and there was no way I would let my
ship sink to the bottom of the standings because of egos. Yet,
I wanted my players to have the satisfaction of knowing that
ASU was not messing with a bunch of sissies. What I needed
most was a plan that would send the Devils a message and, at
the same time, give us a chance to play the game the Bruin way,
while beating the tar out of ASU.

"I tossed and turned most of the night," I told John, "but by
morning, I had decided on a plan that could accomplish these
goals. When I walked into our clubhouse dressing room that
morning, I announced to the players, 'When you're finished
suiting up, we'll get together in our meeting room.'"

With the large four-foot-wide, eight-foot-tall photo of
Jackie Robinson hanging on the wall behind me and the players
sitting in folding chairs in front of me, I told them, "I know how

you feel. You want to retaliate and show them that you aren't going to take it anymore. I understand that. But I don't want *you* to do anything. *I* will do something. You just play baseball the Bruin way.

"I must admit, I saw disappointment in the eyes of some of our players. Maybe they had already gotten together and had a plan themselves—I don't know. But I know they could tell that I meant what I said.

"After this brief meeting, we went outdoors to prepare for the final game of the series. We were ranked tenth in the nation then, in a battle for first place in the Pac-10 with USC. We needed this game against ASU to stay in the hunt.

"When our starting pitcher, Pete Zamora, was almost finished with his warm-up pitches in the bullpen, I approached him. I was about to do something I had never done in my past twenty-seven years as a head coach.

"'Pete,' I said, 'I've got a favor to ask of you. I want you to hit the first batter of the game. Will you do that?'"

BEANBALL WAR: PART II

The look on Coach Wooden's face took me back to the day he had glared at me for resting my feet on his desk. Clearly, he didn't approve of what I had asked Pete Zamora to do—hit the first ASU batter who stepped up to the plate.

I continued my story. "I told Pete I didn't want him to hit the batter in the head," I said. "'Hit him in the back or in the ribs, but not in the head. You understand?' My words—even to me—sounded like I was scolding him. He got the message and nodded. 'Okay,' he said."

John asked me why I had chosen to pitch Zamora, if there was a chance he might be ejected. He wasn't the first person to ask me this, after the fact. I had a couple of reasons.

First, I didn't believe Pete would be ejected. He had been our starter in the third game of every series we had played, and I had already announced to the press and to ASU's Coach Murphy that Zamora would start in the third game. The umpires also knew it. If I had started someone else, the umpires would have been suspicious that we were throwing at the hitter on purpose, knowing that anyone else was expendable. I didn't care if Murphy and his pitching coach, Welch, were suspicious; in fact, I was certain that they would know we had done it on purpose. I figured a warning from the umpires would be the worst result.

Secondly, Pete had excellent control. I knew he could hit the targeted area. I had briefly given some thought to one of our other pitchers, but had ruled him out because he was too wild. I was doubtful that he would ever hit the batter, because he had enough trouble hitting his catcher's glove. Besides, the last thing I wanted was to have a wild pitch bean the batter in the head.

When their lead-off hitter, Mikel Moreno, came to bat, I walked from the far end of our dugout to the nearest end, closer to home plate. I watched Pete stare in at our catcher, Tim DeCinces, for a sign. Tim didn't know the plan; no one in a Bruin uniform knew, except for Pete and me. Tim called for a fastball—the pitch Pete wanted—and he set his catcher's mitt just above Mikel's knees, right down the middle of the plate. Pete and I both knew the pitch would not be down the middle.

I watched my left-hander wind up and fire his typical eighty-eight-mph fastie straight in line at the batter. Only one problem—it bounced three feet in front of home plate. Mikel hopped over the speeding ball, and Tim hit his knees to block it from going to the backstop. I remember thinking, *Pete took my lecture to heart. He made sure he didn't hit the batter in the head.*

I listened for any noise coming out of the Arizona State dugout. It was quiet, but my guess at the time was that they were all suspicious. I figured that most of them, including their coaches, knew Zamora had excellent control, and that this pitch in the dirt was no accident. They probably thought it was a message sent from Pete, and assumed that would be the end of the war.

When Pete got the ball back from Tim, he looked for me in the dugout. I moved a step forward and mouthed silently to him, "Do it again."

Before his next pitch, Pete pretended to look for a sign from Tim. Then he wound up, raised his sights higher, and his second fastball hit Moreno in the upper leg.

The plate umpire, Jim Pacheco, flipped his mask off, took

three or four quick steps toward Pete, and in a grand gesture, pointed to the tops of the trees. "Yer outta here!" he said.

No warning was given. He had ejected Pete, and I had lost the gamble. It was hard for me to believe—the umpires had greater cause for ejecting Bradley the day before without a warning. However, I never thought that it would take two pitches to get the job done. This had made our objective more obvious to the umpires.

I raced out onto the field to pay a visit to Pacheco, whom I had a great amount of respect for—and still do. I got in his face pretty good, among other things, and asked him, "Why today, and not yesterday?"

After I finished my heated lecture, Pacheco asked, "Gary, did you order him to hit the batter on purpose?"

I didn't mind him asking, since Pete had already been eject-ed. In fact, I was glad he asked. I just wished Coach Murphy and Coach Welch would have been within listening distance to hear my answer: "Yes, Jim, I ordered it."

When Coach Wooden heard that part of the story, he gave me a surprised look. "Is that when he threw you out?" he asked.

"Yes," I replied. "I knew he would, because is there ever a re-ally good reason for a pitcher to hit a batter on purpose? Hon-estly, John, up until that day, I never knew of one . . . up until that day."

This time, I was pleased to see a look of understanding from Coach.

I had felt no remorse for Moreno getting hit, because I knew he wasn't hurt, only stung. Like most hitters, he didn't rub his leg; he just jogged down to first base, like it was no big deal.

I was satisfied that our message had been delivered to ASU, and that hitting him had not led to a brouhaha on the field, but I did feel badly for Pete, who didn't get to pitch against the team who had been beating up on Troy, one of his best friends. Pete wanted to beat the Sun Devils probably more than anyone on our team.

I also felt sorry for Pete because I knew he would be suspended from playing in the next four games. Since he always played first base when he didn't pitch, it was a stiff penalty, and entirely my fault. My only consolation was that he would be the *only* player on our team suspended. Our players' emotions were running high, and if there had been a donnybrook on the field, there would have been more than just one of our players tossed, and maybe some injured.

After my ejection, I followed Pete to the clubhouse. Pete sat in front of his locker and lowered his head into his hands.

"I'm sorry, Pete," I said. "But I believe what you did sent ASU the message we wanted to send." I didn't tell him the rest of my thought, which was, *And now, I believe our team is going to clobber them on the field and win this game.*

Pete and I watched the remainder of the game from a distance. Still in my uniform, I sat on a bench outside the clubhouse doors, and Pete sat in the stands with his parents and friends.

Despite ASU's lead-off hitter receiving the gift of first base after a HBP, his team did not score in the first inning. When our players sprinted to our dugout to grab their bats, I could see that they were all fired up. We promptly scored four runs, and by the fourth inning, we led 10–0. The game was never in doubt—we pummeled them. The final score was 16–9.

In this final game, Troy Glaus hit a home run, had two RBIs, scored twice, and was on base three times in six at bats. Coach Murphy had said that Troy Glaus had not hurt his team with his bat in the whole series, but in the five games Troy played against ASU, he hit two home runs and two doubles, scored eight runs, drove in six, and was on base fifteen of twenty-six at bats for an on-base percentage of .571.

On Monday, when I went to the athletic department to pick up my mail, my box was filled with messages—more messages than I had ever received before in one day. They were mostly from the media—radio, television, and newspapers, all wanting to talk to me. "Is it really true?" they asked. "Did you really admit

to the umpire that you ordered your pitcher to hit a batter?"

One reporter from the *Los Angeles Times* wrote, "He has been asked not so much why he did it, but why he admitted to it." That same reporter, George Dohrmann, even interviewed Stanford's Mark Marquess, who said, "There have been times when it was implied that a coach ordered a player to throw at a batter. . . . But I have never heard of a coach admitting it."

Despite the bad publicity, I kept on admitting it. I told everyone that I had made a decision to "fight fire with fire." ASU had thrown at us, so we threw at them. The only two differences—and they were huge—between us and them was that we were willing to admit what we had done, and we had made an effort not to hurt anyone seriously.

I also wanted to give notice to the NCAA Baseball Rules Committee to change their policy of suspending the pitcher for four games, while only penalizing the coach for one game. I felt that the onus of a hit batter should fall on the head coach *at least* as much as his pitcher. The suspension for the coach should be so harsh that he would make sure his pitching staff *never* hit a batter on purpose again. He would also be sure to teach his pitchers how to pitch inside *without* hitting the batter. I felt that a stiffer penalty would also reduce the headhunting in college baseball. I made this clear in every interview I had with the media.

I felt so strongly about the NCAA's obsolete rule that I volunteered to suspend myself for four games. I did it before the Pac-10 office officially notified me of my suspension. They even tacked on two more games. "My message was well received," I told John.

On the second day after the infamous HBP, the CBS network in Los Angeles sent their popular sports broadcaster, Jim Hill, out to Jackie Robinson Stadium. With cameras rolling, he interviewed me while showing where the action had taken place.

I knew that my boss at the time, athletic director Pete Dalis, couldn't be pleased with me for the type of publicity his department and UCLA were getting. I made sure that I told all the reporters that I had not consulted with Dalis prior to the incident, or with anyone else at UCLA. It was entirely my own decision to order my pitcher to hit the batter.

After Jim Hill's interview, ABC, NBC, CBS, and all the local channels offered blurbs about "the coach who ordered his pitcher to purposely hit the batter." Some gave no background story or explanations as to why I had given the order. My mailbox remained full, and the phone kept ringing with more messages and requests for interviews. I tried to oblige everyone, because I wanted people to know the *whole* story. But it was impossible to please them all.

I had plenty of time on my hands, because my suspension included not being allowed to coach on the field, even at practice. I also looked at the interviews as an opportunity to get the word out to the public and to the NCAA Baseball Rules Committee about making the coach's penalty as severe as the pitcher's. Perhaps the Rules Committee would listen more closely to the public than to me. I had called Bill Thurston, the chairman of the committee, on two separate occasions. Although he heard me out, he didn't agree that the rule should be changed.

On the third day following the incident, the nation discovered what was happening in college baseball on the West Coast. I became aware of the national interest when I received a phone call from one of my former UCLA players, Chris Pritchett. At the time, Chris was playing AAA in the Pacific Coast League for the California Angels organization. He eventually played in the majors for four seasons.

"Skip!" Chris said excitedly—or maybe he just sounded excited because it was late at night and I was in bed and half asleep.

"Yes," I replied sleepily.

"This is Pritch. I just saw your mug on ESPN *SportsCenter*. I'm in a sports bar in Vancouver and there's lots of noise and I couldn't hear what they were saying on TV about you . . . but

the caption said that you ordered a beanball."

"Yes and no, Chris," I replied. "I ordered my pitcher to hit a batter, but I didn't order him to aim at his head."

I roused myself enough to give Chris a brief account of the story—not nearly as long as the one I gave to Coach Wooden.

There were plenty of other articles written—mostly negative—that my mom saved and put in her scrapbook. A gentleman who wrote a letter to the editor of *Baseball America* was especially kind to me. His last two sentences were among the nicest compliments I received during the whole beanball ordeal: "Unfortunately, television coverage of Adams's stance has been edited down to the clichéd, 'If they're going to hit us, we're going to hit them,' which is inaccurate. Adams simply has the moral fiber to tell the truth and challenge college baseball's ongoing complacency."

I told John about my mom's scrapbook. "It included clippings that looked at Ryan Bradley's side and Coach Murphy's side more closely."

"And what *is* Bradley's and Murphy's side?" he asked.

"They are both intense competitors," I said. "I believe they admitted to that in some of their interviews. Coach Murphy places emphasis on his players playing hard for nine innings, or whatever it takes. I respect that part of it. I ask the same thing of my players. I know Ryan liked Murphy's style, and Murphy liked Ryan's style."

Coach Wooden listened carefully and seemed to have no argument with Coach Murphy's style. I went further to say, "Coach Murphy has a knowledgeable baseball mind, and relates well with his players. But, in my opinion, he is better suited to coach in professional ball than in college ball. Pro baseball teams, particularly those in the National League, show more tolerance toward pitchers throwing at batters."

Coach nodded. "I know of a few managers in the National League who have the reputation of hitting batters intentionally," he said.

"In one of Coach Murphy's interviews, he said that Ryan was a good kid," I said. "I'm not disagreeing with him about that. I've had players who were good people, but just not mature enough to make wise choices, especially during tough, competitive college baseball games. I've had players who have thrown their bats against the backstop after striking out, and others who have slammed their helmets so hard on the ground they've shattered the helmet. I've seen players who have heaved their gloves and belted their fists against wooden and concrete walls in the dugout. As the head coach, I've always believed that these impulsive, immature actions can be rectified, if the coach pays attention to it and disciplines those who do not abide by his rules of conduct—in other words, no temper tantrums on the ball field. Like Coach Murphy, I believe my players are good kids, too. But I hope they understand that they will be sitting on the bench if they do the wrong thing on the field."

With John standing in front of me, I couldn't help but remember that "self-control" was a block in his Pyramid of Success, and that he insisted upon it from his players.

"If there is a defense for Ryan Bradley, it is this," I told Coach. "Ryan may have never given any thought *before* our games that he would try to hit anybody. I know he is not afraid to pitch inside to hitters, and he has been successful doing it. But, like players who haven't yet learned the art of self-control, his temper got the best of him *during* our games. And it's obvious that he has a temper, or the Pac-10 would not have needed to discipline him three times in a period of about six weeks.

"Ryan got off to a bad start in the first game, when we scored four runs off of him and he became the losing pitcher. In the second game, he gave up an insurance run in our victory. He was used to coming into the game and saving them—not losing them. I'm not making excuses for him, but I think his frustration and temper caused him, in the heat of the moment, to be willing to drill Glaus. That's just my opinion, and I know Ryan would say that I'm full of it. He has always denied hitting

Troy on purpose. But I've heard it said that if a dog has a dirty nose, it means he's been digging in a hole.

"As for Coach Murphy," I continued, "he never admitted to ordering the hit pitch. But, in my opinion, he didn't do anything to prevent it. I believed him when he said that their strategy was to pitch Glaus inside. I just can't understand how his pitchers could 'miss' that far inside to Troy. My pitching coaches knew that I was against hitting batters on purpose, but I did believe that some hitters needed to be pitched on the inside half of the plate to keep them from diving into outside pitches. Our pitching coaches made sure that our pitchers practiced the art of going inside whenever they went to the bullpen. We didn't believe it would just happen, without practicing it.

"I also believe Coach Murphy knew the temperament of Ryan Bradley, and he should have monitored it more closely during the intense game situations when Bradley was on the mound. Yes, that's a hard thing to do; we can't read our players' minds. But even before Troy was drilled in the back that last time, probably more than half of the spectators in the stands could have predicted what was going to happen. Murphy should have known, too, and made a trip to the mound to make sure Bradley didn't give in to his temper."

Coach seemed satisfied with my answer. "Did the rules committee change the rule and make the penalty for the coach the same as for the pitcher?" he asked.

"Not yet," I said. "I hope they will."

A year later, in 1997, we played six games with ASU and split with them. We won two of three at our place, and they won two of three at their place—all of them highly spirited and competitive games—without a beanball war. There were no notable incidents that threatened the integrity of college baseball—or our players.*

---

* The NCAA baseball rules regarding hitting batters on purpose remains the same—coaches are tapped on the wrist and told to sit out one game, while their pitchers must sit out four.

TWO GREAT COACHES
TELL THEIR
BABE RUTH STORIES

O ne of UCLA's old-time ball players, Ken Proctor, was inducted into the UCLA Baseball Hall of Fame in 2002. This scrap-
py infielder was not only a star of the Bruins, but he also
became one of the most successful high school baseball coaches
in California history.

On the evening of his induction, Ken told me that one of
his biggest thrills he had while attending UCLA was shaking
Babe Ruth's hand. He had written about it in his book, *Baseball Memoirs of a Lifetime*. Between his book and what he told
me the night of his induction, this is his story, as I've pieced it
together.

In 1948, before UCLA's game with the University of California, Santa Barbara, the Babe was in Los Angeles to supervise
the filming of his life story.

"I can still see the Babe's big black limousine pulling up and
parking right over home plate at Joe E. Brown Field," Ken said.
"Coach Reichle told the team to line up along the first base line,
and warned us not to speak to Babe, because he had cancer of
the throat and it would be difficult for him to respond.

"After we lined up, the Babe, dressed in a long black overcoat
and donning a short-billed cap, walked silently along the line of

twenty players to shake our hands. I was close to the end of the line. When he got to me, he glanced at the number on my jacket and smiled broadly. As he shook my hand, he whispered, 'Hey, kid, you got my number!' Yes, I was number three—the Babe's number when he played those many years for the Yankees.

"It was hard to believe that he had spoken to me. He sat on our bench for a few innings. What an honor to have this baseball legend with us on that day!"

Not long after Ken's induction, I told his story to Coach Wooden. When I finished, Coach said, "Ken played on our junior varsity team the first year I coached at UCLA. We have stayed in touch all these years, and he's a dear friend."

Coach returned our conversation to Ken's story of the Babe. "Wish I'd been there," he said. "I didn't arrive on campus till that summer." Then his face brightened. "Gary, did I ever tell you *my* favorite Babe Ruth story?"

I shook my head.

"Well," John began, "this is how I remember it. Ruth's Yankees were playing the Washington Senators, and there were three players on the Senators' team who were good friends of his. All of them enjoyed drinking beer—as much as the Babe did, I guess.

"The manager of the Senators knew that his three players— one a starter and the other two, benchwarmers—were good friends with the Babe. After losing the first game because of Ruth's damaging hits, he asked his players to take their friend out drinking after the game. 'Get him drunk, so he won't beat us tomorrow,' he told them.

"So the three went out that night with the Babe, and they even challenged him to a beer drinking contest to spur him on. They all drank till the bar closed."

Coach couldn't hide his grin as he said, "Well, what do you know? The next day the Senators players went zero for four, while the Babe had two home runs to beat them."

I smiled and chuckled along with John. "But Gary," he said,

"that's not the end of the story. You see, when Babe hit his second home run and rounded third base on his way to home, he looked into the Senators' dugout, where two of his drinking buddies were sitting with lingering hangovers. The Babe smiled at them and yelled, 'Hey fellas, where we goin' drinkin' tonight?'"

John chuckled again, but slightly louder this time, which was, for him, a belly laugh. "I don't know if it's a true story or not," he said, "but it certainly sounds like something the Babe would do."

Later, I tried to get to the truth of the story and found that one of the Senators players was reputed to be Hall of Famer Goose Goslin—also well-known for his capacity to drink beer. Apparently, the Babe's capacity was greater.

NUMBERS

Coach once asked me, "Why do you wear number thirteen?"

"In 1970, my first year as a head coach at UC Irvine, I ordered eighteen uniforms, numbered one to eighteen," I explained. "I never thought to omit the unlucky number thirteen. Nobody wanted to wear it, so I had no choice. I took thirteen. It's been lucky for me, and I've been wearing it ever since."

"I always assign players their numbers," Coach said. "I don't let them choose their favorites or refuse their least favorites."

I was curious about Coach Wooden's policy, so I did a little investigating into his numbering system. I discovered that, with the exception of John's first year of coaching at UCLA, no player ever wore a number between zero and nineteen. His players wore double digit numbers all the way up to seventy-eight. The most-used number was fifty-five—thirteen players wore that number from 1948 (John's first coaching year) to 1975 (his last year).

I am suspicious that there may have been one time in Coach's career that he made an exception to his rule, and honored a player's request for a special number—that was the case with Walt Hazzard. I was suspicious for two reasons. First, Walt was born in 1942. Second, Walt's idol, Jackie Robinson, had worn number forty-two in the big leagues, and Walt wore the same number in every game he played for the Bruins. I never asked John or Walt whether a request was made, but I believe it is more than just a coincidence that Coach handed Walt jersey number forty-two.

I decided to ask Raymond Townsend about Coach's numbering system. Raymond had played for both me and Coach Wooden. I knew his favorite number was eleven, because he requested that number in baseball.

"When I was recruited by Coach Wooden," Raymond said, "I asked Coach if I could have jersey number eleven. I told him it was my lucky number, and the number I wore all through high school."

As much as Coach Wooden wanted Raymond to attend UCLA, Coach stayed committed to his principles. Raymond told me that Coach Wooden didn't hesitate with his response.

"Raymond, we don't have our players pick their numbers, we *assign* them," he had said.

Raymond laughed when he told me Coach Wooden did him a favor by assigning him number twenty-two. "That's two elevens," Coach had told him.

My policy differed from Coach's. When Raymond asked me for number eleven on his baseball jersey, I checked my returning roster to see if it was available. It was, and Raymond wore number eleven on his back all four years that he played baseball. My policy was to give the player his choice of numbers, as long as a returning player didn't want it.

Although UCLA has retired ten numbers in their renowned basketball history, Coach Wooden was not real fond of the idea. He felt that there were other players who wore those numbers that worked just as hard at being the best that they could be.

Fifteen years after John coached his last basketball game, UCLA retired Bill Walton's number thirty-two and Lewis Alcindor's thirty-three. Six years later, UCLA retired Sidney Wicks's number thirty-five, Walt Hazzard's forty-two, Marques Johnson's fifty-four, and Ed O'Bannon's thirty-one. In 2004, Gail

Goodrich's number twenty-five was retired. During the half-time ceremony of a UCLA basketball game on January 17, 2013, Keith Wilkes's number fifty-two was retired. Within the following month, two more jersey numbers were retired: number thirty-one in honor of Reggie Miller (also O'Bannon's number) and number eleven in honor of the late Don Barksdale, who played in 1946–1947. Of the ten retired numbers, only O'Bannon, Miller, and Barksdale did not play for Coach Wooden. Despite John's feelings about retiring numbers, he had attended the ceremonies honoring each player while he was alive.

Only three numbers have been retired in UCLA baseball: Jackie Robinson's number forty-two, Coach Glenn Mickens's number one, and my number thirteen. Mick gave me permission to give his number to Pete Zamora, when we were recruiting Pete. Mick said, "If that will help get him to UCLA, go ahead and give it to him." Pete turned out to be worth it, as he became one of the best pitchers and hitters we ever had.

As for number thirteen, I feel the same way as Mick—if it will help the baseball team, give it away. There are no records in baseball that show who wore what numbers. No one's ever come up to me and said, "Hey, Coach, you're wearing my number thirteen when I played here." If anyone did wear number thirteen before me, as Coach Wooden said, "I want to share that honor with you."

CHATS WITH COACH

Coach and I often had brief, unplanned chats at different lo-
cations. Sometimes we would cross paths on the walkways
of the UCLA campus. There were chance meetings in the
parking lot near the athletic buildings and sports fields, and
many times, in the building itself—the mail room, the hall-
ways, and even in the vacant offices of coaches who were out
coaching in the fields, gyms, or pools.

There were many times when we would sneak in a quick,
semi-private conversation in restaurants, hotel lobbies, and
basketball games. Those conversations were recorded in my
memory and sometimes noted on scraps of paper or table nap-
kins. Just like the longer discussions we had in our office from
the mid-seventies to the early eighties, our discussions ranged
from local sporting events, such as the Dodgers and Angels, to
worldwide sporting events like the Olympics.

We never talked about politics. Not once did we discuss
who should be our president or our mayor, or if Proposition
13 was a good thing for California. Politics just wasn't on our
agenda. If it had ever come up, I would have done what I always
do when my wife talks politics—listen until she finishes, and
then nod my head up and down. I'm certain that Coach would

have done the same thing.

Religion wasn't discussed, either, except when he told me once that he always held a silver cross in his hand in every game he coached. But I didn't really need to hear that; I knew who he was by the way he lived his life. I'm not sure he knew exactly who I was, though, because sometimes I didn't even know.

What we *did* talk about were our heroes, matters pertaining to coaching, teaching, and everyday life, and, of course, baseball.

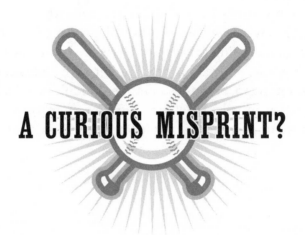

A CURIOUS MISPRINT?

John kept in close touch with UCLA baseball results and some of our statistics, but there was one small detail he knew that surprised me: my batting average in 1962.

One early spring morning, I bumped into John on Bruin Walk, the asphalt pathway leading from the student dorms to the campus. He was coming from the Ducky Drake Track Stadium, where he had just finished walking laps around the track.

"Just a brisk walk, Gary, good for the heart," he said. Then he quickly changed the subject. "When are you going to tell the people who write the baseball media guide to fix the misprint on your batting average?"

I knew he was talking about the page in the media guide that, for years, had listed the leading UCLA hitters for every season since 1958. All of these hitters had averages in the three hundreds, some even in the four hundreds—except me.

"No mistake, John," I told him. "They got it right. I only hit .265."

John studied me closely. Being a kidder himself, I could tell he was trying to see if I was kidding him.

"Gary, you mean you led your team in hitting with a *two*-sixty-five average—not *three*-sixty-five?"

"Yep," I said with a smile, "*two*-sixty-five is correct." I puffed out my chest and said proudly, "It's a record that will stand forever in the annals of UCLA baseball history—like DiMaggio's fifty-six-game hitting streak."

But John didn't crack a smile. "How did you only hit .265, and still lead the team?" he asked.

People had asked me this before, and I was ready with a half-kidding answer: "Tough pitching that year, and no aluminum bats in those days, John."

Coach remained stone-faced. "Gary, aluminum bats didn't come into the game until years later. All the other hitters in your era were above three hundred. Why not you?"

He had me there. I tried a different spin that had worked well in the past with others who insisted on knowing more details about my *two*-sixty-five average.

"If they had kept track of on-base percentage in those days," I said, "I believe my percentage would have been quite respectable."

John nodded. "So, you had lots of walks."

"No," I said, "I really don't remember the walks. But I *do* remember reaching base on a bunch of strike-outs because of swinging at curve balls in the dirt that got past the catcher."

Finally, a smile emerged, then a grin, and finally, a quiet chuckle. With that, I felt satisfied that he finally believed I had only hit .265.

LOW-SCORING GAMES

Most baseball fans prefer the slugging ball games with plenty of home runs, doubles, and action on the base paths. Not so with John. He admitted that he preferred the pitchers' duels in the 1–0 or 2–1 games.

When I asked him why, he bombarded me with so many different strategic situations in a matter of seconds that he left my brain spinning.

"I like focusing on the managers in those low-scoring games," he said. "What are they trying to do just to manufacture a single run to win the ball game? I try to get into their minds—it's like I'm coaching the game along with them. Are we going to take pitches late in the game, and hope for a walk to get things started? Will that make their ace pitcher throw more pitches, and tire him so we can see what they have in their bullpen? Or do we let our hitters swing away on 2-and-0 counts, hoping that they connect on a grooved strike? Are we going to sacrifice bunt with a runner on first and our best hitter at the plate, or will we let him hit away? Why not give the steal sign to get the winning run in scoring position for him?"

John paused only long enough to take a deep breath before continuing. "But Gary, if we do that, will the opposing manager

take the bat out of my best hitter's hands? Will he intentionally walk my best hitter to get to my next batter, who might ground into a double play? If I were that manager, I might do that if the following hitter is a slow runner, has a history of hitting grounders, and is batting a hundred points less than my best hitter."

While John was talking, I could see that he was living all of these various situations. He was managing against himself—and enjoying every second of it.

"I don't understand why major league managers, when their teams have a lead, wait until the eighth or ninth innings to put in their defensive replacements," he continued. "If a manager knows that one or two of his hitters won't be coming up to bat again, and he has a couple of better defensive players sitting on the bench—why not put them into the game in the seventh inning, especially if you are the home team?"

I couldn't come up with a better answer than this: "Well, John, maybe the manager isn't thinking as positively as you, and believes he might need his best hitters in the game in case the opposition catches up to them."

"Yes, I understand that," Coach said, "but I've seen the other teams blow leads only because a player can't make a play that someone on the bench could have made. The unnecessary error results in a sloppier game and more runs. I prefer the neat, clean defensive game with fewer runs."

John was close to convincing me that his type of game was more exciting, but I told him that low-scoring games are a rarity in today's college baseball, in which high-powered aluminum bats are used.

"I preferred college baseball, when the wooden bats were used," he said.

"Well," I said, "if you like low-scoring games, you must have really enjoyed those games our UCLA teams played in the early sixties. We didn't score more than three runs very often, and we didn't have a player on our team hit over .300."

John gave me a knowing smile. "Oh, yes," he said. "I remember, Gary. Those were the years of great pitchers, when you hit a robust .265."

Sometimes I preferred for John to be forgetful.

THE WINNINGEST COACH

Coach claimed that he never used the word "win" when addressing his teams. Every one of his players vouched for this—some even claiming that they doubted any college coach in America could make the same claim.

When Coach and I discussed the topic of winning, he often made light of his reputation. "You know, Gary, I won a sizeable number of games," he said, "but I lost many games, too. One hundred and forty-seven losses at UCLA, which I believe is the second most of all the coaches in UCLA's basketball history."

He smiled and added, "But I can't feel too bad about that, because there is a baseball player who is famous for winning, and he lost a lot of games, too. You know who that is?"

I had no idea.

"As you know, they give an award to the best major league pitcher every year in honor of Cy Young," Coach said. "He holds the all-time record for most wins—over five hundred of them. But do you know how many losses he had?"

"No idea," I replied.

John came a step closer and said slowly, "Three . . . hundred . . . and . . . sixteen. More than any pitcher in baseball history. Can you believe that? They give the best pitcher of the year award in honor of the one who has lost the most games. That record has stood for almost a century and, I believe, it's one that will never be broken."

"Wow!" I exclaimed. "I just assumed he was so great, he didn't lose many games."

John shook his head. "I've told you before, Gary. Winning is overrated, and the effort one exhibits is underrated. What do you think?"

When Coach talked about his losses at UCLA, I couldn't help but think of my losses. "What do I think?" I asked. "Well, John, hearing about your losses and Cy Young's losses, I feel a lot better about mine."

I told John that, at the time I stopped coaching at UCLA, our sports information department claimed that I was the "winningest" coach in UCLA history. They made a big deal out of it, and although I hadn't been aware of that statistic before then, I felt pretty good about it . . . except that I knew I also had the most losses of any coach in UCLA history.

"Thanks for telling me about Cy Young," I said to Coach. "You say his loss record will never be broken; mine at UCLA probably will not be broken, either."

A few years after I retired, my "most wins" record was broken by longtime women's volleyball coach Andy Banakowski. My loss record still stands. That makes two records—one as a player and one as a coach—that I still hold at UCLA that may never be broken.

OUR MENTORS

One morning, after Coach had taken his walk around the UCLA track, I met him in the Pauley Pavilion locker room.

"Gary," he asked me, "who was your mentor? Not when you were a player, but when you were already coaching?"

"You mean, besides you, Coach?" I answered.

He gave me a crooked grin and chuckled quietly. "Yes, Gary."

"Well, I'd say it was the coach who first hired me after I finished being a student here at UCLA—Dr. Don Edwards."

"Doc Edwards," he exclaimed. "You mean the former catcher who's managing the Indians now?"

"No, Coach, not that Doc Edwards. I'm talking about Don Edwards, who was the head baseball coach at the University of California, Riverside. He was an All-American pitcher from Western Michigan University."

"Why do you say he was your mentor?"

"Because Dr. Edwards was a lot like you, Coach. For one thing, I never heard him utter a cuss word—and God knows he had every reason to do so, because we played some lousy ball games our first couple of years. But also, because he knew the game backwards and forwards. He wrote a book, one of the first instructional books ever written about baseball. It had everything in it you'd ever want to know—details from gripping a bat, to gripping a slider, to handling footwork on a double play. He had pictures showing all this stuff in the book, too."

Coach nodded. "Sounds like a good book. You were fortunate to have a man with his knowledge mentoring you when you were first entering the coaching world."

"I was. But it wasn't just what he knew about baseball. He set a good example by his hard work and his determination to get the best out of his players. In those days, we never had the greatest players, but they all gave their best effort because he showed 'em how."

"I had some great mentors growing up and all through college," Coach said. "But once I became a paid teacher and coach, I learned an awful lot from Notre Dame's great football coach, Frank Leahy."

I told Coach that I didn't know much about Leahy, but that I had heard of him when I was a youngster in Ohio. "My mom was Catholic, so she always rooted for Notre Dame in those days," I said.

"Frank Leahy showed me how to be organized in my teaching and my coaching," John said. "He invited me to observe one of his practices at Notre Dame when I was teaching high school in Indiana. I was amazed at how efficient his practices were— he believed that good practices were the key to winning games. His drills went without any delay—one right after another, like clockwork. When I finished watching his practice, I went home with a different outlook. That's when I decided to make my practices short, but efficient."

A HUMBLE REMINDER

After John and I had finished speaking at a coach's clinic, we were walking through the exit doors of our hotel. Suddenly, I felt John's hand grab my bicep and squeeze. In a more high-pitched voice than usual, but not quite a holler, he exclaimed, "Careful, Gary!"

"Huh?" I didn't know what he meant.

"You never know what danger lurks in the outdoors . . . especially near hotels," he said.

I looked at his face. His serious expression suddenly erupted into one of the biggest smiles he had ever given me.

Then, holding onto the smile but letting go of my arm, he told me about an incident that had occurred more than three decades ago.

"I have to admit," he said, "I was elated after we won our first national championship in 1964, beating Duke in the final game by fifteen points. We had just finished our season undefeated. I was walking on clouds and feeling pretty good about myself.

"The next morning—it was Easter Sunday—Nell and I were waiting out in front of our hotel. I was still feeling real good about myself and last night's game. Suddenly, I felt something on top of my head go splat. I reached up and felt a gooey wet spot. I looked at Nell, bent my head down, and asked, 'What's this?' She said, 'It's white . . . sort of.' I looked up to the sky just in time to see a pigeon disappear behind a building across the way. 'Goodness gracious!' I said to Nell. 'The good Lord is trying to tell me something. I must not let this go to my head.'"

BE QUICK, DON'T HURRY

Be quick, don't hurry!" I doubt any baseball coach ever used those famous four words of Coach Wooden's more than I did. I used them before I had read them in any of Coach's books, or had ever heard Coach speak of them in clinics. I used them because I liked what I heard when I was a young student at UCLA, attending Coach's practice sessions in that stinky gym. I used them from my first year until my last year of coaching.

It wasn't until I saw Coach Wooden one day in 2000 that I finally thanked him for providing me with one of the simplest and best coaching tips for an infielder. Coach Wooden's maxim had helped me teach infielders the art of fielding for all of my forty-one years of college coaching, saving more infield errors than anything else I ever taught.

When I said this to Coach, he surprised me with his answer. "Well, Gary," he said, "the first time I ever used that saying was when I coached baseball in high school."

I was stunned. In all the years we had talked, I had always believed that his famous four words stemmed from coaching basketball. John could tell by the way my jaw dropped that he needed to explain further.

"Yes, Gary, those words apply to baseball just as much as

they do to basketball. When I coached baseball, I noticed that most errors were caused by players getting in a hurry to throw the ball before they ever caught it. I used to preach, 'Fielding is a 1-2-3 process. Catch it first, get a hold of it second, and third, throw it.' You can't throw it before you catch it and get a hold of it."

When Coach told me this, I thought of Mike Gallego, a second baseman of mine who had a magical glove. His only weakness in turning the double play was being in a hurry to throw the ball.

I told John, "Mike was one of the first players I ever told, 'Slow down, you're trying to go so fast that you're going 3-2-1 instead of 1-2-3.' Mike became one of the fastest I ever had—and one of the most efficient—at turning the double play after learning your formula, Coach."

Coach smiled broadly. "Glad I was able to help."*

---

* Mike Gallego played fourteen years in the major leagues as a standout defensive infielder—two of those years playing for the World Series Champion Oakland A's. He is currently coaching third base for the A's.

IT'S ALL ABOUT EFFORT

I told you before, Gary, I never talked to my players about winning," Coach Wooden said to me. "It was always about giving
their best *effort*. I made no secret of this. I believe winning is
overrated, and the effort one exhibits is underrated."

Yes, John had told me this many times. Except for Coach
John Matulich, my basketball coach at Riverside Junior College, every coach I had ever played for emphasized winning. Did
Coach Matulich not mention winning because he had played
for Coach Wooden? Too many coaches preach that winning is
the single most important thing when competing in sports, but
John didn't agree, and neither did I.

At the top of my Sphere of Commitment, under the word
"Team," are the words, "The *Effort* to Win." Underneath those
words are: "Play Hard, Give It Your Best, and Hustle"—this is
what I expected from every one of my players in every one of
their games.

I grew up at a time when the great sports writer, Grantland
Rice, was known as the "voice of sports." From my early child-
hood, his words were arguably as famous as Coach Wooden's
are today. Both shared the same belief, but said it quite differently. Rice wrote:

For when the One Great Scorer comes
To write against your name,
He marks—not that you won or lost—
But how you played the game.

My mom and dad never tried to coach me, but sometimes after a tough loss, they did try to console me. They reminded me that the important thing was how you played the game. Coach Wooden fortified that belief when I became a coach.

Grantland Rice died in 1954, John's sixth year as UCLA's head coach. John had yet to win a national championship, and he waited another nine years before winning his first of ten. He once told me privately, and later, said publicly, "As you can see from my record, I didn't learn how to win much in my early years. But once I learned, I got pretty good at it."

FAIR AND REASONABLE

John always enjoyed speaking at coaches' clinics, whether they were for college coaches or high school coaches. He once told me, "I do not expect huge payments for my talks, but I only ask that they be fair and reasonable."

It so happened that we both spoke at a coach's clinic that John felt did not treat the coaches fairly, including him. Although we were handed meal coupons upon our arrival, they only partially paid for our meals, and the coupons could only be used in their hotel. John voiced his concern about this when we had lunch together in the hotel.

When the clinic was over and we had both finished our speaking obligations, Coach and I met at the hotel registration desk to check out. While standing in line with the rest of the coaches, John whispered, "Gary, the clinic was a success. They probably made a sizeable profit. But I won't be coming back. They didn't treat us fairly or reasonably." Though he whispered, I knew that he meant what he said. Although he was invited again, he never went back.

NOTE TO YOUNG COACHES

Coach was a slave to his practice plan, especially when it came to starting on time and closing on time. He admitted to me that he didn't always follow this maxim. When he first started coaching, he would often go "overtime." He said that he learned from another coach whom he respected greatly that the *quantity* of time you spend on something isn't as important as the *quality* of time.

He liked emphasizing this point whenever he spoke at clinics, especially high school coaches' clinics, where many young coaches were in attendance. He said to me, "Whenever I talked to a *young* group of coaches, I made sure to emphasize the importance of having short practices. I told them, 'Don't run practices too late, and go home in a bad mood. It's not good for a newly married man to go home in a bad mood. It just puts your new bride in a bad mood, too . . . which is not good for a marriage, if you know what I mean.' Then I would add, 'Of course, when you get as old as I am, it doesn't make any difference.'"

It was times like these that I had the pleasure of seeing that unique, sly grin that John wore whenever he cracked a joke.

A TOUGH ACT TO FOLLOW

Coach Wooden was the opening speaker at a baseball clinic for high school and college coaches from the western United States. I was part of that large and attentive audience when Coach started the parade of speakers. He spoke for about an hour, then asked for questions. It seemed that everyone raised a hand; although John would have probably kept answering questions all day long, the clinic's director had to stop John's part of the session so that the next speaker could have his share of the platform.

I felt sorry for that second speaker of the day. When he walked behind the podium and looked out into the audience, all he saw were the backs and behinds of people heading for the exit. From my seat in one of the front rows, I turned around and saw the same thing the speaker was staring at.

The scene was a familiar one for me, because of a baseball clinic I had attended in 1973. Bobby Winkles, former Arizona State University head coach and newly appointed manager of the California Angels, was the main speaker that day. Bobby was the idol of many college baseball coaches, especially young ones like me, because he was the first college coach (and the last one) to ever be hired as a manager in the major leagues.

The auditorium was packed with high school and college coaches anxious to hear what the new Angels manager had to say.

When Bobby finished speaking, more than half of the audience began their march to the doors. I planned on joining them. From my front row seat, I stood up and made my way to the aisle, joining the crowded stampede. Then I heard a booming voice say over the microphone, "It looks like a f——g bomb scare hit this place."

Most coaches had already filed out of the auditorium, but those of us who did hear the speaker stopped in our tracks and headed back to our seats. We all thought, *This guy might be interesting to listen to.* It was one of the most ear-catching opening remarks I had ever heard from a speaker. It came from the relatively unknown Preston Gomez, who had just been hired as the Houston Astros' third base coach.

That memory is what kept me sitting in my seat this time, after Coach Wooden had finished, although *this* second speaker's introduction was not as startling as Gomez's. Later that day, I met up with John and mentioned to him that he was a tough act to follow. I also told him the story of how it reminded me of the day Preston Gomez had followed Bobby Winkles on the platform.

I was accustomed to hearing John chuckle over the slightest humorous story, but not this time. John wasn't smiling. I could tell he was unaware of what had happened after he had finished speaking. He had not seen the audience, since it was his practice to walk off the stage and exit through the stage doors. Coach was quite serious when he said, "I'll need to change that."

From then on, whenever he spoke and another speaker followed, he would say something interesting about the next speaker so that the audience would be courteous and the speaker would be heard by all. That's just the way Coach was—always thinking of the other person.

PULLING PITCHERS

When Coach and I had a conversation at a coaching clinic, we came to the subject of pulling pitchers. At first, he seemed surprised when I told him that I had pulled my starting pitcher with only one out to go in a game with a comfortable lead.

I said, "This particular pitcher, Tim O'Neill, took a great deal of pride in completing his games. He was proud of his endurance and stamina—something that he worked on daily so he could finish nine innings with ease. He started and finished most of his games.

"O'Neill started the ninth inning with a big lead, but the opposition began hitting long drives over our outfielders' heads and line drives into the outfield gaps. Although we were still comfortably ahead, I was concerned enough to get the bullpen warmed up. Finally, after several more runs and another long shot against the outfield fence, I left the dugout to take Tim out of the game. I hated to do it; worse, I knew he hated for me to do it. This was not going to be an easy task.

"As I approached the mound, Tim grimaced. He was not happy to see me. Before my foot even touched the dirt on the pitcher's circle, he said in a begging sort of way, 'Coach, I'm not tired at all!' Without flinching, I looked him straight in the eyes and said, 'I know you're not, Tim, but your outfielders are.'"

Coach Wooden came as close to cracking up as I had ever seen him. He said he wished he knew about it while he was coaching.

"Why's that, Coach?" I asked.

"Because I could have used a similar line when I pulled a player out of the game for not sticking with his own man on defense, making all of his teammates tired from having to guard *his* man."

OCTOBER 14

John's birthday is October 14. It is also the birthday of Vince Beringhele, my outstanding and longtime hitting coach at UCLA. Sometimes, when I complimented Vinnie on his coaching talents, he would jokingly remind me, "Well, Skip, great coaches are born on the fourteenth of October."

I relayed this story to Coach Wooden one evening while dining at the Valley Inn. Coach chuckled and said, "Vince isn't the only leader who was born on the fourteenth—General Dwight Eisenhower was born then. William Penn, too."

I told John that I hadn't been aware of that. "My second-oldest daughter, Kimberly, was born on October 14," I said. "That's how I remember your birthday."

He smiled. I think he got my joke. He said, "One of my most memorable birthdays came the year after I retired from UCLA. You might guess what it was, since one of UCLA's best all-time baseball players presented me with a special gift."

Puzzled, I stared at John. He seemed pleased—when it came to baseball, he always loved playing guessing games with me.

"Well, Gary, as you know, I've always been a Yankee fan," he said. "On the fourteenth of October in 1976, UCLA's Chris Chambliss hit a walk-off home run against Kansas City to win the American League championship and send my Yankees to the World Series."

I slapped my knee as I recalled that famous homerun. I also reminded Coach that Chambliss had done the same thing while playing for Coach Reichle's and Coach Mickens's 1969 UCLA team, when he hit a home run against the Trojans to cinch the Conference championship and send the Bruins to the NCAA Playoffs and to the College World Series.

John began describing the details of that October 14 game. "He hit the first pitch in the bottom of the ninth to win it," he said. "Poor Chris. So many Yankee fans came pouring onto the field. He barely made it around the bases—everyone wanted to jump on him and pound him. I think he even fell down once before reaching home plate. And I'm not sure he ever touched it."

Sometime later, I viewed a television clip of the Chambliss home run. Coach Wooden's recollection of Chris falling down was correct. The video clearly showed Chris being body-blocked by a fan as he rounded second base. There was no evidence that he ever touched the plate, because of the crowd blocking his way. In Chris's interview at the end of the clip, he admitted that he did indeed miss the plate and returned a little later to touch it.

The night John and I discussed October 14, neither of us knew that another October 14 alum would become the manager of John's Yankees in 2008—Joe Girardi. Vince Beringhele might be right about that famous birthdate.

THE DEFINITION
OF A HERO

Once, during halftime at a UCLA basketball game, I left my seat in the upper gallery to visit Coach, who always sat in the bleachers about two or three rows up from the floor level. I waited in line with about a half a dozen others before I finally reached Coach. He greeted me with a warm smile and said, "Gary, I found us a good definition for 'hero.'" He surprised me when he said, with a crease of a grin, "I got it from Superman."

I raised my eyebrows. "Superman?"

"Yes, who knows about heroes better than a hero himself?"

"But . . . Superman?" I asked again.

"I think you'll like what he said in a magazine I read." Then he quoted *Superman* actor Christopher Reeve: "I think a hero is an ordinary individual who finds strength to persevere and endure in spite of overwhelming obstacles."

I told John that Reeve would certainly know what he was talking about—he fought heroically in his own battle with paralysis.

John and I didn't talk for long, since there were others waiting behind me. When I returned to my seat, I thought, *Christopher Reeve's definition applies to John, as well.*

THE LATE INNINGS
2003-2010

COACH'S TWO FAVORITE WORDS

On September 20, 2003, ten of Coach Wooden's close acquaintances, including former UCLA coaches and athletes, sat around a dining table at the Valley Inn, having lunch with John. We called ourselves "the Valley Inn Gang" since we always met at the Valley Inn, Coach's favorite dining spot when he wanted something "a little fancy." Actually, we were multi-tasking, firing questions at Coach while watching the UCLA-Oklahoma football game on television. In the middle of the first quarter, John surprised us when he fired a question back at us.

Trying to meet the eyes of everyone sitting around the table, he asked, "What two words in the English language do you believe are the most important?"

We stared blankly at each other in silence. Only the television sounds in the background could be heard. I knew, from talking to John in the past, that one of the words was "love." I did not know the other, so I kept quiet and waited for someone to answer who knew *both* words. Finally, almost simultaneously, two people answered, "love." It was a safe guess.

John grinned approvingly. "And the other word?" he asked.

The table was silent again, longer than the last time. One by

one, people made their guesses, some excitedly, some timidly. Words like "hope," "faith," "trust," and "gentle" were called out. Coach just shook his head from side to side with each wrong answer, the sly grin still on his face. He enjoyed this game.

A couple of players, thinking this second most important word must be one that John had included in his Pyramid of Success, bellowed out the words, "loyalty" and "friendship." But John just shook his head again and waited for more attempts at the right answer.

One desperate player, half-serious and half-hoping to be correct, said, "Win!" We all had a good laugh over that one. It broke the tension, and John did what a little boy might do under such a circumstance.

He leaned forward and challenged us with, "You give?"

I looked around the table and saw nothing but blank faces. Even Jim Bush, the renowned Hall of Fame UCLA track coach, seemed perplexed. I remember thinking, *Maybe Gary Beban, UCLA's only Heisman Trophy winner, who sat with us a couple of years ago, would have known the answer.*

But, alas, we all nodded and surrendered to John.

He seemed pleased that he had stumped us. "In my opinion, 'balance' is the second most important word in the English language," he said. No one at the table openly disputed John's choice, although it did spark my memory. I had heard John speak of the importance of balance on occasion, but I never thought that would be his choice for the second most important word in the American dictionary. Still, John's chosen word stunned all of us. We could have sat there all day and all night without getting it right. By the looks on our faces, John knew that he needed to explain further, so he lectured us on why the word "balance" was so important.

"Physically, emotionally, socially, and spiritually, balance is necessary," he said. He began his explanation with the physical aspect. "Take, for example, basketball. You must be on balance if you expect to defend the man with the ball—fall for a fake and get off balance, and he will dribble right past you. That means keeping your head in the mid-line between both feet . . . lean it too far to one side or too far in front, and you will be off-balance."

John looked at me. "Gary, I think that is the way it is in baseball with a hitter," he said. "Shouldn't his head be in line with the midpoint of his body at the point of contact with the ball?"

I nodded in agreement.

"I also believe the *team* should be balanced," John continued. "You will not win with a bunch of seven-footers on your basketball team any more than you would win with a bunch of five-foot-nine players." Then he asked us, "Do you think we would have won with only a team of Bill Waltons? Of course not. We also needed some adept ball handlers and especially quick players like little Mike Warren. And we would not have won with five Mike Warrens in the lineup, either. We needed Bill Walton to rebound for us and get the ball to our guards, so they could quickly get the ball down court. No, sir . . . without balance on your team, you will not be successful. I always tried to have a well-balanced team. I believe that is why we succeeded.

"You have probably heard me say that quickness is important in athletics, but it is more important for an athlete to be quick *under control*, so that he is always on-balance. I believe that is true for an athlete and for all of us as we live our daily lives. Maintaining balance in our lives is critical.

"Physically, we all have a certain amount of speed, strength, and balance. The first thing that leaves us is our speed. Goodness gracious, most of us start losing our speed and our quickness in our early thirties. It probably has something to do with the fact that we stop trying to run fast at that age. Then, in our late thirties, we begin to lose our strength, although it is more gradual than our loss of speed.

"But we are lucky that our balance stays with us, at least up into the sixties, seventies, and, for the lucky ones, into the eighties. That is when some of us start to fall. But I am not sure

we fall because of a complete lack of balance or because of a lack of strength. I know my legs have steadily grown weaker, and they have a tough time holding me up. Balance may not be the only culprit in older people like me.

"Emotionally, we need to stay balanced all our lives. Some people just cannot handle adversity, and they lose control, either by taking their frustrations out on others or by getting angry at themselves. For example, how many times have you heard of baseball pitchers losing their temper and striking their fist into the dugout wall, breaking their pitching hand? It happens because they lose control over their emotions. Gee-whiz, they don't even have enough control to punch with their non-pitching hand.

"At the opposite end of anger is jubilation. Sometimes athletes get so excited about making a great play that they go crazy celebrating. Have you ever noticed how often basketball players will make a basket and, within seconds of doing so, turn right around and foul somebody? That would not happen if they had a consistent level of emotional balance.

"Emotional balance applies to coaches, as well. Too many get so angry at a referee's call that they lose control. I have seen coaches get technical fouls due to their behavior that have cost their teams the game. Coaches need to maintain their emotional balance as much as their players do.

"Balance is important in your social life, as well. Nothing wrong with going to functions where you meet other people who inspire you and who you learn from. And nothing wrong with just going to a party to have fun. But too much partying gets in the way of sleep, which can affect you not just physically, but mentally and emotionally. For college basketball players, too much partying gets in the way of basketball and, more importantly, interferes with academics. Too much of one thing is not good for anyone. You need a balance."

John concluded by saying, "Even spiritually, you need to be balanced."

The Valley Inn Gang enjoyed listening to Coach spread his wisdom that afternoon, despite our Bruins football team getting clobbered by Oklahoma, 59–24.

Afterwards, I took the time to call John Rouse, who had attended the lunch for the first time. Rouse had been a solid left-handed pitcher for UCLA a couple of years before I began coaching the Bruins. I asked him how he felt about spending that afternoon with Coach Wooden.

"I felt like I was listening to Moses," he replied.

Thanks to Jim Schweitzer, a loyal UCLA fan who organized these lunch and dinner meetings, our gang met regularly with Coach for a dozen years. I always looked forward to these outings and, though I had heard some of his stories before, I always loved hearing them again. There was never a time when I didn't learn something new from Coach.

Not too long after that lunch, when Coach had brought up the subject of spiritual balance but hadn't really explained it, I began thinking about what he might have said if he had. Maybe he felt that the way he lived his life was the best way to explain spiritual balance. He knew that his friends were aware that he went to church every Sunday; yet that alone did not make him a spiritual person. He did not need to wear his Christian religion on his sleeve—he wore it deep inside, in his heart. Everyone who knew him well understood where he stood spiritually. Everyone knew his spiritual life was on-balance. With Coach, it was more about what he *was* than what he *said*.

COACH'S SURPRISE VISIT

My last year of coaching at UCLA brought fond and ever-lasting memories, starting from the first official practice to the final game in the NCAA Regional Playoffs in Oklahoma City.

It is that first practice that stands out most in my memory and, I believe, stands out in the memories of my players. Coach Wooden paid us a visit that day—a surprise visit for my players, but one which was planned well in advance by John, Tony Spino, and myself. My wish for the players that day was that they would be as pleasantly surprised as I was when, in 1959, I first saw Coach Wooden sitting in the stands, watching our team play the Trojans.

That first fall practice in 2003 began at 0600 hours, when I awakened thirty-five groggy players from their slumber by standing on top of the pitcher's mound and blowing a shrill whistle. All of us—players and coaches—had spent a restless and uncomfortable night under the starlight (no tents), trying to sleep in our sleeping bags, which were spread out on the damp infield grass at UCLA's Jackie Robinson Baseball Stadium.

I was dressed in a full U.S. Marine drill sergeant uniform, including laced-up military boots and my Smokey the Bear drill sergeant hat strapped tightly under my chin. As the players moaned and groaned at the sound of my whistle, the stadium loudspeakers blasted the theme song from *Rocky*.

I ordered everyone to "rise and shine." When all were standing, I led them in my favorite warm-up exercises and calisthenics. I could see their breath in the cool October morning air—though it could have been smoke from their fuming insides, since they didn't seem to be enjoying their day so far.

After warming up, we had a camper's version of a continental breakfast: oranges, bananas, jelly rolls, and every athlete's favorite breakfast drink—Gatorade. At 7:00, a chartered bus arrived to take a load of sleepy players to my home in Agoura Hills. The veteran players knew what was planned for the rest of the day, but the rookies weren't so sure what lay ahead. First on the agenda would be a preseason pep talk from their head coach. Next would be a grueling cross-country run up and over the hills of Chesebro State Park, located down the road from my house. Neither one of these items on the agenda seemed particularly appealing to the players. If it weren't for the final event of the day, I doubt many of them would have wanted to board the bus.

That final NCAA-approved event featured an all-you-can-eat barbecue on the front lawn of my home. Barbecued tri-tip and chicken were the main attractions, but salads, western chili beans, corn on the cob, baked potatoes, and apple pie would be served as well. The rookies had heard about this feast from the vets.

Our bus arrived at 7:30, and the players went to their seats on our front lawn. They sat on dew-covered metal folding chairs, which dampened their tired butts. I should have known that my opening line would not fit well with the surly mood of the players. "Did you all have a good night's sleep?" I asked, trying to smile.

I looked at my wristwatch, which read 7:40 AM. Coach Wooden was scheduled to arrive at 8:00. *Perfect,* I thought, *my*

speech is twenty minutes long.

It had no title. I just called it my "Motivating and Inspiring Pep Talk." It was similar to every preseason talk I delivered on the first practice day. But I had never spoken to any of my teams after they had slept (or tried to sleep) on a baseball diamond. From their slinking postures and half-closed eyes, I could tell that this pep talk was lacking one thing—pep.

Halfway through my talk, I sneaked a peek at my watch, which now read 7:50 AM. Coach Wooden would soon be here. I found myself looking over the heads of my players at the road behind them in search of the car that would bring excitement to this dead party. In fact, for the rest of my talk, I only occasionally looked at the players, because I knew they were trying to sneak naps in preparation for the cross-country run they believed would commence after my speech.

By 7:55, I was getting anxious for Coach to arrive. I could feel the excitement in my bones. I knew that, within the next five minutes, these players, who were trying to pretend that they were listening to me, would suddenly be awakened by their celebrity guest. They would experience the same feeling that I had felt as a player almost half a century ago.

Before I knew it, my speech was over. I stood in front of my players, with nothing more to say. My mind was telling me to announce the start of the next event—the cross-country run—but my heart was yelling, "Stay the course!" Then I suddenly remembered that I always set my watch two minutes ahead. Coach could still make it on time!

I looked down the road and saw a car slowing down, with its right-turn blinker flashing to turn into our driveway. As the car pulled into the driveway, the players turned to look at it. They strained to see its occupants, but the early morning sun's glare was bouncing off the windows, and no one could see inside.

I knew who was inside. I breathed a huge sigh of relief. Rather coolly, I said to my players, "Don't mind the car, gentlemen, this is a dead-end street and we get cars pulling into our driveway all the time to turn around." It was true.

Most of the players believed me and turned their attention back to me, but when the engine stopped purring, I lost all of them again. The driver opened the door, and most of the players recognized the face of our trainer, Tony Spino, who walked around the car and opened the passenger side door. Tony bent over and swung his passenger's legs out first, then helped him to his feet, and the face of Coach John Wooden appeared.

The silence was frightening to me. I had expected a chorus of "oohs" and "aahs," and maybe even some cheers, but all of the players seemed frozen in their chairs at that moment as Coach, whose ninety-second birthday was only a few days away, held on to Tony's elbow with one hand and grasped his cane in the other. The two of them walked cautiously in front of the players, where Tony sat Coach in a dry folding chair that I had prepared for him. No one said a word.

Coach Wooden spent over an hour with us, sitting in the chair with that familiar posture, arms folded and legs crossed, answering questions and telling stories—mainly about baseball—and quoting maxims and anecdotes. As usual, he also recited a couple of his favorite poems.

After he left, my wife, Sandy, looked at me with questioning eyes. "The whole time Coach Wooden was here," she said, "I kept thinking, 'Do these boys know how lucky they are to be so close to this man?'"

I decided to ask them that question and also ask how they felt about that day with Coach in general. Their comments were evidence that, indeed, they did realize how lucky they were.

"The mood immediately changed," said sophomore first baseman Brett McMillan. "I guess the only thing I can compare it to is if you were to meet the president or a four-star general. You were at attention immediately, and completely focused on him with your utmost respect. He didn't need to do or say anything to get that reaction; if you knew who he was, you knew he deserved that respect."

Anthony Norman, a sophomore outfielder, said, "Because of Coach Wooden's persona and because he led such a good life—not just about basketball—you listened. He has a mythical thing. It started with basketball, but it became much more than that."

Junior pitcher and first baseman Wes Whisler said, "Being from Indiana, I'd always heard about Coach Wooden. He was our state's hero."

"I will never forget how articulate Coach Wooden was, and how every one of his words was carefully placed," recalled freshman catcher Sam Ray. "Above all else, his humility was staggering—a man who had accomplished so much and is the benchmark for all other coaches, sitting there, unassuming, and seeming to enjoy our company as much as we did his."

WINNING WITH HONOR

In the fall of 2004, after I had coached my last game for the Bruins, I asked John a simple question that led to a thorough and thoughtful answer.

"John, all of your former players say you never mentioned the word 'winning' to them," I said. "What *did* you say to motivate them to win without mentioning that word?"

With a half-smile and a quick wink of an eye, he said, "I'm sure they knew how much I hated losing. I believe my players always knew that winning with honor was the most important thing to me. That means knowing you played honestly and gave your best effort at all times."

"Honestly?" I asked.

"Yes, Gary, honestly. I learned early in my coaching career that winning for the sake of just winning is not important."

Then he told me a story of his first year of coaching college basketball. His Indiana State team won their conference title in 1947, and earned the right to go to the National Association of Intercollegiate Athletics playoffs in Kansas City. John had refused his team's invitation, because they wouldn't allow all of his players to go. John had an African-American player, Clarence Walker, on the team, and John told the rules committee,

"If Clarence can't go, my team won't go." He made it clear that the NAIA was being discriminatory.

When John told me this story, I asked him if he thought his team would have had a chance of winning—with or without Clarence.

He said, "Clarence didn't play that much. I don't know if we would have won or lost, but that is not the point, Gary. The point is doing the right thing. Even if we would have won *without* Clarence, in my eyes, we would have won *without* honor.

"In 1948, we were invited again to the playoffs, but the NAIA still had the rule forbidding blacks to play. I refused their invitation. But this time, Manhattan College's coach heard about our refusal, and he told the NAIA that if Indiana State, including Clarence Walker, couldn't go, neither would his team. I think the officials finally got the message. That was the first time blacks were allowed to play in the tournament."

"Did you win in 1948?" I asked.

"No, Gary, Louisville beat us in the championship game. But I felt like we had won the biggest battle—we won with honor. I believe a coach—not just his players—needs to know that there is a difference between winning and winning with honor."

John's words sparked my memory of the wooden placard perched on top of our athletic director's desk with the words WINNING SOLVES ALL PROBLEMS stamped across it in gold letters. I asked Coach, "When you visited J. D.'s office, did you ever notice the sign on his desk?"

"Gary, *all* UCLA coaches notice that sign."

"I know he wanted to send a message to his coaches that winning was essential," I said. "But Coach, I never believed in those words. I believe winning solves *many* problems . . . but certainly not *all*."

"I always thought so, too, Gary. J. D. probably believed that it solved all of *his* problems, because it kept the alumni off his back. He also didn't have to go to the trouble of firing his coaches for losing too much, and winning made it easier for him to raise money for our programs."

Listening to John, I knew he had thought about J. D.'s sign maybe as much as I had.

He wasn't finished. "If winning solved all problems, then why do universities that win—but get caught cheating—have more problems getting out of the trouble than they would have if they had lost?" He paused momentarily, his eyes fixed on mine. "I'd rather be an honest loser than a dishonest winner," he said.

Coach brought up another example. "Gary, we talked about this before—about coaches routinely taking scholarships away from their players because of poor performance. If we give a scholarship to a player, he and his family should know that he has it until his eligibility expires, usually in four years. Coaches that will take a scholarship away because a player has not lived up to expectations should take a hard look into the mirror. They would see that they were the ones who made the mistake in recruiting that player—it was not the mistake of the player. The coach should live with that mistake until the player completes his eligibility. Coaches who don't realize their mistakes are those who don't care about winning with honor."

Although the NCAA rules forbid coaches from making a *written* promise lasting four years, Coach and I sometimes made the promise *verbally*, and sometimes we didn't need to because our recruits knew our history—we never took scholarships away, unless there was a flagrant violation of team rules.

Coach asked, "What about *on* the field, Gary? Did you teach your players to win with honor all the time?"

It was a question I could not answer immediately, because there were some gray areas in the game of baseball where I permitted myself and my players to play a little "shady."

Finally, I said, "Well, Coach, I do teach the hidden ball trick. And I used it when I played ball. It wasn't exactly honorable when I hid the ball in my glove and asked the opposing runner to step off the bag so I could dust it off—then I'd tag him out."

Coach gave me a crooked grin. I couldn't tell if he thought

the play was honorable or if it was funny.

"That play just seems to be acceptable in baseball because it is stupid for a player to be off the bag without knowing who has the ball," I said.

When Coach gave no hint of approval or disapproval, I made a quick transition. "John," I said, "I would like to have your opinion on a play that went against our Bruins just this past spring. Was it honorable or dishonorable?"

He nodded and said, "I'd like to hear it."

I described in great detail to John what had happened that spring night. Arizona State was beating us by a whopping margin of nine runs in the bottom of the seventh inning at Jackie Robinson Stadium. Our catcher, Chris Denove, came to bat with the bases loaded and no outs. Chris hit a deep fly ball to right field that carried over the fence for a grand slam home run. The score was now 10–5. At least, everyone *thought* that was the score—everyone except the game's base umpire and the Sun Devils' right fielder, Travis Buck.

Travis threw the home-run ball back into the infield, where their shortstop touched second base and threw the ball to the third baseman, who touched third. The umpire ruled that the right fielder had caught the ball, which resulted in a triple play. This was the same umpire who said he had seen the right fielder make the catch, and at the same time, saw the runner (who was behind him) fail to tag up at second base. I told him, "You are the first umpire I've ever met who not only had two bad eyes in the front of his head, but also in the back of his head."

Meanwhile, our captain, Brandon Averill, who was ruled out at third base for not tagging up, was paying similar insults to the third base umpire. In my view, the umpires did not see the ball go over the fence. They did not see the ball being caught. And they did not see the runners leave their bases too soon. I claimed that our base runners at third base were taught to always tag-up on long hit balls to the outfield. I assured them that, if my runner at second base had seen the ball caught, he would have retreated to the bag before going to third. "But my runner saw the ball leave the yard!" I said.

Despite my pleading, the umpires believed that the ball had been caught, and the runners did not tag up. The debate led to my ejection, and also the ejection of Brandon Averill. The game remained 10–1, and eventually ended in ASU's favor, 12–4.

Odds are, ASU would have won anyway without the crazy play that even *Sports Illustrated* wrote about in their magazine a few days later.

How ironic that, twenty years beforehand (in 1984), a video had been produced to show that Shane Mack's double down the left field line at Stanford was truly a fair ball. Now, in 2004, a video once again told the truth when it showed that Denove's blast was clearly a home run.

The game had been recorded by Denove's dad. The video showed the ball clearing the right field fence by plenty, while the right fielder was hanging over the fence without either hand raised to catch the ball.

Although the video showed a large trash bin behind the fence, we could not see the ball once it cleared the fence. We deduced that the ball rebounded off of the bin and landed in Travis Buck's hands. He had made the "smart" play, which turned the grand slam into a triple play. But was it an *honorable* play, and did they win with honor?

I had been asking myself that question long before I asked it of Coach. I knew that, when I played ball, I did some things that were not clearly honorable. I remember, when I was playing second base, a game in which a runner on first took off to steal second with his head down, heck-bent for leather. I rushed to the bag to cover for our catcher's throw, but the ball got stuck in his glove, and all he could do was hold onto it. Meantime, the runner slid headfirst into second and lay on the ground between my feet. I knew he hadn't seen what happened, so I told him, "It was a foul ball—go back to first."

He believed me, and started jogging back to first. Our

catcher, who told me afterwards that he couldn't understand why the runner was running the bases in reverse, nevertheless threw the ball to our first baseman, who tagged out the surprised runner. I'll never forget the look on that runner's face as he delivered an icy glare in my direction.

I rationalized and told myself at the time, "The runner was stupid . . . he should have known better than to believe me." I did it in the name of gamesmanship; I thought nothing about sportsmanship. Even my teammates had pounded me on the back and high-fived me for such a heady play. From then on, I looked for the opportunity to trick another sucker so our team could get an easy out. I kept playing, thinking that was just the way baseball was supposed to be played.

It's amazing how one's outlook changes when he becomes a coach.

Was ASU's Travis Buck, who admitted to his teammates that he had trapped the home run ball against the back side of the fence after it rebounded off the trash bin, guiltier than I was years ago?

Coach's brow furrowed as he pondered my question. "Do you think they won with honor?" he asked. "And did their coach know the truth?"

"Their coach was Pat Murphy," I said, "the same coach we had the beanball war with. But John, I don't know if Murphy did or didn't know what had actually happened. Maybe at that moment, he believed that his player had caught the ball. I don't know if his player ever told him the true story."

"Gary, as soon as ASU came off the field after the seventh, my guess is that Coach Murphy asked his fielder if he had caught the ball fairly." Then Coach paused and asked me, "If your player told you he hadn't caught the ball legitimately, what would you have done?"

I hate hypothetical questions—even this one from Coach, and even one I had asked myself many times, and still ask today. But Coach deserved an answer. It seemed that my hesitating answer did not please Coach, since his eyes widened.

Finally, I said, "I would hope that I would have done the honorable thing and told the umpire the truth." Then I mumbled, "But I really don't know for sure."

Raising my head and meeting Coach's eyes, I wondered if I could read his mind. Maybe he was remembering, as I was, what his dad had taught him long ago, the two-sets-of-threes—the set that said, "Never lie, never cheat, never steal." Those lessons were ingrained in John's conscience.

I knew Coach would have done the right thing and confessed to the umpire that his player had not caught the ball properly and that it was a legitimate home run. John would also tell his team to continue giving their best effort to win, but play the game with honor. *That* is what John would have done. I have no doubt. I still have doubts about what I would have done.

I didn't see John for at least a month after our conversation, but I did receive a letter from him in the meantime that had nothing to do with honor. I was glad to hear from him, since I knew I had disappointed him with my mumbling answer to his hypothetical question.

> *Dear Gary—*
>
> *Congratulations on your thirty years at the helm of the UCLA baseball teams and best wishes in all your future endeavors.*
>
> *You outlasted me by three years, but, of course, I was forced to do my teaching indoors with seventeen of my twenty-seven years confined in the poorly ventilated "B.O. Barn." Quite naturally this brought about a premature retirement.*
>
> *May true joy be with you and yours in the coming years.*
>
> *Sincerely,*
> *John Wooden*

TOP OF THE EIGHTH

When I finished coaching at UCLA in 2004, John was still speaking at clinics, businesses, schools, and anywhere else where it was for a good cause, but he had trimmed his schedule significantly for health reasons. Meanwhile, I was getting used to the retired life of mowing the lawn regularly and staying out of the way of my lovely wife, Sandy, who was busy with our horses. In keeping with baseball language, my friendship with Coach Wooden had reached the late innings—I'd say the top of the eighth. It was, for me, a time to reflect.

I asked myself a question that I am sure anyone who followed John's career and mine might ask: "My goodness, Coach Adams, you shared an office and had a close friendship with the greatest coach of the century—why didn't you win more often?"

It is a fair and understandable question, because it is true that Coach taught me many lessons, offered countless wise opinions, and shared his coaching philosophies freely with me. One would think all of that would add up to a phenomenal winning percentage. I guess my best answer is a simple one: "There is only one John Wooden."

He always told me, "A coach has to be himself. Don't try to

be someone else, because that is impossible. If you try to do that, your players will see through it and you will appear artificial to them."

Although I had listened to Coach's every word in our long friendship, I did not try to mimic him. Coaching is not that simple. Decisions have to be made on the spot, and quickly. Certainly, if Coach Wooden had been like an angel, hovering over my shoulder every moment I coached at practices or games, I would have made wiser decisions and won more often. One thing I do know is that if I had never met Coach Wooden, I would have lost more often.

I decided to check on John's won-loss percentage at UCLA. I knew it had to be a good percentage, but when I read that he won 620 games and lost only 147, I was flabbergasted—his winning percentage was .808. I decided to research the winning percentage of his favorite Big League Manager, Joe McCarthy, who the Baseball Writers of America selected as the all-time third best manager in the history of the game. McCarthy won 2,125 games and lost 1,333 for a .615 winning percentage. I checked to see how that stood up with the two managers whom the writers chose as their number one and two picks, John Mc-Graw and Casey Stengel, respectively.

McGraw won 2,763 games and lost 1,948 games, for a .586 win percentage. Stengel won 1,905 and lost 1,842, for a .508 percentage. It was surprising to learn that the three best managers in the history of the game ranged .193 points to .300 points fewer than Coach Wooden's .808 win percentage.

Knowing John was a big fan of the Dodgers, I checked on Walter Alston and Tom Lasorda, both of whom had managed the Dodgers for most of the years John followed them. Including his time with the Brooklyn Dodgers, Alston had a winning percentage of .558 in his twenty-three years at the helm. Lasorda's win percentage was .526 in his twenty-one years in Los Angeles. These comparisons demonstrate just how remarkable Coach Wooden's winning percentage was in

his twenty-seven years at UCLA.

I had never paid much attention to winning percentages up to this time, but I decided to see where I stood compared to John and the rest of those baseball managers. The baseball media guides showed that I had won 984 games and lost 823 in thirty years at UCLA—a .544 win percentage. That was a far cry from Coach Wooden's record, but I felt pretty good about sharing a winning percentage close to the greats, Lasorda and Stengel (except I knew that Stengel's last four years were spent managing the lowly New York Mets, where his win percentage was .302).

All this talk about win percentages, in my opinion, does not tell the entire story when it comes to coaching at the college level. Professional baseball, basketball, and football are different—it is a business—and winning is the primary measure of success.

I always looked at my job as more than winning—winning with honor, which I learned from Coach Wooden, was more important. Although he won more than anyone, his focus was mainly on the student-athletes he coached. He wanted his players to graduate more than he wanted them to win in sports. He wanted them to understand that they were *student*-athletes. He would often remind me that the word "student" came *before* the word "athlete." Both of us believed that a college coach should be measured on his graduation rates more than his winning rates. John's players graduated at a phenomenal rate. With the exception of a couple of players who transferred into UCLA, *all* of John's players graduated.

Despite the fact that baseball players were eligible to sign professional contracts as juniors, our players' graduation rates were good. I asked Mike Sondheimer, the associate athletic director in charge of recruiting for all UCLA Olympic sports, what my graduation rates were, whether it took them four years or nineteen years to get there diploma.

"Close to ninety percent, Gary," he replied. "Not as good as

Coach's, but better than most colleges across the nation."

There was something else I learned after spending those first seven innings with Coach Wooden—a college coach must demonstrate to his players that he cares about them, not just as players, but as human beings. There was never any doubt in my mind that Coach Wooden cared deeply for his players. Coach said, "My players are my children. I am committed to helping them with their problems and their lives."

Having five daughters, I am often asked if I wish I'd had a son.

My answer has always been the same: "No, I never have wished for a son, because I have five daughters who are as beautiful on the inside as they are on the outside, and I dearly love each one. Besides, I have sons—many sons—whom I've had the pleasure of coaching every day."

My "sons" have always made me proud by the way they've conducted themselves on the field. They played hard and, whether they won or lost, always shook hands with their opponents. They played the games without giving the umpires any guff. I only remember two players in all of my forty-one years of coaching who were ever ejected from games. Both times, I felt that the players were justified in their protest . . . but also that the umpires were justified in ejecting them.

John and I both realized that we hadn't gotten where we were without the help of many people, but, mostly, without the help we had from our players. When I was inducted into the UCLA Athletic Hall of Fame, I made sure that I recognized my players in my speech. I said, "I'm like the turtle who suddenly found himself sitting on top of a fence post and said, 'I didn't get here all by myself.'"

Off the field, I never had to worry about opening up the newspaper and reading about so-and-so arrested for this or that. Yes, sometimes they were ornery, but they were good young men, upstanding citizens, and their behavior always made me—and hopefully, all those associated with UCLA—proud.

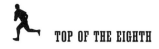

Coach once told me how he felt about his players. "I like them all differently," he said, "but I love them all the same." That's how I feel about my players, too.

FINISHING
THE BILLY KILMER STORY

Before sitting down to dinner with John at the Valley Inn one night, I asked if he remembered me telling him about the line drive I had hit against Billy Kilmer's shin.

He smiled and said, "Of course I do, Gary."

I told him that I had something for him to read. I handed him a newspaper clipping that had appeared in the *Los Angeles Times* on September 10, 2005. Although his hands were shaking a bit as he read, he managed his way through the article.

CAUTION DOESN'T ALWAYS PAY

Former Bruin Billy Kilmer, who went on to star with the Washington Redskins, will be UCLA's honorary captain at tonight's game against Rice. Kilmer, before visiting Bruin practice Friday, recalled the week before the 1959 UCLA-USC game, when he was a junior.

"I was a P.E. major and had a baseball class," Kilmer said. "They were extra cautious about me getting hurt, so I couldn't play baseball. They had me umpire, and I had to stand out on the mound behind the pitcher. So what happened? I took a line drive off my right ankle and suffered a hairline fracture.

To the rescue: Kilmer said he sat out the first half of the game that weekend, but with UCLA trailing, 3–0, at halftime, he asked Coach Barnes to put him in. Kilmer, a single-wing tailback, told Barnes he could at least throw even if he couldn't run. "But I ran for a first down to set up the winning touchdown in a 10–3 victory," Kilmer said.

When John finished reading, a noticeable grin appeared on his face as he said, "Oh, goodness gracious, Gary. Seems like Billy doesn't remember who hit him with that line drive. That's probably a good thing."

THE MOST-ASKED QUESTION

Who is the best player you have ever coached?" John and I agreed that this was the question we were asked most often after our coaching careers had ended—and the most difficult one to answer.

Coach said, "Sometimes people asked the question and, at the same time, also answered it. They would say, 'Who was your best player ever? Bill Walton or Lewis Alcindor?' So I would answer them with a question myself: 'Who do you think would be better at bringing the ball down the court under pressure—Mike Warren, Walton, or Alcindor? I think the two big guys might have some trouble dribbling past the quicker and smaller defensive guards. Don't you?'

"If that didn't satisfy them, I would say, 'Walton and Alcindor usually scored the most points, but they couldn't have scored as often without guards like Mike Warren passing them the ball. Sometimes that satisfied them, sometimes it didn't. On occasion, they would reply, 'So, you think Mike Warren is your best player ever.' I would then tell them, 'Well, I doubt Mike would have rebounded as well as Bill or Lewis.'"

Coach disliked answering that question, and he wanted to know how I handled it.

"I copied you, John. I told them, 'Even Coach Wooden wouldn't answer that question. I can't, either.'"

Coach smiled and said, "You had some pretty good ones, Gary. I'm sure there were players that people believed were your best, like Karros, Glaus, and Utley."

I admitted that those three players were always suggested to me. Like Coach, I enjoyed answering with a question: "Who do *you* think was my best player?"

"They would pick the guys that had made a name for themselves in the big leagues," I said, "like the three guys you mentioned, Coach. But I took pleasure in asking them if they had ever heard of Eric Valent, or Alex Sanchez, or Paul Ellis, or Jim Auten. Most people had never heard of them, so I filled them in. 'Valent is UCLA's all-time home run leader, while Sanchez had the most wins by any pitcher through 2010. They were outstanding players while at UCLA, even though they didn't see much action in the majors.' Then I'd add, 'The other two never made it to the majors, but Jim Auten was an All-American who broke the NCAA home run record in 1979, and Paul Ellis was selected by the Division One college coaches as the Player of the Year in 1990.' Coach, there are a lot more players I could add to those four."

Coach told me at a gathering in 2010 that he believed a better question, and one he didn't mind answering, was, "If you could design the perfect player, what would he be like?"

I noted those qualities as Coach rattled them off:

1. He would know why he was at UCLA—a student-athlete who understood why the word "student" comes before the word "athlete."
2. He would be a good defensive player who stays on-balance. Doesn't leap to block a shot before he is absolutely certain the shot will be taken.
3. He would understand that he is responsible

for guarding his man, but will help his teammates when needed.

4. He would be a good offensive player. Unselfish and doesn't shoot all the time, but when
he does, he makes them.

   a) He looks for the pass first. ("I like the
player who could pass and would pass,"
Coach said. "I've had some that could and
wouldn't, and I've also had some that would
but couldn't.")

   b) He can shoot *accurately* from anywhere on
the court—inside and outside.

5. He would be a good rebounder, and take pride
in the art of rebounding. Assumes every shot
will be missed. Works hard to get into position.

6. He would be gracious and acknowledge his
teammates when they make an assist that
leads to his basket.

When John finished, I was surprised that he had a player in
mind when he described his perfect one.

He said, "Keith Wilkes would fit that list the best."

It was the closest he ever came to answering the question
most often asked . . . without quite answering it.

ATTEND COLLEGE
OR SIGN PRO?

Every June, hundreds of baseball players from high schools, junior colleges, and universities are asked to make tough decisions. They ask themselves and their parents and advisors, "Should I sign a professional baseball contract, or should I go to college?"

The Cincinnati Reds and the Chicago Cubs offered John a pro contract after watching him play summer baseball for his town team in central Indiana, and for his freshman team at Purdue University. Each pro team dangled a respectable amount of money in front of him in an attempt to convince him to give up his college education and basketball at Purdue.

His basketball coach, "Piggy" Lambert, made him look at the big picture. John wanted to be a teacher someday, and Piggy helped him understand that he couldn't do it without a college education.

"Besides," John told me, "I liked the chances of our basketball team winning a national championship. I couldn't have faced my teammates if I had signed."

In my case, when Lou Cohenouer, the Kansas City scout, came to our house to sign me, he probably thought it would be an easy sign—he had signed my twin brother, Gene, the year before, and he had gone on to hit .302 in the California league. Gene's success in his first year of pro baseball made Lou even more anxious to get my name on the dotted line. I told him that Coach Reichle had just offered me a graduate assistant coaching job at UCLA to pursue my master's degree, and I had made a commitment to accept. Lou argued that this would be my last chance to follow my dream to play in the big leagues.

"Lou," I said, "I've looked in the mirror and, at best, I see myself as only a double A player. I'm not a major leaguer."

He must have thought he could change my mind when he argued, "Charlie Finley [the innovative owner of the Kansas City A's] would love to have you twins playing together at shortstop and second base in the big leagues. You would be a big draw for the fans."

That did it for me. I told him, "Lou, I wouldn't want to play in the big leagues if it was because I was a twin, and my brother wouldn't, either. I'm not signing."

He stomped out of the house in a huff. It took some time, but we eventually renewed our friendship.

I recently asked the highly successful head baseball coach at the University of Arizona, Andy Lopez, why he didn't sign pro after being drafted. I was his coach at UCLA when he turned the pros down. His decision at that time surprised me, because he had already completed his college baseball eligibility.

Andy explained that he only needed one more quarter to complete his credits and earn his diploma. "After playing for two years at UCLA, I was drafted by the Detroit Tigers in the ninth round. My father, who was born in Juarez, Mexico, had made it very clear to me that he would support any decision I made, yet he shared his feelings about his desire to see me obtain my degree from UCLA. No one from my mother's or father's families had gone to college, so I would be the first to graduate with a college degree."

Andy added, "My decision to not sign came down to my father's heartfelt desire to see the first in his family graduate, and an honest self-evaluation of just exactly who I was as a potential major leaguer. I will be forever thankful for my father's honesty with me in both categories. Although it hurt in the short-term, I am thankful that he was a loving, honest dad to his youngest child. It pains me that, after thirty-six years of being a head baseball coach, I have seen many families who are not honest or realistic with their sons when it comes to the professional draft. I really don't think I would have been a ten-year big league shortstop. I would not have told you that in 1975. The truth was brought out by my father. I am very thankful for a loving, honest father full of wisdom in his son's life."

There's no doubt that Andy's decision proved to be the right one. He has over a thousand career wins as a college coach, has been selected National Coach of the Year three times, and has won two national championships, his most recent in 2012 with the Arizona Wildcats.

Andy also mentioned the remarkable pension benefits that major league players receive. I checked up on the details of those benefits and discovered that, once a player accrues ten years of major league service, the pension becomes fully vested, yielding a player $185,000 a year, beginning at age sixty-six. There aren't many college graduates that can equal that plan after spending only ten years at their job.

Drafted high school players have a tougher decision to make than those drafted in college. One clear advantage of choosing college is that *you* are in control of getting your degree— you go to class every day, listen closely to your professors, do your homework at night, and persevere for four or five years, and you will be handed a diploma. There are no guarantees in professional baseball. Hard work, high batting averages, and low earned run averages help, but if the top brass believes you aren't good enough, no one is obligated to hand you a major league contract.

Another advantage of choosing college baseball over professional minor league baseball is the mode of travel to road games. At UCLA, we traveled by airplane to eight of our nine league opponents' sites. We only rode the bus about twenty miles to USC, and not much longer when we traveled to the local powerhouse baseball colleges in Southern California. Occasionally, we flew to great scenic spots like Hawaii, Miami, and New Orleans.

There are still minor league teams that make their players ride in old worn-out buses for miles and miles to play in places they'll never want to visit again. One of my best all-around players at UC Irvine, Rocky Craig, told me this story about his minor league days.

"I was trying to get some shut-eye in the overhead luggage rack of the bus on one of our long road trips," he said. "Sitting underneath me, also trying to sleep, was one of my teammates. He muttered to me, 'Rocky, when I make it to the bigs, the first thing I'm going to do is spend my money on a bus just like this one.'

"I couldn't believe my ears. 'You gotta be kidding!' I said to him. 'Why in the heck would you do that?'

"'Because then I'd set it on fire and watch the damn thing burn down,' Rocky said."

There are good objective arguments for going to college immediately after high school. My good friend and sports attorney, Jeff Blank, investigated the major league rosters in 2012, and the results were quite informative. The study revealed that 387 players (51.6 percent) were drafted and signed out of college; 177 (23.6 percent) were drafted out of high school; and 173 (23.1 percent) were international free agent signs.

Many high school graduates are tempted to get started in pro ball as soon as possible, so they can follow their dream to play in the major leagues. Most are not aware of Blank's research, which shows that college players reach the big leagues about one year quicker than players drafted (and signed) out of high school. Still, they hear and read about the rewards of making it to the majors. A minimum salary in 2011 was $480,000;

the average salary in 2010 was $3,014,572, and every player received at least $92 for meals per road day. These are impressive numbers not only for the young player, but also for his parents.

But the long road to the majors is a rough ride. Before those lofty dollar figures can be reached, the rookie minor leaguer has to live on a minor league salary of $1,000 a month for six months. The other six months, he must find a job to pay for rent and food. He tries to eat a wholesome breakfast, lunch, and dinner on road trips, with a total of $20 in meal money—$72 dollars less than major leaguers.

In contrast to the minor leaguers, most Division One college players have a scholarship worth twenty-five to one hundred percent of their basic college expenses. In 2004, when I finished coaching at UCLA, our players received $40 per day for meals—twice as much meal money as the minor league players.

Unless a high school graduate is fortunate enough to get a huge bonus to help him through those minor league days, he has to watch his pennies closely. He also has to maintain a deep, heartfelt passion to play the game, while never losing hope that one day his dream will be realized. Many lose hope and drop out on their own. Others keep grinding their way through single A, double A, and triple A without ever being called up to the majors, and with no job waiting for them when they return home.

It's not easy to stay hopeful. Only five out of a hundred players who sign professional contracts ever get to play a single game in the major leagues. Even the top draft choices aren't guaranteed an automatic spot in the majors. In 2011, the *L.A. Times* reported that, of the fifty players the Angels and Dodgers drafted in the first five rounds since 2007, just one is in the major leagues today.

Coach Wooden and I were on the same page. Coach told recruits more than once, "Education is going to be with you for the rest of your life. The average life in the NBA is less than four years."

Major League Baseball was smart when they created the College Scholarship Program (CSP). It is one of the best arguments the pros have to convince a player to sign. The team that provides the CSP to the player is responsible for the payment, as long as the player begins college within ten years after signing his contract.

There are special cases when the best decision is to sign professionally. It is a no-brainer to sign pro when a player from a poor family has not been offered a substantial college scholarship, or when his high school grades don't qualify him for a four-year college. The junior colleges come into play when grades are lacking, and when the pro offer is not enough. But many baseball players will forego college and sign pro for a small sum because they want to follow their dream. The $480,000 minimum big league salary that the pro scouts dangle like a carrot in front of a young man's eyes is inviting—not many college graduates ever make that in one year.

I once saw a cartoon called *In the Bleachers*, written and drawn by Steve Moore, that made me laugh. A giant-sized youngster in basketball shorts, towering over his fellow smaller teammates, said, "I want to turn pro right away, but my stupid dad says I need to finish fifth grade first so that I have something to fall back on." The way things are now in college basketball, Moore's cartoon is not too absurd.

Coach Wooden didn't like the current NCAA rule, implemented in 2006, which prevented a high school basketball player from signing pro until he was nineteen years old or had attended college for at least one year. John preferred the old rule of not allowing a high school graduate to sign pro. It also required a player to play four years of college basketball.

"Gary, how many players do you think will return to college and get their degree once they sign pro after one year of college?"

He never expected an answer, as he answered it himself. "Close to zero," he said firmly. "They will not have the incentive to go to class like they would have if it meant staying eligible to play for their college basketball team. Half of them will probably be married—some with children—by the time they finish pro. I don't think their wives will want their husbands to go to school while they work to pay for their education. It is a bad rule, Gary. The 'one-year-and-done' rule should be abolished. The chancellors and presidents of the universities are kidding themselves if they believe it will increase graduation rates. It is only going to lower them."

I told John that recruiting in college baseball is a risky proposition every year. It can turn out to be disastrous at times. A coach might believe he has recruited the best class in the nation . . . until the pro draft is held in the first week of June. By summer's end, he might have one of the *worst* recruiting classes. In 2007, all seventeen high school players drafted in baseball's first round ended up signing pro. Most of them had signed letters of intent to attend college. If a coach had two or three scholarships from that group committed to his school, he's not able to replace them with players even close to their caliber. Most good players have committed to other schools. The cupboard is bare.

In 2012, college baseball coaches received a big gift from professional baseball when they revised the deadline date for amateur players to sign. The new deadline date is in the second week of July—a big change from the old rule when I coached, when players could wait all the way up to the first day of school. Before this new deadline, Major League Baseball had adjusted its deadline to August 15—an improvement on the old rule, but still too late for coaches to recruit top players.

When Troy Glaus, our top high school recruit, was drafted in the second round of the 1994 draft, I was so paranoid about Troy signing pro that on the first day of school, I made a trip to his first class and sneaked a peek inside to make sure he was there. I didn't let him see me, but when I saw him, it was the first sigh of relief I gave since the day he committed to us.

One of my former players, Lindsay Meggs, is the head baseball coach at the University of Washington. He told me how he lost his top recruit in 2011. He signed a potential ace pitcher to a full scholarship, and the pros drafted him in the first round. On the final signing date of August 15, his recruit called Lindsay on the phone at ten minutes until 9:00 PM Pacific Standard Time—just before the signing deadline. He told him, "Coach, I'm not going to sign. They are very far apart from what I'm asking."

Lindsay felt great. He had landed a blue-chip pitcher who could step on top of the mound and win for him right away. It was a glorious and joyful time for Lindsay and his family. At five minutes after nine, Lindsay got another call from his pitcher. This time he said, "I signed." When Lindsay finished telling me his story, he said, "I know it's happened to you more than once."

"Yeah, Lindsay, it has," I said. "I'll never forget a call I got from a high school player whom I believed would become an outstanding college shortstop—All-American potential. He called me the day before school started and said he had signed with the Angels two days earlier. I'll never forget the date of that call—September 4, my birthday. Not one of my favorites."

I never told Lindsay the rest of the story. My lost player made it to the majors quickly, only two years from the time he signed. He had been traded to the White Sox in that short time and played in five or six games that year with only three at bats. That was the end of his big league career. I always wondered what he would have done if he had come to UCLA and played baseball.

The best strategy is for college coaches to recruit good players, but not so good that they will be drafted in the first round. Even those drafted in the second round are risky recruits. But how does a coach know what round his recruit will be drafted?

Coach Wooden asked me this question one Sunday afternoon in 2010.

I told him, "We aren't savvy enough to predict the draft. I've signed players to letters of intent that I thought would be drafted in the fifth or sixth rounds, and they ended up in the first two rounds. I've also signed players whom I thought would be in the fifth or sixth, and they ended up past the twentieth round." I teased, "We aren't all wizards like you, John." He smiled and made a fist in front of my face.

How does a coach look a player in the eye and sell him on going to college, when that player is being offered millions of dollars to play a game he loves? It's not easy, but coaches who believe strongly in the value of a college degree still try their best to convince their recruits. I was one of those coaches, and so was John.

Coach Wooden made a good point: "I don't care if it's baseball or basketball, if you are a good player out of high school, most likely you will be better after three or four years of playing college ball. If you are not any better out of college, it probably means you would not have been any better in three years after pro ball, either. In that case, you will be released by the pros— and absent a college degree. *With* college, even if you don't get better at your sport, at least you have your degree."

Every statistic I have seen regarding a comparison of salaries of college graduates compared to high school graduates shows a sizeable greater salary for the college grad.

At UCLA, I have had 163 players sign pro baseball contracts. Most of those signed professionally after their third year of college. A few have not yet returned to finish, but the vast majority have returned for their final year of education and earned their degree. When a college player signs pro after three years of his education, he can see the light at the end of the tunnel. Finishing up his one last year is an easier task to confront than that of the high school player, who signs and has a four-year trek to a college degree.

UCLA players who signed after their third year but did not return to school were usually the ones who signed for big bonuses and spent substantial time in the major and minor leagues. Troy Glaus was one of those. Even so, I tried to encourage him to get his degree almost every time I saw him.

I told Coach about the time I saw Troy at one of our alumni baseball games. "Troy saw me walking toward him, and from past experience, he knew what was next," I said. "'No, Skip, don't even ask,' he declared. 'I haven't gone back to finish school, and I'm not planning to.' He said it with a smile, just having fun with me, but I also knew he meant what he said. Nevertheless, the next time I saw him, I pestered him again, even though he had been a first round draft choice who signed for a huge bonus and made millions playing in the big leagues. He probably will never finish his last year of school."

John shook his head. He didn't care about the millions of dollars. "An education stays with you forever," he muttered. "Money has a way of disappearing."

In defense of Troy, I said, "Troy is an exception, Coach. He won't let his money disappear, because he is a man who will take good care of his family."

Coach smiled. "Glad to hear that."

Most of my players have finished school, and not just because of my prodding. UCLA has a great, unique program called Final Score that enhances their will to return to class. This program not only speeds up the admission process, but also provides counseling and tutoring services for returnees—just as if they were still student-athletes participating in their sport. Many colleges have similar programs now—even USC.

In college baseball, where the NCAA only permits 11.7 scholarships on a typical roster of thirty-six players, it is rare for a student-athlete to be awarded a full ride. Many college baseball players are on partial scholarships that only pay twenty-five percent of their educational costs. College and university presidents would do themselves a favor if they increased the number of full scholarships in baseball. More players would attend college. Baseball is becoming a big income producer for

the athletic programs, so it would be worth it to them to raise the limit, at least to the same level that women's softball enjoys (thirteen full scholarships).

The last time Coach and I discussed the choice between attending college versus going pro, he said, "There is no guarantee, even with a college degree, that you will be successful, but it does increase your odds. Why not choose the best of two worlds and do both—go to college first and sign pro afterwards?"

BUILDING A CAR AND A TEAM

Of all the books written by or about Coach, my personal favorite is *Wooden: A Lifetime of Observations and Reflections On and Off the Court*, by Steve Jamison and John. This book contains lots of Coach's pearls of wisdom, and one analogy he delivered that landed so deep in my glove, I could never throw it out. I kept that analogy stored away until 2008, four years after I finished coaching baseball at UCLA.

The first team to hear me tell Coach Wooden's story of how a team is built much like one would build a car was our UCLA alumni team, ages 35 to 69.

The team had only practiced together one time before departing for Australia to compete in the Pan-Pacific Senior World Games—where ten thousand male and female athletes from over thirty-seven different nations competed in a variety of sports for gold, silver, and bronze medals. We were the only representatives from the USA.

I believed our Bruins, with such wide-ranging age differences and from different eras of UCLA baseball, needed to know their roles and what kind of a team we needed to build in order to compete with teams that had played together for a long time.

I thought Coach Wooden's analogy would fit perfectly for

this group, so I told John's story while on the field just prior to our first game. Using almost his exact words, I told the team, "We as a team are like a powerful car. Maybe a Chase Utley, Eric Karros, or Jackie Robinson [John used UCLA basketball names Bill Walton and Kareem Abdul-Jabbar] is the big engine, but if one wheel is flat, we're going no place. If we put brand-new tires on that car, but the lug nuts are missing, the wheels come off. What good is the powerful engine without the lug nuts? It's no good at all.

"A lug nut may seem like a small thing, but it is not. We must make sure that when we put the lug nuts on, we tighten them properly. Each and every one of us must play a role. We may aspire to what we consider to be a larger role, or what we *think* is a more important role, but we cannot achieve that until we show that we are able to fulfill the role we are assigned. It's the little things that make the big things happen. The big engine is not going to work unless the little things are being done properly."

Before I finished, I told them exactly what Coach Wooden had reminded his players. "The car also needs a driver behind the wheel, or it will just go around in circles or smash into a tree. The driver is me."

Coach Wooden's analogy had a great impact on the players, and they remembered its message throughout the seven-day tournament. We had a couple of big engines in former eight-year major leaguer Mike Fyhrie and iron man pitcher Tim O'Neill. The rest of the team consisted of fully inflated wheels and firmly tightened lug nuts.

From the first day of the tournament to the last, the Bruins alumni team played like a well-tuned, powerful car, winning the gold medal. It was the second gold medal our team had won in four years—our first being in the Paris International Tournament.

After the Australia tournament, I heard our players talking about getting T-shirts with a big lug nut insignia on the chest that read, "I'm a Lug Nut—Proud of It!"

I told the team that I had hoped at the beginning of the tournament that we could build a simple but powerful Ford. I didn't realize that what we built was even more than a Mercedes—we built a gosh-darn made-in-America *tank*!

I am grateful to Coach Wooden for his leading role in helping us build that tank.

THE PYRAMID OF SUCCESS

During the summer of 2008, I had breakfast with John and a few other friends, including his son, Jim, at his favorite breakfast place, VIP's, in Tarzana, California. Jeff Moorad, a UCLA alum and, at the time, a partial owner of the Arizona Diamondbacks, asked John a good question that morning. "Coach, is there anything you would change in your Pyramid of Success?" he asked.

John looked up from his usual plate of two eggs over easy, crispy bacon, and an English muffin, and answered, "No, not really. Maybe I'd put some of the blocks in different places, but I wouldn't change the titles of those blocks." He added emphatically, "I would *never* change the two cornerstones, industriousness and enthusiasm. You need those two because, without being enthused with what you are doing you certainly won't work hard at it. And you definitely need to work hard if you want to get better."

Little did John or any of us know that, within a year, there would be a significant change in his Pyramid of Success. That's a story for the bottom of the ninth.

Once John had told me, "Take either of those out, industriousness or enthusiasm, and the pyramid would crumble."

John's words never left me, and they triggered thoughts to all the players I had coached who embodied these two characteristics. In over forty years of coaching college baseball, I have had many players who were industrious and many who were enthusiastic. Some played for me at the University of California, Irvine in the early seventies. Most of those Irvine players were not on athletic scholarships; they simply played for the love of the game. But they played just as hard and as enthusiastically as any of their opponents who had scholarships, and any of my UCLA players. They used to joke that, with a nickname like "the Anteaters," they had to play harder than other teams. I could write another entire book about those Anteaters and the glorious years they gave me.

Ninety-nine percent of my players were good examples of John's two cornerstones. In fact, their tremendous effort inspired and motivated me.

I find it peculiar that so many of my coaching peers who quit coaching would often ask me, "Gary, how can you keep coaching today's players? They're so selfish and lazy now." Some of the coaches were more harsh, claiming that they got out of coaching "because kids don't care about anybody except themselves and don't know what it's like to play hard—the way we used to play in the old days." I never truly believed this line of thinking, because I found that the players I coached from 1963 through 2004 were as hard-working, dedicated, and enthusiastic as the players when I played college ball at UCLA in the "old days."

After that breakfast with John in 2008, I gave a lot of thought to who I would select as the best representatives of John's cornerstones, industriousness and enthusiasm. I decided to choose players only from UCLA, because John would have a better recollection of them than he would of my UC Irvine players. I considered my candidates for almost a year, always with the thought of who John would choose if he were in my shoes.

When I visited John at his home in 2010, I told him that, ever since he had told me his favorite sport was baseball, I had started taking notes of what he said. Some I wrote down, and some I kept in my head. Most had something to do with baseball.

"I hope you won't mind if I put those notes and memories together and write a book about your love for the game of baseball," I said.

I didn't have to wait long for his answer.

"Gary, I do not mind at all," he replied. "You will be writing about my favorite sport. No one has ever written a book about me and *baseball* before. Tell me more about it."

My heart was pounding. I was happy to oblige. "Well, John, for one thing, I was thinking of using some of our UCLA baseball players as positive examples of your Pyramid of Success— in particular, the cornerstones of your pyramid, industriousness and enthusiasm."

"Do you have some players in mind?" he asked.

"Lots of players, John. But I've given much thought to those who stood out, and I've come up with three players for each of your cornerstones. If you approve of my choices, I'll include them in my book."

INDUSTRIOUSNESS

RICH AMARAL

The first player I discussed with John was Rich Amaral, a second baseman who played for UCLA in 1982 and 1983.

"John, you would have loved to watch him play. Rich hustled on every play, whether it was on defense—diving for ground balls—or on offense—bursting hard out of the batter's box after hitting a pop-up. Rich didn't just jog like most ball players do after popping up, he ran as if every pop-up he hit was a potential double. John, I'm not exaggerating, Rich looked like his life depended upon making it to second base."

"I like him already," Coach said.

I had just begun. "When Rich raced around first base on a sure pop-up *out,* his teammates would say things like, 'There he goes again, bustin' his butt on a sure out.' It wasn't that they were against *hustle,* exactly. They just thought that Rich was hustling unnecessarily. Finally, when I heard one of our players mutter something about Rich's 'unnecessary hustle,' I told the whole bench, 'You wait and see, one of these days Rich is going to be standing on second base with a double because of that unnecessary hustle—and it just might help us win a ball game!'

"Sure enough, in 1982 we were playing at the University of Nevada Las Vegas, and Rich hit a high pop-up where the second baseman was camped under it for what looked like a routine out—to everyone except Rich. As usual, Rich tore out of the batter's box and roared around first base, headed for second at full throttle. But, as the ball was coming down, the Las Vegas desert wind caused it to drift just beyond the second baseman's reach. By the time the second sacker picked up the ball, which was very near the second base bag, Rich was standing there with a double. It was a big play that led to a three-run inning in a game that we won, 13–11."

I didn't tell John that Rich had four hits in six trips to the plate that day, because I didn't remember that part of his performance until I checked an old box score. To me and, I believed, to John, the best part of Rich's performance that day was the pop-up-hustle play.

After hearing about Rich's hustling ways, Coach said, "The way Amaral hustled on everything he hit . . . that is *true* hustle, not *false* hustle. I don't like false hustle."

I stopped Coach right there. "What do you mean by false hustle?" I asked.

"Well, Gary, some players are all talk. They chatter a lot— even yell at their teammates to hustle—but they don't do it themselves. Now, there is nothing wrong with a player who chatters and, at the same time, plays hard and always hustles. He is backing up his words. Take Bill Walton, for example. Bill talked a lot on the court—to me, to his assistants, and to his teammates—a regular chatterbox. But he backed up his chatter by the way he played, and he did it every day. In practice, he put forth as much effort as he did in a game. Guys who do not practice hard and claim that they are 'gamers'—meaning they will turn it up in games—are also false hustlers."

I thought of how similar Rich Amaral was to Bill Walton, and yet so different from him. They were both the same when it came to industriousness, but different in their manner. Coach said that Bill was a chatterbox. Rich, on the other hand, was quiet and led his team mainly by his example of hard work.

Shortly after I had talked with John, I discussed the pop-up-hustle play with Rich when we attended a funeral for his UCLA keystone partner, Vince Lopez, in 1983. I asked Rich if he felt he played with that same kind of hustle in pro ball. He replied, "I took it with me, Coach."

He then went on to tell me what he and his teammate, Alex Rodriguez, did when the two of them had played with the Seattle Mariners. "Alex and I used to have contests with each other to see who could get the closest to second base before the pop-up reached the fielder's glove."

When he told me this, I was sure of one thing—Rich would win this contest, hands down. I said, "Well, you won every time, right?"

"No, I didn't, Coach. He won most of the time. You see, Alex was so strong that his pop-ups were twice as high as mine, and he always got closer to second base before the ball came down to anyone's glove." I wish I could have related Rich's story to Coach. He would have had a good chuckle over it.

When I first recruited Rich from Orange Coast Junior College, I knew he was a hard worker, because his coach, Mike Mayne, had told me so. I trusted Mike's opinion because I knew him quite well. He had been our third baseman when I was the assistant coach at UC Riverside. Mike knew what he was talking about because he was a hard worker himself. He deserves much of the credit for molding Rich into the player he became. (Mike Mayne was the pitching coach for Fresno State when they won the College World Series in 2008.)

Rich's industriousness earned him the respect of his teammates, and they elected him co-captain in 1983. I told Coach that if he could have seen Rich play as many games as I did, he would have witnessed the effort Rich delivered and had given him a grade of "A" in *all* of his games. I was confident in telling him that, because Coach often said, "At the end of the game,

the score that should matter most is the one that measures your effort."

Rich's effort and competitiveness were never more evident than in that 1982 game I talked about earlier against the University of Nevada, Las Vegas Rebels. I didn't tell Coach Wooden about the donnybrook that broke out in that game, in which Rich played a leading role. In the later innings of a game that seesawed back and forth, the Rebels had a runner on first base and no outs. A ground ball was hit to our third baseman, Lindsay Meggs. Lindsay made a perfect throw to Rich to start the double play. The UNLV runner, however, came sliding hard into second base with his spikes flying high. Rich got off the throw but took exception to the runner's aggressiveness. He landed on top of the runner, and got in a few uncomplimentary words.

I was standing in our dugout, pleased with the double play Rich had just turned, but there was no time to gloat—the scene at second base turned ugly. Rich and the UNLV runner were wrestling in the dust. Rich told me afterward, "I popped up on my feet, and so did the Rebel player, with the intention of maybe duking it out. That's when Brian Graham came flying in from right field and tackled him."

I was in the middle of my sprint to stop the fight when I saw Brian's body flying parallel to the ground, hat twirling in the wind and arms outstretched, before making contact with an unknowing human being. When this human missile met the standing legs of the Rebel, it looked like a football lineman sacking a surprised quarterback. (Actually, Brian had experienced this plenty of times while playing football in high school and coming to UCLA on a football scholarship.) Brian's tackle resulted in both benches emptying and pouring onto the field. In a flash, the two-man tussle became a full-fledged brawl. Players were piled on top of each other as both coaching staffs tried to peel them off. Then, solitary duels broke out in other spots on the infield, and even on the pitcher's mound. Those duels quickly became other piles of wrestlers in the dust.

I don't know how the umpires and coaches stopped the brawl, but it did end with no serious injuries and, amazingly, no one was ejected. When Rich and I, along with a few other team-mates, reminisced about the Las Vegas brawl at a get-together at a Dodgers game in 2010, we all remembered it the same way—but Rich did add this bit of news to the story: "When the runner and I stopped wrestling on the ground and both of us popped up on our feet to duke it out, I had not noticed how *huge* he was, standing up." Then, with a big smile, Rich added, "I was glad Brian tackled him." That story went untold the day I was with Coach, but I did tell him more about Rich's industriousness.

As our second baseman, Rich liked polishing up his foot-work on the double play, and he practiced it almost every day. One time I wrapped a blindfold around his eyes and handed him the ball as he stood on second base. I said, "Now, throw it accurately to your first baseman." I watched as he threw the ball too wide, too high, too short, and mostly out of reach of our first baseman with his first dozen throws. But, eventually, he got the feel of where the ball should go, and his throws became more accurate.

No doubt, Rich thought that this drill was a bit over the top, but he plodded through it industriously, without complaining. I told him, "If you can make the throw blindfolded, you can make it easily with your eyes open." I don't ever remember Rich making a bad throw after that.

I told John that Rich was not drafted by the pros after high school, but after being drafted from UCLA, he ended up playing ten years in the major leagues (1991–2000), eight years with the Mariners and two with the Orioles. His lifetime batting av-erage in the majors was .276, quite respectable for a good base runner and dependable defensive player. But it didn't come easily or quickly, as he spent eight long years in the minors, working hard at polishing his skills. A lot of minor leaguers would have quit by then, but not Rich. He learned how to play every position on the field except pitcher and catcher. With all

his hard work, he became one of the best utility players in the major leagues.

Rich demonstrated his industriousness every day and every year that he played ball. He managed to tough it out, and persevered through all the hard times. I remember reading a quote by a man named William Feathers, who said, "Success seems to be largely a matter of hanging on after others have let go." Rich never let go, but even he will admit that he had help in hanging on from his partner and wife, Michelle. She stuck by him and encouraged him through all those years that Rich labored to achieve his dream. She helped him hang in there because she, too, respected his industriousness.

Although I only told Coach Wooden pieces of Amaral's story, he agreed that Rich displayed all the qualities of industriousness. I wish I had thought to tell Coach about Michelle. Coach would no doubt have been reminded of the way his beloved Nell stood by him throughout his high school and college years, the navy, and his long coaching career.

ERIC KARROS

Coach Wooden once said, "Character is doing the right thing when nobody is looking." Eric Karros was a great example of this. He worked hard, no matter what the score was, no matter what the situation was, and no matter who was looking. Whether working on his academics or on the ball field, Eric Karros's industriousness was limitless. He went about his business seriously and with purpose.

When I told Coach that Eric Karros would be one of my choices for the Most Industrious list, John acknowledged that he had followed Eric's career very closely. He said, "Having seen Eric play at UCLA, I was happy my Dodgers drafted him so I could see him play again. Eric reminded me of the late Gil Hodges—both of them were big, strong, and consistent performers who went about their business without saying much."

I agreed with Coach wholeheartedly, and began telling him how I witnessed first-hand Eric's commitment to hard work. When I told Coach that Eric was a walk-on recruit (no scholarship), he gave me a you-can't-be-serious look. I explained how I came to recruit Eric.

His dad, George, called me on the phone asking me if he could bring his son to a weekend game at UCLA. He wanted to know if I would have time to talk to them before or after the ball game. Eric was a senior in high school, and a player I had never heard of until his dad called. George didn't brag about his son, but he did say that Eric's grade point average was 3.7. That got my attention. I told him I'd find time to talk to them.

As soon as I hung up, I called Eric's baseball coach at Patrick Henry High in San Diego. Immediately after that, I called a friend in San Diego who followed the high school baseball circuit quite closely and knew about most of the top prospects. Neither one gave me glowing reports on Eric's skills, but they did praise Eric's work ethic and character.

On the day Eric and George visited, I talked with them through the chain-link fence on our field before the game. Eric said he'd like to attend UCLA because of its excellent academics and its sports programs. He asked me what his chances would be to make the team next year.

I wasn't too optimistic, but I did give him one small guarantee. "Eric, I promise that you will have all fall to show us what you can do," I said. "I usually cut walk-ons after the first two weeks, but I promise that I won't cut you from the team—if I do cut you—until the end of our fall tryouts."

"You said *that* to Eric Karros, Gary?"

I smiled. "Yes, John, but I didn't know he'd become a star. I didn't want to make any promises I couldn't keep—this promise, I knew I could keep."

John shook his head. "And he came anyway," he said.

Still smiling, I said, "Despite my lousy recruiting, Eric showed up for fall tryouts. We had close to seventy players trying out,

counting our recruits and returning players from last season—
only thirty-five could be on the team. Most of the walk-ons were
nameless to me, including Eric, although I knew he was the
young man from San Diego to whom I had made a promise.

"The second day, I hit ground balls to the infield candidates.
Eric stood with a half-dozen other second base candidates in
the back of the line. His six-foot-four frame towered over his
much smaller competitors. He was not the typical mold of a second baseman. After two or three ground balls to Eric, I yelled to
him, 'Hey, big guy! Move over to third base!' He seemed happy
to do so, as he jogged to the other side of the infield.

"No one worked harder than Eric through the fall training
camp. Early in the fall, our coaching staff discussed the possi-
bility of red-shirting Eric for a year, but the more we saw what
he could do with the bat, the more that idea vanished.

"At the end of fall tryouts, it was time to let Eric know
whether or not he had made the team. When I told him he
made it, he didn't jump up or down or show any sign of excitement. In fact, he acted like he expected it. I think he knew we
wouldn't cut one of our leading hitters in the fall."

I told John that the only thing Eric lacked was foot speed.
I've heard scouts say, when they put their stopwatches on runners, "Hey, he's faster than he looks when he runs." I believe
most pro scouts who watched Eric run looked at their watches
and said, "Hey, he's *slower* than he looks when he runs."

Like Rich Amaral, Eric was not drafted out of high school.
Besides being a slow runner, his feet weren't exactly agile. Some
scouts put it another way: "He's clumsy." But I had seen clum-
siness in young players I had coached before—like Pat Dodson,
Tim Leary, and Don Slaught—and when their feet caught up
with their bodies, they ended up playing in the big leagues. I
was positive that Eric, with his tremendous work ethic, would
become a solid all-around player before he left UCLA. I told my
friends and coaches at the time, "Eric is a colt who's going to be
a stallion someday."

"Did you think Eric would turn out to be the kind of hitter he became?" John asked.

"Yes. Despite his lack of foot speed and coordination when he was younger, his hands were amazingly quick and strong. Put those two things together, and you have what pro scouts look for in all hitters—good bat speed. Eric had awesome bat speed, which translates into being able to hit with power and catch up to the fastest pitches."

John said, "If I were a scout, I think I would pay attention to a hitter's hand-eye coordination, too. I've seen hitters with good swings before, but too often they'll miss the ball."

"You bet, John. Eric's hand-eye coordination was superb. His swing may not have been the prettiest swing I'd ever seen, but, by golly, Eric always had a knack for hitting the center of the baseball with the sweet spot of his bat."

Coach and I talked some more about Eric's baseball career, but John also wanted to know more about Eric's character. I told him that Eric was mature beyond his years. He had a realistic view of his priorities. He ranked academics as high as he ranked baseball. He was a B+ student, majoring in economics. His biggest reason for choosing UCLA was because of its academic reputation. He wasn't offered a scholarship to play ball, and he never asked me for one, but I gave him a scholarship after his first year because he earned it.

"John, even though Eric signed a pro contract after his junior year, I never had any doubts that he would return to his classes and get his degree. He proved me right when he earned his degree within one and a half seasons of pro baseball. It takes hard work and determination to accomplish that at the same time one is playing professional baseball. I had a player who became my assistant coach for fifteen years, and it took him *seventeen* years to get his degree—Vince Beringhele."

John nodded and said, "I admire Vince's perseverance. That's a heck of a lot better than not trying at all."

I was anxious to tell Coach more about Eric's character. One

of the best examples was how Eric had dealt with an infamous topic in the 1990s and early 2000s—anabolic steroids.

"Coach, I used to read the articles written by the sports writers, and they never seemed to be satisfied with the number of home runs Eric hit," I said. "They complained that Karros only had warning track power. They were correct that he did hit an abundant number of fly balls to the warning track—about ten feet shy of going over the fence—and I witnessed many of those long outs. I remember talking to Eric about it one day, and he said that he wished he was just a bit stronger so more of his long-ball outs would leave the yard. This was during a time when many players were using steroids to get that extra boost of strength to hit the ball farther. I admired Eric for not giving in to the temptation to use steroids, despite the criticism he received in the newspapers and despite the fact that other players around him were using them. He just believed that his hard work would keep paying off. As you know, it did. Eric became the all-time home run leader in Los Angeles Dodgers history, and he did it without cheating."

John made no secret of his feelings about athletes using steroids. "Gary," he said, "do you remember what I wrote underneath the word 'industriousness' in my pyramid?"

"Something like, 'Nothing comes easy—work hard,'" I said.

"Close, but not exactly. It says, 'There is no substitute for work. Worthwhile things come from hard work.'" John spoke firmly as he added, "Steroids are a shortcut."

John was right. Eric never took shortcuts. That is why, to this day, Eric Karros is one of the most respected names in the long history of Dodgers baseball. Los Angeles baseball fans respected the fact that Eric played the game honestly and gave his best effort every time he took the field. Most of them understood that it was Eric's determination and drive that took him places no tape-measure home run ever could. His name is also one of the most respected in UCLA athletic annals. He was named a member of the school's prestigious UCLA Athletic

Hall of Fame after becoming one of UCLA's all-time great hitters and an All-American in 1988.

The value of a ball player cannot just be measured by his statistics. Yes, Eric's stats were outstanding at UCLA, but his intangibles were just as remarkable. "I can still picture him on the field as a calming influence for the rest of the players," I told John. "As our quiet captain, he was the first to go to the mound to give words of encouragement to his pitchers."

With a wrinkled grin, John said, "That reminds me of what happened to Sandy Koufax when Gil Hodges made a visit to the mound during Sandy's first year with the Dodgers. Sandy had walked about seven or eight batters, but the Dodgers were still leading in a high-scoring game when the big first baseman strolled to the top of the mound and stared Sandy in the eyes. Normally, Hodges didn't say much, but he did this day. He told Sandy, 'The rest of us out here all like to win, son, and we need to feed our families. Throw strikes!'"

Eric's quiet and methodical way of going about his business every day was inspirational. He brought a quality to our team with his intense industriousness. His teammates knew that, because of his hard work, Eric was a self-made ball player—not a God-gifted one.

I was a bit hesitant to tell Coach Wooden my next story about Eric which, at the time, demonstrated quite the opposite of industriousness.

"John, I hope this next story doesn't exclude Eric from your list of Most Industrious Players," I said.

Coach waved his hand at me, as if to say, "Go right ahead."

"Well," I continued, "there was an instance in one game out of all the 136 games that Eric played at UCLA when I believed he had a lapse of effort on the field."

I explained to John that we had already cinched an NCAA Playoff birth, so this particular game may have seemed meaningless to the casual fan. John, of course, understood that this was USC we were playing. No game against our crosstown rival

is ever meaningless!

It was 1987, Eric's sophomore year, and it was our last league game that we were playing at USC. I was coaching third base when Eric came to the plate with no outs and no one on base. He hit a long fly over the center fielder's head, and the ball rolled to the deepest part of the outfield. I thought his hit had the potential for a triple. Eric, I quickly learned, had other ideas. He ran as hard as usual out of the batter's box and continued running hard until he approached second base. I was yelling and waving my arms for him to come to third, but he was paying me no attention. He coasted into second base and contentedly stood on the bag.

I was shocked. This was not the Eric Karros I knew. It didn't take long for my shock to turn to anger toward the satisfied young man standing at second. I tried to justify his actions, knowing that there was a traditional unwritten rule in baseball that says you never make the first out of an inning at third base. But, as hard as I tried, I could not excuse Eric. I was absolutely sure he would have easily made it to third base, had he only tried.

As I stood fuming in the third base coach's box, I hoped that our next hitter would execute properly and hit the ball to the right side of the field so Eric could advance to third—where I could give him an earful. Our hitter executed the play perfectly, grounding out to the second baseman. Eric now stood on third base. It didn't take me long to come over and stand alongside this player, who once claimed that Pete Rose ("Mr. Charlie *Hustle*") was his favorite player.

Now, I'm not the type of coach that normally gets in the face of his players during a game, particularly not in full view of everyone in the stadium. But this was an exception, and I said quite a few things during Eric's stay at third that left little doubt I was not pleased with his effort. Eric didn't say a word. He just stared and listened.

Eric and I have talked about this incident in the years that followed. He told me that, even in the locker room after that game, I had reminded him of his lack of hustle. He said, "My dad was waiting for me after the game, and asked me what took me so long. I just told him, 'Coach chewed me out some more.'"

A few days later, I found out that the double Eric hit that day at USC was his twenty-first of the season, which broke the UCLA all-time season record for doubles. He hit two more doubles in the NCAA Playoffs, and that record stood until Eric Byrnes broke it ten years later with twenty-four.

When I finished my story, John asked, "Did he know that double would break the record?"

"I'm not sure . . . but probably," I said.

John cracked a slight grin. "You know, Gary, there are players who have great speed and are capable of stretching doubles into triples," he said. "Maybe Eric's one of those guys whose lack of speed only makes him capable of shrinking triples into doubles. Did you ever think that, being as slow as he was, maybe he just assumed it was another double?"

I had to chuckle at Coach's use of the word "shrinking." It's common parlance in baseball to describe a speedy player stretching a single into a double or stretching a double into a triple. But, before Coach had used the word, I had never heard of a slow runner shrinking a triple into a double.

I later investigated Eric's UCLA batting records and discovered that he had never hit a triple up to that time, and had only hit one triple in his entire career at UCLA. Coach Wooden was probably correct—Eric stopped at second base simply because he didn't believe his foot speed would ever get him safely to third, since he had never made it that far in the past. Also, not having confidence in his speed, he wanted to make certain that he didn't make the first out of the inning at third base. Thanks to Coach Wooden, now I regret being harsh with Eric.

Eric played in the major leagues for fourteen seasons, mostly with the Dodgers. Just like Rich Amaral, Eric took his industriousness from UCLA to professional baseball. Dodgers manager

Tommy Lasorda praised the way Eric worked to improve his defensive play at first base. He was amazed at Eric's eagerness to work, and to learn how to hit the ball to all fields—and how to hit curveballs.

Tommy once said, "I must have thrown him a million curveballs. He'd stand out there till his hands would bleed. Look what he went through to get to the big leagues! He didn't even get a scholarship at UCLA."

Because of his industriousness, Eric became a proficient first baseman and a consistent doubles and home run hitter. I think it was remarkable that Eric hit more than twenty doubles in each of his eleven full seasons with the Dodgers, and collected double-digit home runs in every full season that he played in the majors.

As I mentioned earlier in the book, at the top of Coach Wooden's Pyramid of Success is the block marked "competitive greatness." Like Torey Lovullo, Eric Karros is a prime example of what John meant by that block. One particular event in the summer of 1999 illustrates perfectly the type of character Eric possesses. I did not tell John this story because Eric had told me about it in confidence. Eric later gave me permission to write about it.

That summer, I opened the sports page of the *Los Angeles Times* and read that Eric was going to take a leave of absence from the team for a couple days. This was in the middle of the season. I couldn't understand why Eric was taking this time-out. Nothing more was said in the papers, and no reason was given for Eric's absence. After missing only one day, Eric quietly returned to action and played in the remaining games.

I was certainly curious about Eric's absence. Not too long afterward, I had a chance to ask him why he missed that day of playing. Though I noticed some hesitation in his answer, he explained briefly, "Trish [Eric's wife] was in the UCLA hospital, giving birth to our first son . . . and he died." I felt horrible for him, and this information left me momentarily speechless. He told me that it had been much more important to be with Trish at that time than to be with his team. Eventually, I asked him why he never made mention of it to the sports writers and the public. "I wanted Trish to have her privacy. It was such a hard time for her." He also admitted that he didn't want the sports writers to make a big deal about it. "I didn't want to make any excuses if I didn't do well the rest of the season," he added.

Well, here's what Eric did in that 1999 season: he hit .304 with 176 hits, forty doubles, thirty-four home runs, and 112 RBI. All these numbers were the highest in his fourteen-year major league career.

Although we had kept in touch, I never brought up this fragile subject with Eric again until ten years later, when Eric and I saw each other at the annual UCLA golf tournament. While out on the golf course, we talked about his career and, eventually, the remarkable season he had with the Dodgers in 1999. He said, "Yeah, it was my best year, baseball-wise."

I knew what he meant by "baseball-wise." From Eric's personal standpoint, he and his family had to face a tragedy that year that no mother or father ever wants to face. He went on to say, "After my son died, my outlook changed 180 degrees. I realized baseball wasn't the most important thing in my life."

Eric told me that even he couldn't quite understand why he had played so well after that tragedy. I think perhaps it was because he discovered that, although he still had a passion for the game of baseball, it wasn't a life or death matter. From listening to Eric, it seemed to me that he played that 1999 season more like he had played the game when he was a kid. I really don't know if that was the reason, but I do vividly remember Eric telling me, "I played the rest of the season with my son's initials in my cap."

In Coach's Pyramid of Success, underneath the words "competitive greatness," John wrote, "When the going gets tough, the tough get going." He had borrowed that phrase from one of his mentors, coach Frank Leahy.

Eric Karros certainly had to be tough as he stood by Trish's side and endured the loss of their son as best he could. In my opinion, Eric not only demonstrated competitive greatness, but also the type of character that embodies the spirit of what John intended for his Pyramid of Success.

CHASE UTLEY

John's reaction to my recommendation of Chase Utley for one of the Most Industrious was amusing. "Why does he always have to play his best games against my Dodgers?" he wondered aloud. "He seems to find ways to beat us with his bat, his glove . . . even with his base running." He tried to conceal a grin. "Gary, I'm sorry. I cannot approve of Chase for your book."

I had seen that sly, mischievous grin many times before. "I have watched Chase enough to know how hard he plays," John continued. "If you insist, you can put him in your book." This time, John didn't hide his genuine smile.

I once heard someone say about how people treat hard work, "Some turn up their sleeves, some turn up their noses, and some don't turn up at all." Chase Utley turns up his sleeves whenever he's on the ball field.

I am not alone in saying Chase is one of the most industrious players to ever play the game. His coaches—both former and present—would agree with this. Even the tough-to-please Philadelphia Phillies fans admire the way he plays. Philadelphia is a town of mostly blue-collar workers, and Chase is one of them—a blue-collar worker on the baseball diamond.

Those same fans would describe Chase's style as gritty, gutsy, and spunky. When many of those fans come home after a hard day's work, they have grease under their fingernails and oil or paint stains on their clothes, and they reek of sweat. Chase is no different from them. After a ball game, he looks like Pig-Pen from the *Peanuts* cartoon, with dirt and grass stains hiding the red-and-white Phillies colors. No wonder his number twenty-six

Phillies uniform is the best-selling jersey in the whole city. Moms never have to wash it, if they really want their sons and daughters to follow in the footsteps of their role model.

Phillies coach Mick Billmeyer once said, "Chase takes a thousand grounders and hits early every day." Even if it's not quite a thousand grounders, we get the idea.

"I could not attend your games when Chase played because of my knees and other health issues," Coach Wooden said to me. "So tell me, Gary, did he play the same way when he played for you as he does with the Phillies?"

"John, I fungoed ground balls to Chase every day at UCLA," I replied. "He could never get enough. 'One more, Skip!' he would holler to me. I wore out before he did. And he would yell to me, 'Hit it farther away from me, Skip!' But I was reluctant to do it, because I knew he would dive recklessly into the dirt with no concern for his body, trying to flag down everything between first and second base. I honored his request only occasionally. I didn't want him to get hurt. We needed him in our lineup."

I told John that Chase had a problem with his feet during his freshman year. Our athletic trainers treated him before and after each practice for a long time, but nothing seemed to help. Finally, they called in a foot specialist, who molded special-ly-fitted arch supports to ease the pain. No one could tell he was in pain when he ran all-out to first base. It was only when he hobbled back to the dugout on his aching feet that it was noticeable.

At the beginning of the season every year, I required my players to join me in a long run. My purpose in having the run was to keep the players from getting out of shape during the nearly month-long Christmas vacation. I figured that, by hav-ing a grueling run over the hills near my home in Chesebro State Park, the players would consider doing some running on their own when they were home for the holidays. Their main incentive to run was that, if they didn't finish the three-mile run in less than twenty-eight minutes and forty seconds, they

would have to run it again in a couple of days—and they would keep running it until they made the allotted time. Most of them made it the first time, but there were always four or five who didn't make their time and had to run it again with me. Some had to run it three times before they made it under the allotted time.

Troy Glaus was one of those who barely beat the clock each year. Troy just wasn't built for cross-country running, but he worked extra hard preparing for the run, and it paid off. He was smart and made it a point to come visit me during the vacation period, when we could run those park trails together.

Had it not been for his feet, Chase would have been perfectly built for distance running. They were so bad that, even after the holiday vacation, I couldn't in good conscience ask Chase to pound his feet in that long run. We had another player, Brett Nista, who was also injured. I told Chase and Brett that they wouldn't have to run, but they must ride their bikes around the hilly course twice as far as the runners. Well, at the time, I *thought* it was a good plan.

It had rained the night before. I realized the trails would be muddy in certain areas, but I figured the runners could sidestep most of those soggy spots. I had run through some of those spots and dodged others without collecting too much heavy mud on my shoes. What I had never done before, however, was ride a bicycle through the mud. I gave no thought to what Chase and Brett would be up against on their ride, but I did provide directions for the two bike riders and the runners. I posted the directions on the trail to show my players where they would need to make certain turns.

Since I would be accompanying the runners, I knew I could prevent my players from making a wrong turn and getting lost. But Brett and Chase had no one with them to show them the way. They were sent on their ride five minutes earlier than the rest of the team, and were on their own in a strange park with only my signs to direct them.

There was another factor I did not consider—the wind. I didn't know that a strategically located sign I had thumbtacked to a tree had blown away before the race began. Instead of making a left turn at that point, Brett and Chase kept going straight ahead, missing the sign that would turn them in the direction of our home base. They were lost on a hilly and muddy trail that went five miles in. A search party consisting of my daughter and some neighborhood friends was sent on horseback to find them and guide them back.

When I talked to Brett afterward, he didn't complain, but instead just stated the facts. "It wasn't the mileage that killed us," he said. "It was the mud. There was no way we could ride up those hills, so we had to push our bikes through the mud to the tops of the hills. Our backs and legs were killing us."

So, even though I had tried to make things a little easier on Chase and Brett, both players ended up working harder than the players who ran. Like Brett, Chase never complained, although they did take some ribbing from their teammates for getting lost. As for me, I felt bad for the two players and faulted myself for not obeying one of Coach Wooden's golden rules: "Failing to prepare is preparing to fail." I failed to factor in the wind, rain, and mud for the bike riders. As far as I was concerned, my players all passed the cross-country run that day—but I flunked the course.

I try to follow the careers of the players I coached who made it to the major leagues by reading the newspapers and watching their games on television. One night, I was watching a game between the Phillies and the St. Louis Cardinals. I especially wanted to watch this game, because it was during Chase's remarkable hitting streak in 2006. His consecutive streak had reached thirty-three games, but he had gone hitless when he came to bat in the ninth inning. He was facing Randy Flores, a former USC pitcher, who got Chase to top a grounder slightly to the third base side of the mound. It was supposed to be a routine out for Flores, as he looked the runner back to third base

and then threw to first. What Flores seemed to forget, however, was the character of the runner going as hard as he could down the first base line. Flores's throw to first was late. As Eric Karros described it on FOX-TV that night, "That's a hit all the way!" Of course, Eric and I had the extra pleasure of knowing that a former Bruin had just beat a throw by a former Trojan rival. Who better to judge a good hustling hit than Eric Karros, another industrious player?

I called Chase that night and left a message on his cell phone, saying, "Great hustle, Chase!" I didn't want to mention his consecutive game hitting streak for fear of jinxing him (that's just another baseball superstition). I was glad that, the next day, Chase had three hits in six at bats to extend his streak to thirty-five straight, tying him with Ty Cobb's thirty-five in 1917, and Luis Castillo's in 2002. His streak ended at thirty-five.

I told John that Chase never wanted out of the UCLA lineup. He always wanted to play, despite his ailing feet, his aching arm, and the usual blisters, bruises, and abrasions that resulted from his extra hitting, diving, and sliding. Chase played in 126 consecutive games at UCLA, a remarkable feat for a young man who played as hard as he did. In his sophomore year, he played in *every inning* of all sixty-two games; in his junior year, he played in all sixty-four games, but not every inning. I only took him out when we had a big lead, but he hated it.

"I coached my share of players like Chase, who hated coming out of games even for a few seconds," John said. "I did not mind it at all. I wanted my players to have that intense desire to play. I even hired two of my biggest complainers—but best competitors—as my assistants later on, Jerry Norman and Denny Crum."

John was surprised to hear that college baseball didn't come easily for Chase in his freshman year at UCLA. He struggled at shortstop, the position he played in high school. Usually, it was his throwing that got him into trouble. He didn't have great arm strength from the shortstop position—nothing like the rifle-arm of the shortstop preceding him, Troy Glaus. Chase especially had trouble making the throw in the six-hole, the longest throw any infielder has to make.

Knowing his arm was not the greatest, Chase would often be in such a hurry that he didn't look the ball into the glove or set his feet before trying to throw. As a result, he booted ground balls and made too many throwing errors.

I often used Coach Wooden's famous words, yelling to Chase, "Be quick, don't hurry!" Although this had worked with other infielders, the long throw from shortstop continued to cause him problems. By the end of the season, I moved him off the infield and made him our designated hitter. I felt bad for him, because it wasn't due to his lack of effort. I even wrote him a letter during that time, asking him not to give up, because I wouldn't give up on him—he would always be in my lineup. I wanted him to see my commitment in writing.

Actually, it was a *qualified* commitment. The following year, I moved him to second base. I believed he would worry less about throwing from second and could concentrate more on just catching the ball. I also believed he would relax more on defense, which would make him even more productive at the plate. Chase was right at home playing second base. With his quick hands, he turned the double play as well as any second sacker I ever had, and he did it *quickly* and without *hurrying*.

I don't recall ever teaching Chase anything about hitting. I've always believed in the expression, "If it's not broken, don't try to fix it." Coach Vince Beringhele, arguably the best college hitting coach in the country, had the same philosophy. He helped Chase with the mental aspect of hitting, always making sure Chase had a plan of attack on the opposing pitchers. But, like me, Vinnie rarely messed with Chase's swing.

"Chase's dad is the man who had the most to do with his success as a hitter," I told John.

Knowing that Chase had been a good hitter most of his life, I asked his dad, Dave, what he had done to teach Chase to swing

the bat like he did.

Dave grinned. "I will take credit for one thing," he said. "I made him bat left-handed. He was a natural right-hander."

"Wow," I said, "That's something. You showed a lot of foresight, knowing left-handed hitters have an advantage over right-handed hitters."

"No, Gary, I didn't do it for that reason," Dave said. "I did it because I was lazy."

"Lazy?" I asked, puzzled.

"That's right. You see, when he was five years old, we'd go out in the front yard and I would pitch to him. Right-handed, Chase would always hit the ball down the street, and I would have to run after it. That got tiresome. I made him bat left-handed so that when he hit the ball, it would rebound off of our house and come right back to me."

Let that be one of the best coaching tips for fathers in this book.

On August 12, 2008, Chase left tickets for me and my family to attend a night game between his Phillies and the Dodgers. Chase hit a home run, but the Phils lost, 4–3. After the game, my family and Chase's family all met him inside the stadium. As we talked, Chase was constantly hounded by kids, parents, grandparents, and Phillies and Dodgers fans of all types and sizes. They wanted him to sign their caps, T-shirts, programs, and baseballs. He never refused a single person, smiling as he signed his autograph while still keeping up with the conversation of both families.

As we were getting ready to leave, I told Chase, "I'm impressed that you took the time to sign your autograph for all those people. You didn't refuse a single one."

Chase looked at me and said, rather matter-of-factly, "Oh, it's never a problem, Skip. But I have learned to shorten my signature so it doesn't take so long, and I can do it for more people."

Chase's response reminded me of what Coach Wooden had once told me a long time ago. "I used to sign autographs 'John R.

Wooden,'" he said, "but I don't write very fast and didn't want to take up people's time, so I eliminated the 'R.' from my signature." I've watched John sign many autographs for people. He does it methodically and meticulously. It takes him longer than the NBA's twenty-four-second clock to sign his name on paper, and when I have asked him to write his signature on a baseball, it takes him longer than college basketball's thirty-five-second clock. But whatever he signs and however long it takes, it is a beautiful signature. *Los Angeles Times* sports columnist T. J. Simers once wrote, "You'd think that John was signing the Declaration of Independence when he signed his autograph." John confessed to me that his careful signature was the result of his strict third grade teacher, who expected all students to inscribe each letter carefully and precisely.

One time, when we were having breakfast together, people kept approaching John for his autograph. I asked him if he ever got tired of people interrupting him and asking him to sign things. "No, Gary, quite the contrary," he said. "I am honored that people would even want my autograph."

When Chase took the time to do the same thing John had done for years, I thought of how similar these two were in the way they treated everyone around them. The way Chase handled the situation that evening was the same way he had handled things at UCLA—he was always considerate and respectful to others. Nothing changed when he became a superstar in the major leagues. In only six years of playing, Chase started in five consecutive All-Star games, tied with Reggie Jackson for most home runs in a World Series with five, and was on the road to becoming a Hall of Famer, due to his consistent play. I told Coach, "The only thing that would keep him out of the Hall of Fame would be injuries."

Off the field, Chase is also a superstar. He and his wife, Jennifer, established a charity, Utley All-Star Animals, to bring awareness to animal cruelty and to educate the community about the proper treatment of animals. Chase gives most of the

credit to Jenny, saying, "My wife has had the majority of that on her shoulders."

Chase Utley is truly an industrious player. As Coach Wooden often said about his players, I'm so pleased with his performance, and honored that I had the privilege to coach him.

* * *

When John and I finished discussing the three Most Industrious Players, he said something that made me think these players were not at all unlike John himself. "Gary, I believe all three of these young men have an intense love for the game of baseball."

John's words reminded me of something I had said to the fans in my farewell speech, prior to coaching my last home game at UCLA. It was a quote from an anonymous source that had always hit home with me: "Get a job you love, and you'll never have to work a day in your life."

When I quoted this saying to John, I waited for his look of unequivocal approval . . . and waited.

Finally, he said, "I don't agree, Gary."

His explanation was simple. "To think that just because you love your job it will eliminate hard work is quite misleading."

Although I was surprised and offered no response, I felt a bit foolish that I had not thought of that before. For a moment, I wished John would have told me this before I had used this "wise and profound" quote in my farewell speech. Then I told myself, *Probably no one even noticed the flaw in that quote. I mean, how many John Woodens are out there, anyway?*

Since John's criticism, I've given some thought to that quote and decided that it would be more correct if it read: "Get a job you love and, even though you will work hard at it, it will *seem* like you never work a day in your life."

ENTHUSIASM

Your heart must be in your work. Stimulate others." These are the words Coach Wooden inscribed underneath the "enthusiasm" block in his Pyramid of Success. Many names came to mind when I began thinking of which three UCLA players most epitomized this characteristic.

ERIC BYRNES

The first UCLA player I thought of happened to be sitting next to me and across from Coach Wooden at the breakfast table one summer morning in 2008. Eric Byrnes was now the regular left fielder for the Arizona Diamondbacks, and his style of play in the big leagues was just as enthusiastic as it had been when he played the outfield for the Bruins from 1995 to 1998.

Jeff Moorad, who was sitting next to John, was complimenting Eric. He told John, "Eric is your type of player, Coach. A real 'Charlie Hustle' type, and he does it every day, every play." John smiled and gave an approving look over to Eric, whose face turned almost beet-red from embarrassment. It was the first and only time I ever saw my former player embarrassed, and I've seen him a lot since that morning breakfast—at UCLA golf

tournaments, at his wedding, and on television as a baseball broadcaster for ESPN and the MLB network. Eric does not embarrass easily, even though he often says things that would make most people want to hide under the table. That's Eric, though . . . he's never afraid to say what he thinks, even if it's unpopular.

Eric is a very bright person who always did well in his academics at UCLA. He worked hard at getting good grades, and I never had to worry about him skipping classes and slighting his academics. Vin Scully was fond of telling his listeners, "Eric can recite, in exact order, the names of every president of the United States—and he can do it forwards and backwards. Yes, Eric is smart, and he is enthusiastic at just about everything—but especially about baseball."

Eric follows baseball news like a newborn colt follows its mommy—very closely. When Coach Wooden asked Moorad what he thought of the Manny Ramirez trade from the Red Sox to the Dodgers only a couple of days prior, Jeff admitted that the Diamondbacks hadn't been interested in making that deal. Eric interjected, "Manny is the best right-handed hitter I have ever seen. He's amazing, but he's really a space cadet."

I couldn't help myself. "Eric, it takes one to know one," I said. But he wasn't embarrassed in the least by my quip.

While I was trying to decide on my three most enthusiastic players, I asked another former Bruin, Adam Melhuse, who was the most enthusiastic player he had ever played with while at UCLA or during the eight years he was in the major leagues.

"At UCLA, it was D. R. [David Roberts]," Adam replied. "I never played with D. R. in the bigs, but he said that Eric Byrnes, my teammate on the Oakland A's, was easily the most enthusiastic player he ever played with *or* against. Eric was intense—he played like his hair was on fire."

As I mentioned earlier, Vin Scully was impressed by Eric's enthusiasm, too. One day, while I was out pulling weeds in my yard, I was listening to Vin describe a play Eric was involved in. After talking about Eric's dramatic follow-through, when he had somersaulted to the ground on a throw he made to home plate, Vinny told his listeners, "Eric certainly puts everything into everything he does—and he does it every time I see him play."

I said to John, "You often hear coaches say of their players, 'He's always the first player on the field, and the last to leave.' Well, John, when Eric played at UCLA, he was not only the first *player* on the field—some days, he would beat all the coaches, including me, and even the groundskeepers to the field. Eric didn't sleep much in those days. He told me and his teammates, 'I only need four to six hours of sleep at night, and I'm ready to go.'"

Eric was atypical of most college students, who love to sleep in whenever they have a chance. Not Eric—he loved getting up early and going over to our ball field to practice his hitting.

There were many mornings when I arrived at the ball field and heard the sound of "ping . . . ping . . . ping." It was Eric in the batting cage, blasting baseballs off the batting tee with his aluminum bat. Official practice was still hours away. It was this kind of enthusiasm that rubbed off on his teammates—and on me, too.

I told Coach how Eric's sleeplessness paid off for him on one occasion, while he was a student at UCLA. One night as he laid in bed, he heard the sounds of an intruder climbing through his bedroom window. He told me and some of his teammates afterwards, "I pretended I was asleep as the guy wandered about in my room. I laid there thinking that I could just keep pretending I was asleep until he left, or I could do something." Knowing Eric, we all knew he would do something.

"I decided to take action," he said. "I leaped from my bed, made a flying tackle, and started pummeling the guy with my fists. I think a right hook knocked him out for a while. I yelled to my roomie to call 911, and held the guy down till the police came."

I told Coach, "That night, we played USC and Eric got the game-winning hit. A newspaper headline the next day read,

'Byrnes KOs Intruder, Then S.C.'"

"You know, Gary," Coach said, smiling, "near the top of my Pyramid, along the left side, I wrote the word 'fight.' Underneath that word, I wrote 'effort and hustle.' Maybe we can use Eric as an example for that category, too."

I told Coach that things did not always go smoothly between me and Eric. His intense desire to play and my impatient desire to see him reach his full potential clashed on occasion. I wanted Eric to use his speed more, not just his strength. He loved to hit balls over our fence at Jackie Robinson Stadium. It looked to me as if that's what he was trying to do on every swing. In fact, he would grunt loudly whenever the bat met the ball. Sometimes, even in our games, the opposing players, especially the pitchers, heard his grunts. I knew they didn't like it; they thought he was trying to show them up, which is an unwritten no-no in baseball. But that was not the reason Eric grunted on his swings. He was just letting out his intense effort, believing it helped him hit the ball harder and farther. "Hey, weight lifters do it all the time," he would say.

Coach's eyebrows rose when I told him I had benched Eric for a short time during his sophomore season to send him a message that strength wasn't the only thing a player needed. I believed he was wasting his other God-given skill—the gift of speed. He was our fastest player, but I told him, "You need to learn how to bunt, to make more consistent contact, and hit more ground balls so you can use the gift you are blessed with." In short, I wanted him to improve his on-base percentage.

I don't think Eric made any argument against what I said, but I knew he wouldn't like the idea of sitting on the bench. I hadn't forgotten what Coach Wooden always said: "A coach's best ally is his bench. Put a player on the bench, and you have his undivided attention."

Coach reminded me of the power of the bench that day, saying, "It is the most underrated assistant coach known to sports, Gary."

Well, putting Eric on the bench certainly got his attention, and the way he reacted got mine, as well. He didn't know that I intended to bench him for only two games. I thought that if I told him it was only temporary, the message would lose its impact. After I informed him of being benched, he headed back to his apartment at full speed and told his roommates he was quitting the team.

That same night, as I was sitting at my clubhouse office desk, the phone was ringing off the hook with calls from Eric's teammates. Basically, the message was, "Skip, Eric is going to quit. You gotta talk to him again." None of the players criticized me for criticizing Eric (at least, they didn't admit it to me), but they wanted me to call him up and ask him to come back to my office for another talk.

Eric got to my office at around 10:00 PM, and the two of us tried again to straighten things out. We talked until close to midnight, but this time it was much more cordial. When all was said and done, Eric did not quit the team. His teammates had the most to do with Eric's change of heart. I told Coach, "I'm thankful to them for that."

Eric only sat out for two games, and never missed another game as a starter the rest of his UCLA career. I don't know if my sitting him out did any good, but his On-Base Percentage did improve in his final two years, from .378 and .397 in his first two years to .426 and .405 in his final two years. In addition, he reduced his strike-outs significantly. Eric used his speed quite well, going from thirty-two stolen bases in his first two years to forty-nine stolen bases his final two years. Of course, this improvement might have happened anyway, without my interference, simply as a result of Eric's hard work and determination to improve.

Eric and I have reminisced over the little "battle" we had, and we both agreed that we gained more respect for each other. It brought us closer, and added to our lasting friendship. I look forward to his Christmas card every year with a picture

of his family, including his three bulldogs—Bruin, Bella, and Mr. Hitch.

Eric had an eleven-year career in the major leagues, and was a fan favorite everywhere he played because of the *way* he played. To say Eric wore his enthusiasm on his sleeve is a huge understatement. His enthusiasm came from his heart and was visible where his teammates, opponents, and fans could always see it. He played every game as if it were his last, crashing into walls while chasing fly balls and diving headfirst into a base as if he were tackling it. He came the closest to Pete Rose's style of play than any player I ever coached—including the way he knocked over catchers who stood in the way of home plate.

Just like his UCLA teammate, Chase Utley, Eric's uniform looked like it had been through a dust storm after every game he played. In fact, the Arizona Diamondbacks sold Eric Byrnes T-shirts in their concessions that had fake dirt printed all over them. It was a best-seller; I even have one that I wear only occasionally, because I want to keep it in good condition as a memento of Eric.

Eric made my coaching job easier, because his enthusiasm was contagious to his teammates. Just watching Eric's approach to daily practices, the other players didn't need a constant barrage of pep talks from me—watching Eric and listening to Eric was inspiration for us all.

John was a fan of Eric's before he ever met him. He remembered him as a star player at UCLA, and he liked his style of play when he watched Eric on television, except for his occasional dive into the first base bag. John said, "I have seen him dive headfirst into first base on close plays. You didn't teach him that, did you, Gary? I don't think it is the quickest way to get there, right?"

"That's debatable, John," I said. "But no, I didn't teach him that. I did teach him to dive *back* to the base headfirst when pitchers were trying to pick him off." We didn't bother to debate diving into first from the direction of home plate.

I told John a story that demonstrated Eric's big heart and his love for people. When he played for the Arizona Diamondbacks, the city of Phoenix built a ball park they were supposed to name Eric Byrnes Field. But when it came time for Eric to give his ceremonial speech, he surprised everyone by saying he wanted the field to be named Saulo Morris Field instead. Saulo was a local high school student who had died of leukemia, whom Eric said was "the most selfless person I have ever met." *The Arizona Republic* newspaper reported that this young man, whom Eric had befriended two years earlier, had donated $6,750 to help victims of the war in Sudan.

Eric was quite emotional at that dedication as he struggled to express his feelings about Saulo Morris. "Saulo's approach toward life, his attitude, his selflessness, was something that I think we all could learn from."

I could tell by the look in John's eyes that he found an even deeper respect for Eric after hearing that story. I could see that he was thinking about it before he finally said, "Gary, those are the kind of players we like to coach—hard and tough on the court and field, but soft and big-hearted off of it." Coach Wooden has coached players very much like Eric, such as Bill Walton, with his same intense enthusiasm and big heart. But both players will always be remembered as playing as if their hair was on fire.

When John sat across from Eric at breakfast that morning, he grinned every time Eric talked—Eric's enthusiasm showed through his excited voice and borderline hyper actions. I could see that Eric was enthralled with being in the presence of Coach. Eric told me afterward, "That was awesome . . . Coach Wooden really fired me up!"

I told Coach what Eric had said. John said, "Eric got so excited talking about how anxious he was to get back into the Arizona lineup (Eric had a pulled hamstring at the time) that I thought at any second he might hop on top of our table and start doing jumping jacks." I told Coach I wouldn't have been

surprised if he had.

In 2010, when Coach and I discussed my nominations for Most Enthusiastic Player, I informed him that I had decided one of them was Eric Byrnes.

Coach said, "That does not surprise me, Gary."

JACK GIFFORD

My friend and former teammate at UCLA, Jack Gifford, told me once, "You can take the man out of the little boy, but you can't take the little boy out of the man." I always knew Jack was describing himself when he said that. Like Coach Wooden, Jack *loved* baseball, and he *lived* it until he died suddenly in 2009, on his sixty-eighth birthday. Jack was the second UCLA player I discussed with Coach for his extraordinary example of enthusiasm.

I gave Coach Wooden a quick glimpse of Jack's love for baseball, starting with his involvement in the sport in the years just before his death. I told Coach that, soon after Jack became the CEO of Maxim Integrated Products, Inc., he organized a company baseball team—the Maxim Yankees. He not only sponsored the team, but was also its field manager and first baseman. Some of his players affectionately referred to Jack as "Little George Steinbrenner." Although they meant it in a complimentary way, they were afraid to say it to his face. Like George, Jack was passionate about his team and gave generously to make it better. Like Eric Byrnes, Jack's enthusiasm was contagious amongst his players, and they all respected him. Some even loved him.

Coach Wooden's eyes brightened when I told him that Jack patterned his Maxim pinstripe uniforms after Steinbrenner's Yankees—the "NY" design was identical to the Yankee uniform, except that an "M" took the place of the "N."

Coach smiled. "So Gifford was a Yankee fan, too," he said. "You know, my favorite major leaguer today is Derek Jeter. He's enthusiastic about playing baseball, but it's less visible than Eric Byrne's style."

I agreed with John, then continued talking about Gifford. "Jack recruited his players from some of the best college baseball teams in the nation—particularly from his alma mater. In fact, he was accused by more than a few of his associates for hiring some Maxim employees based on their baseball-playing ability."

In 2004, when Jack was 63 years old, he became the oldest player ever to play in the National Baseball Congress Tournament that began in 1934. He continued to play for the next five years, until he passed away. Jack did not just make brief appearances on the field and then managed from the dugout. He played first base regularly, alongside college-age players and former professionals. He played and coached with the enthusiasm of a little boy playing with his friends in a sandlot ball game—except he played almost as if winning the game was a life and death matter.

Although John had watched plenty of our UCLA games, he didn't remember seeing Jack play, so I began telling him a little about Jack's playing career. I told him that I met Jack Gifford on UCLA's Joe E. Brown Field at our first practice in 1960. What caught my attention was the wooden slide rule sticking out of the back pocket of Jack's uniform.

Jack majored in engineering, just as Coach Wooden did when he was a freshman at Purdue University, so Coach was familiar with a slide rule. The dictionary's definition of a slide rule is quite complicated. Suffice it to say, that it serves the purpose of what a math calculator does today.

Jack told me he didn't know what a slide rule was until his first math class at UCLA. "My math professor said if you don't know how to use a slide rule you better learn it fast or get out of engineering." So, Jack took advantage of every opportunity to practice using his slide rule . . . even on the ball field.

Most days at practice, I saw that slide rule sticking out of

his uniform's back pocket. One day, Coach Reichle caught him using it, and that ended that . . . or so Coach Reichle thought. Afterward, Jack hid his slide rule in the corner of the dugout. Jack would sneak into the dugout whenever Coach Reichle wasn't looking to practice on his slide rule.

I explained to Coach why I thought Jack deserved to be included among the examples of enthusiasm. Jack's boundless energy on the ball diamond, even during practice, was a picture I still remember—Jack running with his glove thrust out in front of him, chasing pop-ups in foul territory with no regard for our dugout or the adjoining chain-link fence. I can see him bouncing off of that fence and landing on his back. Sometimes he would even climb the fence to catch a ball, looking much like a monkey reaching for the highest banana in the tree—just to catch a *batting practice* foul ball!

Enthusiasm. If anyone ever wanted to see what it looked like, all they needed to do was stand on our ball field when Coach Reichle yelled, "Your turn to hit, Gifford!" The way Jack ran in from the field to grab his bat and raced to the left-hand side of the batter's box reminded me of the way I used to run home when I knew mom had just baked a chocolate cake. Oh, how Jack loved to hit!

Jack was a chatterbox on the field, always yelling encouragement to our players, especially to our pitchers. Playing to the right of him at second base, I heard his constant chatter before each pitch as he pounded his first baseman's mitt. He kept all of us in the ball game. If he thought we weren't in the game, he let us know.

Before many a pitch, I heard him yell over to me, "Hey, Adams, I can't hear ya!" Sometimes he would get so mad at our quiet infielders that he would yell loud enough for everyone in the bleachers to hear. "Hey, let's hear some chatter in this dang infield!" Although he only stood at five feet seven inches tall, he was a husky lad who grew up in one of the toughest neighborhoods in Los Angeles, the son of a dock worker at the San

Pedro harbor. Nobody wanted Jack's wrath upon them, because they knew he would take on anyone in a wrestling or boxing match. So when Jack yelled for more chatter, we all knew he meant it and we'd better do it.

Coach Wooden got another good chuckle after I told him about a play that Jack made in a game at Fresno State, although our Bruins team, especially Jack, did not chuckle at the time.

In the bottom of the ninth inning, we were leading 3–2 with two outs and a Fresno runner on second base. A routine grounder was hit to my brother, Gene, at shortstop. As all second basemen are taught to do, I went over to back up first base in case of a bad throw. I admit that I was not traveling at full speed, because Gene almost always was on target with his throws. So, as I casually jogged in the direction behind first base, I was thinking, *Hot dog! Another win for the Bruins!*

Speaking of hot dogs, Jack was about to demonstrate a hot dog play with all the trimmings: mustard, ketchup, relish, sauerkraut, chili, onions—the works!

Gene's throw, as I expected, was perfect. The ball was headed dead center for Jack's chest. All Jack needed to do was hold his glove steady in his right hand and squeeze the ball when it landed safely in the pocket of his glove.

But Jack did not hold his glove steady. What he did then is a common practice today, especially for major league players when they catch a ball for the final out. His enthusiasm got the best of him in the anticipation of our victory, and he hot-dogged it. Jack swiped his glove rapidly across his chest, like he was batting at a buzzing fly. He might as well have used a baseball bat when his glove met the ball. As I watched in awe, the ball appeared to go into Jack's left ear and shoot like a bullet out of his right ear. The next instant, I was chasing the ball as it whistled its way down the right field line.

I am not one to use profanity, but that night, while desperately trying to catch up to the ball, a few choice words occurred to me. I vividly remember the surge of blood filling my head out

of anger at Jack Gifford. Now the score was tied, 3–3, with the batter who should have been out standing on second base. The game ended shortly afterwards when the following batter hit a shot against the left center field wall to score the winning run.

I got over my anger before we played our next game. No one who played that night felt as badly about our loss as Jack. In fact, he felt so bad about his error that immediately after he made it, he ran down the line, trying to catch up and pass me to get to the ball before I did. I never realized he was right behind me until I turned to throw the ball back to the infield. He was standing there, looking like a little boy who had just lost his puppy. It was the only time I ever felt sorry for Jack. But I never let him forget that play.

I told and retold this story in a humorous way every year we held our UCLA alumni game. I doubled as coach and public address announcer for those alumni games, because I knew all the players and could tell stories about each one as they came to bat or stood in the field. Whenever Jack came up to bat for the first time, I described what happened that sorrowful night in Fresno. His reaction was always the same. He would step out of the box and look at me, imitating sadness as much as he could muster, and then break out into a wide smile as he mouthed the words, "Not again, Gary, not again."

Many former UCLA baseball players have heard this story—at least all those who have attended our alumni games. I admired Jack for showing up at those alumni games and taking his "punishment." I don't recall that he ever missed a single alumni game in all my thirty years of coaching at UCLA.

When I finished the Jack Gifford hot dog story, Coach Wooden grinned and said, "Gary, he *must* have loved playing baseball to come every year and take your abuse."

I told John, "Yes, but I do have one regret about telling that story. I had always planned to tell Jack someday that he wasn't the only one responsible for that loss in Fresno. You see, John, I went 0 for 4 and stranded two runners in scoring position that night. If I had done my job, those runs Jack gave up wouldn't have made a difference. Jack never thought to pin the blame on me . . . at least, he never mentioned it."

Until the day Jack died, he not only loved *playing* baseball, he loved *talking* baseball, especially hitting. He treated hitting as if it were a science. Anybody who was a proven hitter in Jack's mind was fair game to talk about the science of hitting. He didn't like talking about hitting with someone who didn't play much baseball. He once said, "I could tell you how to hit a baseball until I am blue in the face, but unless you go do it, you'll never learn how."

He would grab former UCLA major league players Todd Zeile, Billy Haselman, Eric Karros, and Eric Byrnes every chance he got to discuss hitting.

Minnesota Twins scout and former All Pac-10 UCLA short-stop Vern Followell told me about a debate he once had with Jack regarding the "rising fastball" myth. He said, "Jack insisted that a fastball rises. As hard as I tried, I couldn't convince him that scientific studies have proven the ball does not rise. I kept telling Jack that the ball only appears to rise in the batter's view, but actually stays level longer when thrown overhand with great velocity. Jack was stubborn and wouldn't concede. A couple of weeks after our discussion, I received a phone call from Jack's secretary. She said, 'Jack wanted me to give you this message: Vern, you're right, it doesn't rise.' Apparently, Jack did some research of his own."

His favorite target was former major leaguer Doug DeCinces. Doug did such a great job of teaching his son the art of hitting that Tim became one of the best clutch hitters in UCLA baseball history. Doug and Jack talked hitting for hours upon hours and though they didn't always agree, they became very close friends. There's no doubt in my mind that their friendship started and flourished because of their respect for each other's hitting knowledge. I was witness to some of those discussions, and I had to laugh every time Jack popped out of

his chair, grabbed an imaginary bat, and planted his feet into his batting stance.

For a guy who knew so much about hitting, he had the ugliest and most unorthodox stance of any hitter I have ever seen from Little League to the big leagues. I referred to it as the "Jack Gifford Leaning Tower of Pisa Stance." He didn't use that stance when he played college ball, but somehow he managed to make it work for him after he finished his career at UCLA. He would often tell me, "Gary, I wish I knew then what I know now about hitting . . . I would have hit over .300 every year." I'd always reply, "Would you have had the guts to use that crazy stance of yours?" That would always get a bit of a rise out of him.

Jack never played professional baseball, but he kept an eye on the sport, especially following the ball players who used to play at UCLA. He received his bachelor's degree in electrical engineering in 1963, and not long afterward became one of the founding fathers of the analog industry. When he retired as chairman, chief executive officer, and president of Maxim Integrated Products, Inc. in early 2007, Maxim had over ten thousand employees and reported revenues of over two billion dollars.

The more I talked about Gifford, the more Coach was pleased with "our" selection for an example of enthusiasm. He put it this way: "Many times, I would not say if a player of mine—even a team of mine—was successful until years afterwards. It is like judging a president of the United States during his term. One never knows if his decisions were the right ones until years later . . . sometimes many, many years. It is not just what you do in college. It is also what you do with your life afterward."

I nodded and began telling Coach how Jack ran his company—much like the way he ran his baseball team. He expected his employees to be as enthused about their jobs as he was about his. I didn't recite all of the quotes attributed to Jack that his employees had to listen to, but I did remember a couple that I thought Coach would like. One had to do with success, something Coach spent most of his life talking about.

Jack told his employees at a company meeting, "I believe that success does not come with eight-hour days or lack of anxiety." Coach nodded and mumbled his approval.

Jack also told his employees, "Any organizational mistake, people remember. It's just like a bad call from an umpire. People don't remember the good calls. They only remember the bad ones."

When John heard that, he said, "So true, Gary, so true. But, I always *tried* to forget those bad calls. Problem was, the more I tried the more I remembered."

There are many wise and humorous quotes attributed to Jack that I heard on the day I attended his memorial in Palo Alto. I didn't relay those quotes to Coach on this day, but they do paint a picture of Jack's personality and his enthusiasm toward life.

One of my favorite Gifford quotes is: "Japan put guys on torpedoes to steer them when they had a really tough target. Not only were they going to die, but they had to hold their breath." He said this while he attended a meeting *in Japan.*

Another Jack Giffordism occurred when he and his vice president, Rob Georges, had just sat down in Jack's small Learjet preparing for takeoff to Dallas. Rob was much taller than Jack, and made a comment to Jack that it would be nice if the interior of the jet was about two inches taller. Jack's reply was, "It would be cheaper to get a new vice president."

At his memorial in 2009, his daughter, Tracy, told about her dad's penchant for winning. "My dad didn't like woodpeckers because they pecked holes in the side of our house and the 'peck-peck-peck' noise was disturbing. So, every once in a while he would take his gun and shoot them. They would fall with a splat on our driveway. He never picked them up and would leave them lying there on the concrete for days. My mom finally asked him, 'Jack, when are you ever going to clean up this mess of woodpeckers?' His reply was typical Jack: 'Not yet. I

want to send them a message.'" Jack was a funny guy, without trying to be funny.

I told Coach that Jack was a giver, not a taker. Jack's enthusiasm for baseball, especially college baseball, never waned. Year after year, Jack made large contributions to his alma mater. He and his gracious wife, Rhodine, would host our UCLA baseball team at their home every year when we played at Stanford. Rhodine did most of the planning and the cooking although Jack did help with the barbecue steaks between hitting in his backyard batting cage. That batting cage was Jack's pride and joy.

He would invite the players to take some swings off his pitching machine, which he enjoyed cranking up to ninety miles per hour. Somehow, someway—despite Jack's Leaning Tower of Pisa stance—he hit the fastest pitches off that machine as well as any of our young players. After several line shot hits, he would beam with pride as he left the cage and bragged to the next hitter, "That's how it's done."

Speaking of batting cages, in 2008 the Giffords sponsored the construction of the Jack and Rhodine Gifford Baseball Training Facility at UCLA. This is a state-of-the-art structure where UCLA players can take batting practice underneath a lighted roof and where they can field ground balls at the same time. Jack was proud of the facility and knew it would contribute to the success of the UCLA baseball program. I guess he was proven right because two years after it was built, Coach John Savage and his UCLA team were runners-up in the NCAA College World Series.

Besides UCLA, Jack and Rhodine gave substantial donations to baseball programs at other universities such as Stanford, Cal Berkeley, Hawaii, Santa Clara, and San Jose State. When I was coaching UCLA, I asked Jack, "Why do you give so much to us and to the other college baseball programs?" He replied, "It's payback. If Coach Reichle hadn't given me a scholarship to play baseball at UCLA, I would have never gotten to where I am. College baseball saved me."

Coach Wooden really liked what Jack said about the giving back. "You know, Gary, we all owe so much to the schools we come from. I am not just talking about Purdue University, where I graduated. I'm also talking about my grade school and high school. I'm not rich enough to help them in a financial way, but I try to visit them as much as I can. I give speeches and tell them how grateful I am."

I told John that Jack did more than just give money—he gave himself. Jack was convinced that youths exposed to athletics were more likely to succeed in life if they received a solid education. This led Jack to establish the Hawaii Kalaeiki Baseball Youth Clinic in 2004. The clinic was held in Kona, Hawaii, offered to ages seven to eighteen, and was free to all! As many as 350 youth attended the four-day event annually which featured volunteer coaches from the major leagues and Division I universities.

I've coached and lectured at many camps and clinics in my day, but I personally believe Jack's clinic was the best I've ever participated in. Jack was not cheap with the gifts he gave to every youngster attending. Some years he handed out brand-new fielding gloves, sometimes aluminum bats, and often he gave them batting gloves and equipment bags. Every player, every year, received a high quality major league hat.

The biggest gift Jack gave was the gift of himself. No one worked harder or displayed more enthusiasm on the field under that hot Hawaiian sun. He was relentless in teaching those youngsters how to play baseball, focusing especially on—what else—hitting. It was Jack's enthusiasm that motivated and inspired me during those long, hot days. I'm sure the other coaches felt the same. I believe with all my heart that Jack's enthusiasm stemmed from his genuine love of Hawaii and its youth and also his love for the game of baseball.

When I finished telling John portions of these stories about Jack, he said, "I believe you miss him, Gary." He was right—and

I still do miss him. John agreed with me that Jack was a perfect example of a person whose enthusiasm inspired and stimulated others.

DAVID ROBERTS

When I told John that David Roberts was one of the first people I thought of for the enthusiasm cornerstone, he said, "Oh yes, I remember Dave Roberts. He was a good left-handed pitcher in the major leagues."

"No, John, he was an outfielder for our UCLA team," I said.

"Oh, *that* Dave Roberts," Coach said. "Yes . . . yes, of course, I remember him playing for you, a little guy who stole a lot of bases. If it were not for him, the Red Sox would never have won the World Series."

"That's the one, John."

"You know, Gary, there was another Dave Roberts who was a left-handed pitcher in the big leagues, and he was a pretty good one, too."

I hadn't known that, but when I got home that night, I Googled Dave Roberts and, sure enough, there was a lefty pitcher who pitched for eight different major league teams from 1969 to 1981 and almost won the coveted Cy Young Award one year. I did not remember him, but John, at ninety-nine years old, did remember.

The two of us talked for quite some time about Dave Roberts's famous stolen base. Coach said he watched that game on television and was "on the edge of my seat from the time Dave Roberts went into the game until it ended in the twelfth inning." I was watching, too. What each of us saw and heard on Sunday, October 17, 2006, of Game Four of the American League Championship Series—plus inside information from David Roberts—is described below.

"Now running for Millar . . . number thirty-one . . . David Roberts!" Boston's Fenway Park loudspeakers boomed the announcement over the capacity crowd of 37,402, mostly Red Sox fans.

As David Roberts quickly donned his helmet and jogged to his spot on the first base bag, every knowledgeable baseball fan in the stadium and the millions of Americans watching and listening on television and radio knew exactly why his manager had put him in the game. Terry Francona wanted to get the tying run into scoring position as quickly as possible. No player in the American League had a better chance of accomplishing this feat than the speedy David Roberts.

The thirty-two-year-old former UCLA outfielder was perfect for just this situation. With his 135 steals in only six big league seasons and ninety-three percent success rate, there wasn't a better base-stealing threat in the American League.

Time was running out for the Red Sox. The score was 4–3, in favor of the mighty Yankees with Boston down to their last three outs in the bottom of the ninth. Worse yet, they were facing the best closer in Yankees history—perhaps in all of Major League Baseball history—the great Mariano Rivera.

This ninth inning was crucial for the Sox. The Yankees had won the first three games of this American League Championship Series. If the Red Sox couldn't score at least one run in this inning, it would mean another year without a chance for a World Series championship. A total of eighty-seven years had passed since their last one.

Before the game even started, "D. R." (David's nickname when he played at UCLA) was with one of his coaches down the right field line, working on the art of base-stealing. It was a regular ritual prior to games. His coach pretended to pitch from the stretch position and D. R., with eyes focused intently on his pitcher, readied his body to jump at the first slight sign of movement. Would the pitcher's move be to first base, or would it be to home? In either case, D. R.'s reaction would be a quick one, either back to the imaginary first base or headed for the imaginary second base. This was repeated until D. R. was

confident in his reads and jumps. When D. R. told me about his routine preparation, I was reminded once again of Coach Wooden's popular phrase, "Failing to prepare is preparing to fail." D. R. had prepared, even though he had not seen action in the past ten games in a row.

Just before the game started on this chilly Massachusetts night, manager Terry Francona talked to D. R. "Dave, be ready to pinch run in the eighth or ninth innings." D. R. knew he had to keep his legs ready, so throughout the game he would go beneath the stadium and run in the tunnel to keep his legs warm. But even he admitted it wasn't nearly the same as being out there on the field, playing every inning. When Francona winked at D. R. sitting on the bench after Kevin Millar got his lead-off walk in the ninth, D. R. knew his coach was summoning him to pinch run.

When D. R. got to the base, the first thing he did was look for a sign from his third base coach. To his surprise, he saw the sacrifice bunt sign, and so did the batter, Bill Mueller. D. R. didn't like it. He wanted to run. Although he did admit that the sacrifice bunt in this situation was the *safe* thing to do, he didn't want to waste an out on a sac bunt.

He told his first base coach, Lynn Jones, "I'm going to steal this base." Coach Jones looked over at the third base coach, Dale Sveum, and then both coaches looked at Francona with expressions that said, "He wants to steal it." D. R. stared intently at his manager, who stood on the top step of the dugout.

Francona acted quickly, erasing the bunt sign and giving the okay to steal. Coach Jones stepped over to D. R., put his hand on his runner's shoulder, and whispered, "Okay, Dave, do your thing." D. R. described the next few moments to me like this:

"When I was with the Dodgers, Maury Wills told me that one day I'd probably be in an important game where everyone in the park knew I would try to steal. It would be a pressure steal in a pressure situation, and I would have to discard all fear of failure and do what I'd been trained to do. Maury told me,

'Don't be afraid to steal.'

"I wasn't planning on going on the first pitch, because I wanted to get the feel of the game and get my legs underneath me. I had a lot of nerves going through me at first.

"Before Rivera threw his first pitch, he tried to pick me off. I easily made it back safely. Then he picked a second time and almost got me. But when he picked a third time in a row on another close play, in which I dove back head first, it fired me up. That's when I decided to steal on his first pitch to the plate. You see, all those picks helped get rid of my jitters, and now I felt like I had played nine innings. I was in the flow of the game, and after he picked that third time, I knew I had him.

"At that time, I flashed back to a game we had had in September at Yankee Stadium, when I was on first and Mariano was pitching in the ninth. We were down by only one run. In that game, Jorge Posada (the same catcher who was catching now), went out to talk to Mariano, and I learned what their strategy was to deter me from stealing. When Mariano came set, he tried to 'freeze' me by holding onto the ball a long time before delivering to the plate. Well, in that game, I stole it anyway. I ended up scoring the tying run on a sacrifice fly, and we won that game in extra innings.

"I told myself that if I ever faced Rivera again, his strategy would be the same—to hold the ball a long time to get my legs antsy and prevent me from getting a good jump. I also had a gut instinct that he would pitch to the plate this time and not throw over to first base.

"Sure enough, that's what he did. After he came to a set, he held the ball, and held and held. I felt like it was an eternity. But I had done my homework and was prepared for it.

"Once he went to the plate, I broke with a great jump. Posada's throw to second was a good one, but going head first into second, I was able to get my hand to the bag before Derek Jeter put the tag on me. When I stood up on the bag, Jeter patted me on the butt and said, 'I don't know how in the heck you just did

that.'" D. R. told me he thought Jeter was referring to how cold it was and all the attention they gave to him to prevent him from stealing.

"Two pitches later, Bill got a ground ball base hit up the middle, and I tore around third base and beat the throw home with a pop-up slide. I was so happy I jumped and twirled my body in mid-air. My teammates mobbed me, and the Sox fans went crazy. I thought then that the tide had turned in our favor."

When D. R. described all this to me, he was as enthusiastic as if he was doing it all over again. That's D. R.

He didn't need to tell the rest of the story; most baseball fans know what happened next. The Red Sox soared back to win that game on David Ortiz's two-run homer in the twelfth inning. From there, the Sox went on to win the next three games, becoming the first team in history to win a series after losing their first three games. They advanced to the World Series, where they swept the Cardinals in four games to break their eighty-six-year-old jinx. Finally, they were world champions! Most sports writers agreed that when David Roberts entered the game to pinch run, it proved to be the turning point for the Red Sox.

Boston fans had their heroes throughout the playoffs and World Series, including David Ortiz, who hit .387 and had three clutch home runs, and outstanding pitching from Curt Schilling and Derek Lowe. But in 2006, "the Steal" was recognized by the Red Sox Hall of Fame as one of the most memorable moments in their history.

In 1951, I watched the final playoff game between the Brooklyn Dodgers and the New York Giants on national television. The winner of this game would go to the World Series. It looked like the Dodgers would win, with their 4–1 lead going into the bottom of the ninth inning, until Bobby Thomson hit his dramatic, game-winning home run that baseball people have referred to as "the shot heard round the world." Who doesn't remember broadcaster Russ Hodges screaming into his microphone, "The Giants win the pennant! The Giants win the pennant!"

David Roberts's steal of second base was the equivalent event, from a base runner's perspective. At the end of the Red Sox-Yankees game, it would not have surprised me if the Boston announcer had yelled, "The Red Sox steal the pennant! The Red Sox steal the pennant!" Baseball historians will forever refer to D. R.'s steal as "the steal of the century." Without that steal, Boston's "miracle" never would have happened.

The Red Sox fans never forgot what David Roberts did for their city. When he played for the San Francisco Giants a few years later and they played in Boston, the Red Sox fans gave him standing ovations every time he came to bat.

A few years after D. R.'s "miracle steal," his manager, Terry Francona, said, "Dave Roberts's theft of second base was maybe my single most favorite moment since I've been in the game."

John's eyes perked up when I told him that. "Gary," he said, "that single moment of glory took Dave Roberts many years of hard work, and without his enthusiasm, he would have lacked the industriousness to ever make that moment happen. Maybe you should think about putting him in both blocks of the Pyramid?"

It was a question, but I knew how he felt about it. "If you think so," I said.

Like Eric Karros, David Roberts was another walk-on recruit from San Diego County. If it were not for Butch Smith, his high school coach, I would have never invited D. R. to visit UCLA. I thought my recruiting for the up-coming season was finished, until Butch phoned me one summer morning in 1990.

I listened to what Butch had to say about his outfielder, who was "as fast as lightning" and had only one serious scholarship offer—the Air Force Academy wanted him to play football and be their option quarterback. But David wanted to play baseball in college—not football.

Three things Butch said excited me. First, I knew his player

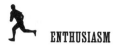

was a good student, or else he wouldn't have been accepted to the Academy. Secondly, his dad was a master gunnery sergeant in the U.S. Marine Corps, and that meant D. R. qualified for a partial scholarship to any college of his choice. Thirdly, David was fast—something my team would be lacking in the next couple of years.

So, I invited Coach Smith and his player to come up to UCLA and visit our campus. I made no promises at that time because I wanted to meet his player face to face and check him out. I wanted to make sure David knew he might not play much his first year. I was hopeful that he wanted to be a Bruin badly enough to have the patience to sit on the bench for a while.

When I saw David and greeted him during his visit to UCLA, he had a beaming smile that still lingers in my memory. That smile hasn't changed a bit in all the years I've known him. It is so genuine, it goes straight up into his eyes.

Speaking of those eyes, I didn't need to look up or down at them, they were straight in front of me. He was short, like me, about five foot eight, maybe five foot nine in a stretch. I always chuckled when I read our UCLA roster each year and D. R. listed his height as five foot ten his freshman year, then it went to five foot eleven his sophomore year. I wondered if he'd be six foot and six foot one by his junior and senior years, even though I still looked him straight in the eyes.

As I forecasted, D. R. did not play much his first year, having only five at bats and appearing in only nine games, mostly to pinch run. But he sat on the bench and rooted for his team while waiting patiently for his turn to play—just like he said he would.

D. R. was an unselfish player who set the table for the hitters who followed him in the batting order. I always preached to him that his job was not simply to get on base a lot, but to make good outs. That meant making the opposing pitchers throw at least five or six pitches every time he went to bat. That's a tough assignment, because he often hit with two strikes against him before ever taking a swing, and he had to pass on some fat pitches, especially when the count was two and zero. But he did it willingly, knowing the hitters that followed him would get a good long look at the different types of pitches they would be seeing when they came to bat. Besides, the more pitches the starting pitcher threw, the sooner we would get to see their second-liners from the bullpen.

I would always compliment D. R. whenever he got those six pitches, even when he made an out. I remember once that he came back to the dugout and I said, "Way to go, D. R., you got *seven* pitches that time." He stopped in his tracks, gave me that contagious smile of his, and said, "*Eight*, Skip. I got *eight* pitches." He was right. There were games when he got even more.

Of course, D. R. got plenty of walks, too, and for him that was like a double because of his success at stealing bases. Those number two and number three hitters loved him for that, because they could gear up for the fastball knowing that catchers would be calling more straight fastballs to give them a better chance to throw out the stealing Roberts. Also, with D. R. standing on second base, our hitters had a good shot at driving in a run.

Like Eric Byrnes and Jack Gifford, D. R.'s enthusiasm rubbed off on his teammates. I asked several of D. R.'s UCLA teammates who was the most enthusiastic player they had ever played with. One of those I asked was former All-American and six-year major leaguer, Ryan McGuire. He took about one second to answer: "D. R." Then, expounding further, he said, "I never saw D. R. hang his head when he was in a slump. He never pouted or moped. He was always up and happy."

Adam Melhuse, who nominated both Eric Byrnes and David Roberts as his most enthusiastic players, told me, "No one ever had to pick up D. R. He always picked us up. Just watching the energy D. R. played with was contagious."

I could quote every UCLA player who played with D. R. from 1991 to 1994, and they would make similar remarks to those of

Ryan and Adam. If I were to put D. R.'s teammates' sentiments into one sentence, it would be: "D. R. made you feel good about playing just by being around him."

No one I talked to ever saw D. R. dejected, disappointed, or depressed. I was in that same company until one day, when D. R. came to visit me in my clubhouse office at Jackie Robinson Stadium. He came walking in with his smile missing and asked if we could talk. "Of course," I said. "Have a seat."

"Skip, what do I have to do to show them I can play?" I knew he was referring to the professional scouts. The 1993 Major League Baseball draft that was finished the day before had not selected D. R. until the 47th round—the 1,434th player chosen. I had never seen him depressed and frustrated, as he was that day.

Part of his frustration was that seven of his teammates, also juniors, were drafted ahead of him, and he knew that most of them would sign pro quickly. My answer to his question was rather simple. I told him he needed to bunt more, hit more grounders (no pop-ups), and steal more bases. If that sounds familiar, that's what I had also told Eric Byrnes. On defense, I told him he needed to strengthen his throwing arm, learn to get rid of the ball quicker, and field base hits closer to the infield so he wouldn't need to throw so far. In the end, I gave him some encouraging words that seemed to perk him up a bit. "D. R., you have the potential to be the perfect lead-off man. Every major league team needs a player like you. You don't have to be one of the best players in the nation to be drafted higher. All you need to be is one of the *thirty best* lead-off men in the nation. If you can do that, one of the thirty major league teams will find you."

So, D. R. returned for his senior year. He worked harder than any senior I've ever coached. His peers elected him captain, mostly because of his positive attitude and work ethic on the field. Every day in practice, his outfield coaches, Vince Beringhele and Don Tamburro, worked with him on his outfield play, especially his throwing and getting off his throws quickly, without hurrying. He spent hours polishing up his bunting skills until he became a master at placing bunts on either the first base or third base side of the diamond.

With a little negative reinforcement from me, he stopped popping up as often. Every time he popped up during batting practice, I terminated his "b.p." for that round. He learned quickly, as any hitter would, because no hitter wants to be cheated out of his normal quota of cuts. But he did thank me later, when he returned after his first year of playing pro ball. At our 1995 UCLA alumni game, he said, "Skip, you saved me some money last season." I didn't know why until he explained further that his minor league manager fined the fastest players on his team five bucks every time they popped up.

D. R. made the most of his senior year, leading the Bruins in batting average (.353), hits, triples, runs scored, walks, and on-base percentage. He also shattered the UCLA single season stolen base record with forty-five stolen bases, a record that still stands.

His success at UCLA paid off in the draft the next season, as he was selected in the twenty-eighth round by the Detroit Tigers. Being a senior and a low draft choice, he had no leverage to bargain for a large bonus, but he was more than happy to sign for a whopping $1,000. Although he was drafted higher than the year before, nothing forecasted stardom for him in pro baseball.

When D. R. was in the minors, we talked on the phone occasionally, sometimes when things were going well for him and sometimes when they were not. One day, when he was playing in the California League for Visalia, he called me. His tone on the phone reminded me of the day he visited me in my office. He was really down and, in his mind, his chances of ever making it to the major leagues looked bleak. Here he was, after four years in pro ball, still at the single A level. All I did during that phone call was remind him of what I had said a long time ago:

"Every team needs a lead-off man. You only need to be one of the thirty best, and a team will find you."

In his sixth year in the minors, he was traded from the Tigers to the Indians, and that was when he finally got his big break. When Kenny Lofton, the speedy center fielder and lead-off man for the Indians, was injured, D. R. got called up to the big leagues, where he played for the next ten years. Every team he played for (he played for five big league clubs) appreciated the intangible qualities that D. R. brought to his club.

Peter Gammons, the highly respected sportswriter and baseball critic, named D. R. to his five-man list of the Most Valuable Team Players in the Major Leagues (Eric Byrnes was also on his list). In an article in the 2002 *Baseball World Series Magazine*, sports writer John Maffei named D. R. as one of the best hustlers and lead-off men in the game. D. R. was quoted in that story saying, "Ichiro Suzuki brought back the importance of the lead-off hitter. He's the best in the game." D. R. also praised a couple of other players who were great hustlers, David Eckstein and Darin Erstad: "Their teams feed off their energy. They're all foxhole type guys that I really respect."

I'm not sure D. R. was even aware that *his* teammates felt the same way about him.

* * *

When Coach and I finished discussing Byrnes, Gifford, and Roberts, I was left with a good feeling. I knew John was pleased with all three former UCLA student-athletes chosen to represent his block of enthusiasm. At the end of our discussion, we both agreed that Roberts deserved a spot in both cornerstones, industriousness and enthusiasm.

LIFE AND DEATH

John always said, "I am not afraid of death, but I'm not intentionally going to speed it up, either." He made it clear that he was not afraid because he believed in heaven. "That is where I will be with my Nellie once again," he said.

In his later years, he attributed his longevity to living a balanced life. He told me, "I ate a balance of fruits, vegetables, and meat on the farm when I was in my youth, and I try to keep a balanced diet in old age. Except for one time at Purdue, I never drank alcohol, and I stopped smoking early enough that my lungs didn't quit on me. I try to treat life with balance, too. What I mean is, I never get too excited when things go well for me and—except for when Nellie died—I never get too low when things go badly. Life is full of peaks and valleys. You might as well accept that fact and be willing to treat each one the same, if you want to stay healthy."

In his late years, Coach gave speeches to a variety of groups—from large corporations to elementary schools. He told me about a speech he delivered at the request of one of his former players, Swen Nater, who worked for Costco.

"After I finished speaking, I opened it up for questions," he said. "A middle-aged man asked me, 'Coach, are you afraid of

death?'

"I replied, 'Now, that's an odd question to ask a ninety-five-year-old man.' Of course, everyone laughed, including me."

John said that the man's question reminded him of something he had read on a tombstone:

> *As you are now*
> *So once was I*
> *As I am now*
> *You're sure to be*
> *So may I say*
> *As here I lie*
> *Prepare yourself*
> *To follow me.*

Under that, John said, someone had scratched:

> *To follow you*
> *I'm not content*
> *Until I know*
> *Which way you went.*

I heard John recite that tombstone story over and over again in his old age, and every time he finished, he genuinely cracked up. I believe he actually enjoyed making fun of death. Not just because he didn't fear it, but because he almost welcomed it so he could once again join his Nellie.

A TRUSTED FRIEND

While newspaper reporters, broadcasters, and John Wooden fans across the nation wondered how he was faring in his latter years, a friend of John's helped keep that secret. No one outside of John's family knew more about John's daily life than a quiet, humble man named Tony Spino.

On August 2, 2008, during breakfast at VIP's in Encino, John told me, "A *trusted* friend is special, and should be cherished." He was talking about his longtime friend, fifty-eight-year-old Tony Spino. I had just finished telling him that, although we had wonderful trainers for our baseball team at UCLA, Tony was the best.

We could always count on Tony's ability to treat our injured players and, if a player needed more care, he quickly sent them to a specialist or to get an X-ray or MRI for further diagnosis. Before Tony came along, injured baseball players were sent to the end of the line with the other Olympic sport athletes to see doctors or get X-rays and MRIs. Tony wasn't afraid to tell the top brass that baseball players deserved the same kind of medical attention as football and basketball players. He always followed through to make sure that happened. Our players respected Tony not only for his ability in treating them, but also

for sticking up for them. We all trusted him to do the right thing.

I wasn't the only coach who trusted Tony as he performed his training duties for men's and women's coaches in eleven different sports at UCLA. All of them would heartily agree that he not only worked *for* them, but *with* them, to help their teams succeed. While a student at UCLA, he served Coach Wooden as a student-trainer for five years under the direction of head trainer "Ducky" Drake. Tony also assisted, in some capacity or another, the eight basketball coaches who followed Coach Wooden. The list, in chronological order, included Gene Bartow, Gary Cunningham, Larry Brown, Larry Farmer, Walt Hazzard, Jim Harrick, Steve Lavin, and the current coach, Ben Howland.

One time, when Tony and I were talking about Coach's ten national championships, I asked him, "How many UCLA national championship teams were you a part of?"

He lowered his head, looking slightly embarrassed, and answered, "Twenty-five."

"That is amazing," I said in awe.

He quickly added, "That doesn't count the ten that Coach won, because I was only the *assistant* trainer then. Ducky was the head trainer, so those ten belong to him. The only basketball championship I count is the one in 1995, when I was the head trainer with Coach Jim Harrick."

It took many years to cultivate the trust that Tony and Coach Wooden had in each other. Certainly, they celebrated the glory of UCLA's success in basketball, but it wasn't only the victories that built their trust. There were defeats along the way that cemented it—and a serious accident Coach experienced that might have resulted in his death, had it not been for Tony.

Tony told me, "For twenty-five years—ever since Dr. Todd Grant [team doctor for UCLA athletics] asked me to take care of Coach's injured shoulder from a fall—I would stop by Coach's condo three times a week on my way to work at UCLA. I usually arrived around six o'clock in the morning, and visited with him until nine o'clock. On this particular Thursday morning

[February 28, 2008], I arrived earlier than usual.

"I opened the front door and noticed that there were no lights on. That was unusual. I called for him. No answer. I walked down the dark hallway to his bedroom. He wasn't in bed. Not in his bathroom. I turned around, and on the way back down the hallway, I almost stepped on him. He was lying on the floor between his den and the hallway.

"'I'm freezing,' Coach murmured. I went down on my knees, and when I rolled him over to lift him, I noticed he was lying on top of his wrist, which was bent in a crooked position, and his collarbone was protruding more than it should. I lifted him up and carried him to his bed. He was so cold . . . his whole body was shivering. I was worried about that more than anything, afraid he would go into shock. I wrapped my arms around him and held him close to warm him.

"Coach said, 'Don't call anybody.' I didn't want to do *anything* until his body had warmed up.

"Finally, he felt warmer, and I called Nan [John's daughter] who had stayed with John until 10:00 PM the night before, and Caryn [John's granddaughter], who was scheduled to look after him later that morning. I told them to come over *now*." These two ladies, along with John's son, Jim, were all part of the team that had been faithfully taking care of John in his late years.

Tony continued, "They called an ambulance, which took him to the hospital. He was treated for a broken left collarbone and a fractured left wrist. They also gave him a couple of blood transfusions, because he was anemic. He stayed in the hospital for twelve days."

As Tony relived this ordeal, his voice trembled, especially when he talked about Coach being so cold.

"Coach had an unbelievable desire to live," he continued. "Even Jim, his son, said, 'If he had really wanted to die, he would have then.'"

I asked Tony, "Why do you think he fought so hard to live, after what he said about wanting to join his Nellie in heaven?"

"I think he felt he was the true glue of his family."

"Then why was Coach living alone in the first place?"

"Because that's what he wanted," Tony answered, without hesitation. "He didn't want people fussing over him every minute of the day. He was constantly afraid of losing his independence and, with it, his dignity, so he refused to have anyone stay the night with him."

I knew that Nan and Jim spent a lot of time looking after their dad, despite Jim working full-time and Nan having a family. Their dad had fallen before and spent some time on the floor. John told me and others that Nan had even made him promise to get an emergency medical alert device. "Reluctantly, I gave in to her and wore it," John said, "but when they found me after another fall and asked why I didn't press the alert button, I said, 'I promised I would wear it; I didn't promise I would press the button.'"

After that scary fall in 2008, John finally consented to having someone spend the nights with him. In the book he wrote with Don Yaeger, *A Game Plan for Life,* John wrote that he had some wonderful family companions to keep him company throughout the day and night.

John's daughter, Nan, who had already spent much of her adult life looking after Coach—much like her mother, Nell, had done when she was alive—was a regular in his home. John's son and granddaughter, Jim and Caryn, took turns each week staying all night with John. John was truly grateful for his family's support and companionship—as well as their demonstration of love—through this difficult period in his life.

This was also a time for Tony Spino to step in and help. John recommended his trusted friend to stay with him twenty-four hours a day, nearly seven days a week. John's family and the UCLA administrators agreed that it was in John's best interest. They all knew it would be difficult to find anyone else whom they could trust more.

But that would take some doing. As much as Tony wanted

to help John, he had his own wife and daughter at home, so there was more to think about. According to Tony, his family was okay with it. "Coach loved Sandy and Kim [Tony's wife and daughter], and they loved Coach. They told me to go ahead and take care of him, if that's what Coach Wooden wanted. They never once complained. Hey, they always knew where I was. I owe them so much. They never asked me to get someone else to do it."

Although UCLA administrators wanted Tony to stay with John, they hoped he would serve as one of the football trainers during the day, because they were short of trainers for football at that time.

"I told them I couldn't be a football trainer and at the same time take good care of Coach. They didn't realize that when I stayed overnight with Coach in the past when he was ill, I was up sometimes three or four times a night. Not much sleep. I knew I wouldn't be up to par during the day if I had to treat football players, then drive back to Coach's place and be at my best with him. Everyone at UCLA understood. 'Okay, just stay with Coach and we'll pay your salary as long as it takes.'"

Tony agreed, provided he could have his job back at UCLA whenever he was ready to come back. From then on, Tony spent Saturday afternoon through Friday evening taking care of John, twenty-four hours a day. Coach's son, Jim, drove up from Orange County to stay with John on Friday night and Saturday morning, until Tony returned on Saturday afternoon. Nan and Caryn continued to check in on John to make sure he was doing okay.

"I never left Coach alone in the condo," said Tony, "except for one hour on Saturdays to go to four o'clock mass. I always made Coach promise to stay seated in his chair while I was gone. I didn't want him to try to get up and fall again. He never moved." Tony shook his head. "I never knew him to break a promise.

"Starting when Coach was in his early nineties, I gave him

full body massages and exercised his legs—holding them with my hands and pumping them back and forth—because his knees ached continually. I think if the doctors had given him knee replacements, he wouldn't have needed a wheelchair and he would have kept his independence, which is what he longed for. He might have lived to be over a hundred if he had been able to keep walking longer."

"Why didn't he have the knee replacements?" I asked.

"Because of Coach's age," Tony replied quickly. "No doctor wanted to be the guy to operate and have him not wake up."

I asked Tony if he was a "caretaker" or a "caregiver" for John. He answered emphatically, "Neither. I was his *friend*. I don't have a caretaker's certificate or anything. I'm not qualified. I have a lot of respect for *non-abusive* caregivers."

He added, "Although I spent a lot of time with Coach and his family, I never thought of myself as 'family,' either. His family was Jim and Nan and all of his grandchildren and great-grandchildren." Then he repeated, "I was just his friend."

And what a friend he was. I will never forget what Tony told me happened on January 30, 2008. Coach was ninety-seven years old at the time.

"I have spent the last eighteen of twenty-one nights with John, seeing to his needs," he said. "He's gone from a limp, to a cane, to a walker, and yesterday I had to put him in a wheelchair.

"When I was putting Coach to bed last night, he said, 'Tony, I've had a long journey. And it's been wonderful, but I am ready to go. I don't need to wake up in the morning.'

"'Coach,' I said, 'don't think that way—it's negative—because if you do wake up, you'll be disappointed.'"

On December 17, 2011, I met Tony for lunch at Coach Wooden's favorite place to eat on special occasions, the Valley Inn. Most of our conversation was about Coach and his love for baseball.

Tony said, "Coach and I got along so well because we both loved baseball and Western movies, which we often watched together. But I think his favorite movie was *Goodbye, Mr. Chips* with Jimmy Stewart."

Coach and Tony shared something that rarely occurred in baseball—both were offered major league contracts, and both turned them down. As mentioned previously, Coach turned down a Pittsburgh Pirates offer to manage their team on the field. Tony turned down a Red Sox offer to be their head trainer. Instead, he took a job with the Milwaukee Bucks pro basketball team.

"We both loved talking baseball," Tony said, "especially baseball trivia. Coach would go way back in baseball history and ask me questions." Tony smiled. "I think he was amazed when I occasionally came up with the answers. Lou Gehrig was Coach's favorite old-time player, but he believed that Ruth was the greatest player he ever saw. Isn't that something? Coach was old enough that he actually *saw* Ruth play. I asked Coach, 'Why do you think Babe was the best? Was it because of all the home runs?'

"Coach said, 'No, Tony. Ruth never made a mistake. He anticipated the next play, and he never threw the ball to the wrong base. And he knew how to play the hitters. That, I think, was because he used to be a pitcher.'

"But Coach thought Josh Gibson, the great player in the Negro leagues, would have been as good as Ruth, if given the chance. Coach saw Gibson play, too. He told me, 'Gibson was phenomenal.'"

Tony and Coach also talked about their favorite big league managers. They both had tremendous respect for Walt Alston of the Dodgers, whom Tony got to know well when he served as the Dodgers' bat boy when he was seventeen years old.

"Coach loved Alston," Tony said, "partly because he worked with one-year contracts, just like Coach did for twenty-seven years."

"And because Walt was a high school teacher, just like John," I chimed in.

"Coach thought Joe McCarthy was the greatest manager ever, because he won at every level—in the majors and the minors," Tony said.

I believe there were other reasons, besides McCarthy's winning records, that Coach liked McCarthy. First of all, he managed John's favorite American League team in those days, the New York Yankees, for fifteen full years (1931–1945). Secondly, John knew that McCarthy cared deeply for his players, especially John's favorite, Lou Gehrig. According to old news clippings, McCarthy once said to the dying Gehrig, "It was a sad day . . . when you . . . told me you were quitting as a ball player because you felt yourself a hindrance to the team. My God, man, you were never that."

I also believe Coach admired McCarthy for allowing umpires to make their calls without any interference or complaints from him. On controversial calls, he usually kept his seat on the bench—just like John always did. He once said about umpires, "You can't expect them to be as perfect as you are."

Tony and I were almost finished with lunch, but he had much more to say about Coach's love for baseball. I had set a small recording device between the two of us so I could get his times with Coach word for word. He said, "Coach loved to go to the Dodgers and the Angels games."

Tony drove Coach to many ball games in Los Angeles—if one believes that the *L.A. Angels from Anaheim* play in Los Angeles. Coach was invited to throw out the first pitch of the 2002 World Series in Anaheim. Tony said, "I had to talk Coach into it, because he didn't want everybody seeing him gimping out to the mound with his cane. But he did it, and threw the ball quite well."

Tony and John were there as the guests of Major League Baseball's commissioner, Bud Selig. The two sat next to Bud and Peter Ueberroth and their wives. Sitting behind them were Tommy Lasorda and, as Tony put it, "Lasorda's entourage."

He continued, "I was talking to Mr. Selig about Coach's love for baseball and his knowledge of the game. I mentioned that Coach can name the greatest players who ever played, position by position, and each one's statistics. And he can tell you *why* they are the best.

"Bud looked at me and said, 'He used to be able to do that?'"

"When Coach heard Bud, he said, 'I can do that right now if you want me to.'"

The day Tony and Coach visited Angel Stadium to watch the Angels play the Yankees, manager Mike Scioscia invited them to sit in on their pregame coaches' meeting.

Tony described it this way. "The meeting lasted one hour and forty-five minutes. At the end, Scioscia turned to Coach and asked him, 'What do you think, Coach?'

"Coach gave Mike a short and simple one-sentence answer. Scioscia was astonished and said, 'That sums it up!' Then he told his staff, 'We wasted an hour and forty-five minutes. Coach gives us a one-sentence answer, and it makes more sense than anything we just said. We could have been out of here in one minute.'"

I asked Tony, "So what was Coach's answer?" Tony looked down at his empty plate, then looked up, smiling and embarrassed. "I can't remember. But Coach would remember. He had a great memory."

Night after night during Coach's last two and a half years, Tony put his friend to bed, turned off the lights, and went to his tiny bedroom, where he switched on the baby monitor so he could listen for any signs of trouble in the bedroom next door. Usually two, three, or even four times during the night Tony would hear rustling or moaning on the monitor, meaning Coach needed help to go to the bathroom or needed a drink of water. Often Tony just went in to comfort Coach.

"He lived with a lot of pain toward the end," Tony said, "but I never once heard him complain. I saw how tough Coach was when we played up at Oregon in 1973. I was the assistant trainer for Coach's team when we were playing in Oregon's arena,

called "the Pit" because the fans are so close and have a reputation for being wild and rowdy. Well, some crazy fan threw an
apple at Coach, and it landed hard against his chest. I saw Coach
double over, but he didn't fall. He didn't complain, just kept
coaching as if nothing happened. Like I said, he was tough."

They tried four or five different caregivers to come in on
weekends and help Tony with Coach. None of them lasted long.
One of the younger ones quit after only two weeks. Tony said
proudly, "I started and I finished. I heard it said that caregivers have the toughest and most stressful jobs in America. On a
scale of ten being the worst, they are a ten."

I thought back on what Tony said about Coach living past a
hundred years if he had been able to have knee replacements. I
thought, *Yes, that may be true, and if John hadn't had a friend like
Tony to be with him, he wouldn't have lived as long as he did, either.*
John would have lost most, if not all, of his independence and
dignity if some stranger had been watching out for him. John
looked at Tony the same way Tony looked at him—as a trusted
friend who was always there. Tony helped give Coach his last
bit of independence and dignity.

John often said, "There is no greater joy one can receive
than the joy of helping others." Sometimes, in his later years,
he was reminded of that quote when he was the one on the
receiving end. He would retort, "That's true, but I don't like *receiving* it."

Tony kept giving it. "Not for the money, not for the recog-
nition, but simply for the love of my friend," he said. "And I am
truly grateful to Coach's family, Nan and Jim in particular, for
trusting me."

One night, during the last days of Coach's life, Tony asked
him, "What am I going to do when you're gone?"

"Go back to your family and take care of them," Coach said.

During our conversation at the Valley Inn, Tony told me,
"Gary, you were lucky. You got to sit with him. I never really
pulled up a chair and sat and talked with him. We always talked

while on the move. Whether it was dressing him in the morning, bathing him, or assisting with his exercises, we were always moving. And when we did sit down in restaurants for breakfast, lunch, or dinner, people would always be coming up, wanting to talk to him. He always obliged.

"But our favorite time was when the two of us were alone in the car. He called it his 'quiet time.' He loved this time, when he could tell me something he wouldn't tell anybody else.

"He told me, 'With you, I can say whatever is on my mind and not worry about it going any further.'" I knew Tony didn't tell me all of Coach's thoughts, either.

This reminded me of a quote by one of Coach's favorite authors, Ralph Waldo Emerson. I used the quote in one of the children's books that I authored: "A friend is someone with whom I can be sincere. Before him, I may think aloud."

No doubt about it—Tony Spino was that kind of friend to Coach.

A MISUNDERSTOOD FRIEND

People who read the sports pages of the *Los Angeles Times* know about T. J. Simers and his controversial column on page two. Some take delight in the sharp-witted writer's words, while others probably end up throwing their newspaper in the wastebasket before ever reaching page three. The same reader may find T. J. skillfully arousing his sentimental feelings one day, and causing the blood to pound against his veins the next day.

One thing is certain—his readers know that he is unabashedly fearless. With biting words, he is unafraid to attack just about anyone in the sports field—whether they're professionals, such as owners of the Dodgers, Lakers, or Clippers, or stars, like Kobe Bryant, Andre Ethier, or Blake Griffin. T. J. will even take a nip or two at the amateur sports—UCLA and USC, and especially their coaches and athletic directors—which are not immune from his poison pen.

But there are two popular men residing in Los Angeles that have never been struck by his blistering words. Although T. J. has poked fun at John Wooden and Vin Scully, they have remained safe. T. J.'s fun-loving teasing and kidding of Vin and John was never more evident than on the night of June 13,

2008, when he interviewed the two men in front of a live audience at the Nokia Theater in Los Angeles.

T. J. was the director and emcee of the show—the engine that made it run. His purpose was to raise money to help fund local pediatric cancer-fighting programs, and for research at L.A.'s pediatric hospitals. He called the event "Scully and Wooden for the Kids." No dummy, he knew those two men were the most admired and respected sports figures in Los Angeles—a sure draw.

The theater was filled to capacity. I was one of thousands sitting at home, watching on television, while T. J., Vin, and John awed their listeners with words of wisdom, sometimes bringing laughter, and sometimes tears.

At the time, I never gave any thought that this show would ever be mentioned in my book. Holy cow! Imagine a complete chapter about the irascible T. J. Simers in a John Wooden book! But that was before I had ever talked to Coach about T. J.

A couple of months later, at Coach's favorite breakfast place, the topic came up.

Coach said, "T. J. might be the most misunderstood person I know."

He had his reasons. "T. J. has an uncanny skill of putting into words what people—his readers—may be *thinking*, but would never *say*. I have found him to be quick to pounce on sports figures who make mistakes, and then compound their mistakes by making more of them. Nothing wrong with T. J. doing that—he has every right to his opinion. This is America.

"Some people may think he gets more pleasure out of 'bashing' sportsmen, but I am of the opinion that he prefers to write about the underdog—the guy or gal who admits their mistakes, or even the so-called 'losers' who keep trying their best to win with integrity."

"How many of his readers do you think understand this?" I asked John.

With a half-smile, he said, "One out of three, Gary."

Half-smiling back at him, I said, "If one didn't understand T. J., they might have thought he was a little rough on you that night he interviewed you and Scully."

Coach didn't hesitate. "I think everyone knew it was all in fun."

"Well, John, you looked pretty serious when he opened the show with the comment about George Washington being your classmate."

John laughed quietly. "Oh, Gary, I just glared at him for a few seconds—the audience thought T. J.'s quip was funny, but I think they laughed louder when I didn't say anything and just stared at him. It wasn't meant to be a mean look, anyway."

I admitted that I had laughed with both of them and with Vin for much of the night. It seemed that T. J., John, and Vin were enjoying themselves from the first moment they sat down in their blue oversized armchairs, John seated between T. J. and Vin.

The next thing T. J. said to John was quite complimentary. "Coach, I'm not sure how I should address you tonight. I think 'Saint John,' for some people, would probably be appropriate." His comment received applause.

But, typical of T. J., he followed up with what he knew was a sensitive topic for Coach.

"Aren't you known as the wizard, sir? My personal favorite is the wizard."

"I told you not to say that," John replied quietly.

After a pause, John drove a dagger of a remark back at T. J. "If it were not for this charity thing, I would never be with you."

The audience loved it, and roared its approval. T. J. laughed right along with them—which reminds me of something else John said about T. J. that morning during our breakfast: "T. J. can dish it out with the best of them, but he can also take the dishing. I like that."

It wasn't the only fun-dagger John threw at T. J. that night. T. J. said, "In your books—like, you've never stopped writing them. You're even writing kids books now." John interrupted him and said, "When are you going to start writing?"

T. J. didn't get it at first, and said, confused, "When am I going to start writing books?" Then John's words connected in T. J.'s head and he said, " . . . Or start *writing*?"

Once again, T. J. had to laugh at himself—along with John and the audience—but being the true competitor that he is, he responded with a laughable quip of his own. "I see you got your nap today!" This left hook delivered by T. J. reminded me of another thing John once told me: "I think T. J. likes to say things just to remind you he isn't soft-hearted. He doesn't fool me."

I mention these comedic battles of words so that one can better understand T. J. the way John understood him. I certainly don't know him as well as John knew him—I've never met T. J.—but something he wrote or said once struck me and made me think differently about him: "[John] loved [Nell] after her death more than us whose wives are still alive." It was a great line; it takes a lot of guts to say that when you still have a wife at home.

Vince joined the "war" with a good line of his own that handed Coach one of his biggest laughs of the evening. It, too, came at the expense of T. J.

I don't remember what led Vin to say it, but it came at the tail end of one of his answers to a T. J. question.

The eighty-year-old Vin said, "I am rather emotional just sitting here with you and realizing where my life has wound up."

The audience busted up, and T. J. laughed louder than anyone. T. J.'s back pounded heavily against his chair when he laughed at the jokes aimed at him. I do believe that if he had been sitting in a standard folding chair, he would have done a few backflips on that stage.

With Vinny onstage, of course, the topic of baseball was a continuous thread that wove its way throughout the discussions. Vin told tales of Jackie Robinson, when they both broke

in with the Dodgers at about the same time. He marveled at Jackie's composure, despite the insults he received by the fans and the opposing players.

Vin's baseball stories motivated John to tell a tale of his own that I had never heard him tell in all the years we had talked baseball. "When Casey Stengel was manager of the Boston Braves, they gave an award for the one who did the most for baseball that year. Then, in the middle of the season, Casey was hit by a taxi. His leg was badly injured, and he was out for the season. The taxi driver received the award for the person who did the most for baseball." His story brought more laughs from the audience.

I asked John, "Do you remember what you said that probably brought the loudest laugh of the evening?"

"Gary, I was only ninety-eight years old then," he said with a sly and mischievous grin. "Of course I remember. T. J. got all over me about my screaming at the referees when I coached. He asked me, 'How do you explain that?' I told him that I first wanted to quote Abraham Lincoln: 'It's better to keep quiet and let people *think* you are a fool, than to speak up and remove all doubt.'"

The audience laughed its loudest after Coach's answer, and T. J. laughed along with them for a while, until I heard him slip in a comment that barely caught anyone's attention—maybe not even John's and Vin's.

Quietly, but earnestly, T. J. said, "I have great affection for you two."

I believe these soft and heartfelt words slipped right over most of the heads that were in attendance that night. I heard T. J. say it because I was watching alone in my quiet living room, listening closely to my television.

When the show was over and they stood to receive a standing ovation, I watched John struggle to rise from his deep-seated chair. I heard T. J. say to John, "Let me help you up." Vin went behind John to steady him, and a familiar figure entered the picture. Tony Spino, John's trusted friend, grabbed Coach under the armpits, helped set him into his wheelchair, and then wheeled him offstage as the audience continued to stand and applaud. It was a wonderful event produced by a man that Coach said was the most misunderstood of any man he knew.

Our discussion ended that morning with words from John that only someone with his insight and wisdom would say. "At first glance, [T. J.] comes across as a man without compassion for his fellow man," he said. "But I do believe he is very compassionate—probably more so than most. My goodness, look how he took the brunt of the jokes that night. He did it for the children. He made that sacrifice for what was a good cause."

John added, "People who might have disliked T. J. before that night saw him in a different and more honest light—they may have come that evening to laugh *at* him, but they left laughing *with* him."

COACH TALKS BASEBALL
WITH FRIENDS

In January 2010, I received a phone call from Tony Spino asking me if I would be interested in attending a barbecue for Coach Wooden. It would be held at the home of loyal UCLA athletic booster and alumnus Angelo Mazzone.

"Coach wants to have a small group of 'baseball people' get together with him and his family to talk some baseball," Tony told me.

A couple of days later, I received a call from Angelo Mazzone, officially inviting me to the baseball party.

On Sunday morning, January 31, my wife, Sandy, and one of my daughters, Jessica, walked through the wide-open entrance to Angelo's beautiful home in Brentwood, only a few miles from UCLA's campus. We were greeted by our host, Angelo. Behind him, I spotted the main celebrity of the day, Coach Wooden, chatting quite spiritedly with family and friends as he sat in a large leather chair.

The three of us immediately greeted John with the others before circulating through the expansive rooms, meeting John's large family of children, grandchildren, and great-grandchildren. I don't remember all of their names except for John's daughter, Nan, his son, Jim, and Cori, one of Coach's thirteen great-grandchildren.

We met and talked to most of the baseball people, including Dodgers manager Joe Torre and Angels manager Mike Scioscia. John's good friend, Jeff Moorad, was also there, and had recently become owner and CEO of the San Diego Padres. I hadn't seen Jeff since our breakfast with John over a year earlier. At that time, he had been a partial owner of the Arizona Diamondbacks. UCLA had its baseball representatives in attendance, including former UCLA second baseman and current athletic director Dan Guerrero, and the current head baseball coach, John Savage. Vin Scully was there long enough to talk to Coach and take a posed photo with several of us, but he left before the group baseball discussions began because he had another commitment.

For the first hour, people mingled and exchanged pleasantries while Coach was busy posing for pictures with anyone who asked. After Joe and Mike had had their pictures taken with John, it was my family's turn. John seemed to enjoy having my wife's arm around him, as he smiled broadly for several photos. I also asked John if he would autograph his most recent book, *A Game Plan for Life*, which I had brought with me. As usual, it took Coach quite a while to write his signature.

When John was in the middle of signing my book, I couldn't help but notice his hand trembling. When he finished and handed the book back to me, he apologized. "My signature doesn't look like it used to, Gary." I took a quick glance at it and yes, it wasn't the immaculate signature I had seen in the past, but I told him, "Doesn't matter, John. I can read it."

I watched Coach as he took pictures and signed autographs for everyone, always with a humble smile. John's warm smile had not changed since I had first met him thirty-six years beforehand. It was an easy smile that made his eyes twinkle, accompanied by a sense of humor that made everyone who met him feel like he was their friend. Behind that smile was a simple, unmistakable message that he would remain your friend for a long, long time. I found myself thinking, as I gazed at this man, *It is popular when writing letters to our friends that we sign off with the words "Your Friend Always." Coach truly believed those words*. I was amazed by his energy and enthusiasm at the age of ninety-nine. His cheerfulness and friendliness was contagious to us all. Coach was having fun at his party.

After all the introductions, signings, and pictures, Angelo summoned us to the backyard patio, where several picnic tables were set up for an elaborate meal. I sat down at one of the tables, with Sandy and Jessica on each side of me. Across the table sat Bill Sharman, who had been one of my basketball heroes when I was a teenager. This great USC and Boston Celtic Hall of Fame player spoke barely above a whisper, because he had damaged his vocal cords from too much yelling when coaching the Los Angeles Lakers.

I was not surprised when, instead of talking about basketball, Sharman mentioned baseball. Coach Wooden had told me a long time ago that Sharman was a professional baseball player as well. Coach had informed me of that fact in 1975, the first year we were office mates. At the time, Coach and Bill had just finished co-authoring a basketball book called *The Wooden-Sharman Method: A Guide to Winning Basketball*.

Coach had told me a story about Bill's short stay in the major leagues. He said, "Bill was called up from the minor leagues to the Brooklyn Dodgers late in the season, but never did get into a game. He was sitting on the Dodgers bench that day, when the umpire got tired of hearing all the griping coming out of the Brooklyn dugout. The umpire ejected the entire Dodgers bench, including Bill. It earned him the distinction of being the only player in major league history to be thrown out of a major league ball game, without ever having played in one."

Bill and I only talked briefly, but I did notice that this gentleman, now in his mid-eighties, looked like he could still shoot free throws as well as he had in the NBA many years ago. Bill still holds the NBA record for making fifty-six consecutive free throws in the 1958–1959 playoffs—an amazing accomplishment.

After everyone had eaten and done their share of visiting, Tony Spino brought John and his wheelchair to a spot next to me while Angelo called out to all the "baseballers" to sit near John.

While Angelo gathered Torre, Scioscia, and others to the picnic table, John and I were left alone. It was the perfect time for me to ask him how he *really* felt. All day long, I had been hearing his patented answer to his well-wishers: "Just fine, thank you."

"So, John, how do you *really* feel?" I asked.

He turned to me and said, "As good as it's going to get, Gary."

"Well, I know you've had a rough time of it lately—in and out of the hospital," I said. "But you look okay to me."

His eyes remained on mine and, all of a sudden, I was sent back in time to the days he and I talked privately in our tiny UCLA office. "Thanks, Gary," he said. "I guess the good news is that you can still see me . . . I am still here." Then he smiled broadly. "I think I'm part cat."

In this moment, when we were alone, he asked me, "Do you miss coaching, Gary?"

"I miss the action on the field, John—the practices and the games—and I miss the everyday camaraderie with my players and coaches. But I do get a taste of all this when I coach our alumni team once a year, for a week or two."

His eyes widened. "Alumni team?" I could see that he didn't know I had been coaching my former players once a year in a worldwide competition.

"Yes, John. Our alumni team has played in France, Italy, Spain, and Australia, and this summer we're going to Puerto Rico. Next year we're playing in Prague—the Czech Republic."

"I didn't know we had an alumni team, Gary. Do you play other university alumni teams?"

"No, there aren't any. UCLA is the only one. Maybe someday other colleges will join in—they don't know what they're missing. Our players love putting on the old UCLA uniforms and playing together again."

We didn't get a chance to talk about the alumni team again, as everyone began gathering around the table. Joe Torre and Mike Scioscia sat down directly across from John, and Jeff Moorad sat to the right of him. Dan Guerrero, Coach Savage, and Zev Yaroslavsky, a UCLA alum and the current Los Angeles County Supervisor, gathered around as well. Zev is an avid baseball fan who gave a speech at the ceremonies dedicating UCLA's Jackie Robinson Baseball Stadium in 1981.

After everyone had settled around John, he let the two managers, Joe and Mike, lead the discussion. Joe started it off with a story about Sandy Koufax, the three-time Cy Young Award winner and one of John's all-time favorite players. Joe told about the time he was eating a late-night dinner by himself at the same hotel restaurant where Sandy was eating, just across the way from him. Koufax had just pitched against Joe and his Atlanta Braves that night. "He struck me out three times and popped me up once," Joe said, shaking his head.

Sandy sent a drink over to Joe and told the waitress to ask him to come over and join him for dinner. Joe, not being in the best of moods, told the waitress, "Tell him to come over to me. I came to him all day."

Sandy joined Joe at his table, and they both stayed and had drinks into the early morning. "We both drank way too much, especially since we had an early Sunday afternoon game the next day," Joe said. "I realized my mistake the next day, when I was catching in the Atlanta ninety-degree heat. I looked over at the Dodgers bench and saw Sandy sitting in the shade of their dugout on his day off—smiling at me."

That was just one of the stories Joe told that day that gave Coach a good laugh. I know, because I felt John's hand squeeze my forearm whenever he chuckled.

Joe's story about drinking with Koufax must have sparked

Scioscia's memory, because he jumped right in with a Koufax story of his own.

"Sandy and I were sitting with a few others in a nice Italian restaurant," he began. "I bought a bottle of wine for the table. It cost me about nine bucks. I didn't know at the time that Sandy was a wine connoisseur. When we finished my bottle, Sandy insisted on buying the next bottle for the table. He spoke to the waiter in perfect Italian. Shortly after, here comes the waiter with another bottle. It was great. Best I've ever tasted! After Sandy's wine, mine tasted like it was made from a bunch of dried raisins." Mike shook his head and seemed to be reliving his embarrassment all over again. "Sandy's bottle cost thirty-five bucks . . . I felt a little cheap."

It wasn't until Joe and Mike had finished their stories that I realized today's beverages were all non-alcoholic. I'm sure it was in deference to John's taste in drinks.

John admitted to the group that he had only drunk alcohol once in his life, at a Purdue University fraternity party. We all laughed when he said, "Actually, it was during Prohibition . . . so I guess I committed a felony."

Joe and Mike were not hesitant to make fun of themselves that day. Joe told a story about a major league record he broke when he played for the New York Mets in 1975. The dubious record he set was hitting into four ground ball double plays in *one* game.

"Felix Millan, who hit right before me in the batting order, had gotten on first base with less than two outs his first three times to the plate," he said. "I followed him with three straight ground balls to the infield and, of course, with my speed, those were three automatic double plays." Joe didn't need to remind us of his foot speed. Most baseball fans were aware of his turtle-like legs. I remembered what former catcher Joe Garagiola had once said: "The wind always seems to be blowing against us catchers when we're running."

Torre resumed his story. "It got to the last inning with one out, and Felix was up to bat, nobody on base. I'm in the on-deck circle, hoping he makes an out or hits a double—anything except getting on first base again. So, what do ya know . . . he gets another single.

"I went to bat and hit another grounder to the infield, which was my fourth double play and a major league record, which stands to this day. It just might never be broken!" Joe seemed to take pleasure and even some pride in telling his story, as Coach Wooden and the rest of us chuckled.

A few days after Joe told this story, I checked the major league statistics under the category of "Grounded Into Most Double Plays in a Single Game." There, I read Joe's name, all by himself as the National League's all-time leader. But there was another name that appeared as the American League leader— Goose Goslin of the Detroit Tigers. He had hit into four double plays way back in 1934. Joe is probably right about his record lasting forever.

I was surprised to discover that two of baseball's most celebrated players, Cal Ripken and Henry Aaron, led their respective leagues in grounding into the most double plays of all time. Joe Torre ranks thirteenth. I wished I had known these facts at the time Joe told his story, so I could have told him he was in good company.

Coach sat with his arms folded and listened intently as Joe and Mike did most of the talking. But whenever John spoke, both of the managers would scoot to the edge of their seats and lean forward so they wouldn't miss a single word.

John told his story about the time he was offered the field manager's job with the Pittsburgh Pirates. John had said to the general manager, Joe Brown Jr., "If you hired me, they would fire you first, and then fire me." Although I had heard Coach tell this story a few times before, I laughed with him and the rest of the group when he finished.

Coach had told me more than once that Scioscia and Torre were two of his favorite modern-day managers—"and not just because they managed Los Angeles teams, Gary," he added.

John admired Joe's style when he managed the Yankees, with all those superstars. "It's not as easy as most people think to coach a bunch of stars," John would say. I guess he knew this as well as anyone, having coached Lewis Alcindor, Bill Walton, Gail Goodrich, Walt Hazzard, Sidney Wicks, and Keith Wilkes, to name a few.

John especially liked the way Torre showed confidence in his players—his casual style was devoid of any signs of panic, even in crucial times. Coach once described Joe's style in this way: "If you watched Torre closely during his games, you couldn't tell if his team was winning or losing, or if one of his hitters had just hit a home run or struck out." Sounds a lot like Coach's style . . .

John liked Scioscia's style of aggressive base-running, "especially the way his runners go from first to third on singles." He added, "And his teams always play good fundamental defense."

When Coach talked about the way these two former great players managed, I couldn't help but be impressed again with his knowledge of the game. I believe he would have been just as successful coaching college or professional baseball as he was coaching his *second*-most favorite sport, basketball.

Mike Scioscia was quoted in the *L.A. Times* by sports writer Bill Shaikin as saying, "[Coach Wooden] understood the importance of a secondary lead. . . . He understood the importance of hitting behind the runner, and the importance of taking the extra base. He definitely understood what would help a team win a game."

A popular topic of discussion that day pertained to the changes that have been made in the game of baseball since John played and coached the game. Coach told us that, although there have been some adjustments, one of the main reasons he liked the game of baseball was the fact that it didn't change.

He did mention a couple of modifications that had been made, like the designated hitter in the American League and, in recent years, the practice of managers using their relief pitchers in most games. "In my day," he said, "starting pitchers were expected to go all the way, every game. If they didn't, they felt they had failed their team."

Joe related a story that Walter Alston, the great manager of the Dodgers, had once told him. Alston was faced with the decision of whether to have Koufax or Don Drysdale pitch the seventh and final game against the Minnesota Twins in the 1965 World Series. When Alston chose Koufax, Drysdale came up to him and said, "I want to be the first out of the bullpen." Joe's point was that even starting pitchers in his day were willing to come in from the bullpen if needed.

When Joe finished his story, Scioscia said, "Starters go six innings now and start looking for the bullpen to finish up for them."

"I can't imagine Bob Gibson handing the ball to his manager in the seventh, eighth, or even the ninth inning, when the game was on the line," Joe replied. Joe caught Gibson when they played for the Cardinals. Gibson's history of complete games, especially in the World Series—nine starts and eight completions—speaks for itself.

Coach tapped me on the knee and whispered, "Gary, do you think Sparky [Anderson] would have any trouble taking Gibson out?" He was smiling; we both knew he was referring to the feisty Cincinnati Reds manager who had a reputation for taking pitchers out quickly. Sparky's other nickname was "Captain Hook."

Scioscia was nodding his head in agreement with Joe. He was probably thinking of a couple of other Dodgers pitchers, besides Drysdale, who would have trouble with being taken out of the game in the late innings, including Orel "Bulldog" Hershiser, who pitched fifteen complete games in 1988 and Fernando Valenzuela, who in 1986 was the last pitcher to pitch twenty complete games. Scioscia caught both of them.

Joe told us about one time, when he managed the Yankees,

that they had just lost to the Atlanta Braves in the first game of the 1996 World Series. "We lost in our own yard, and George [Steinbrenner] was deeply concerned about the next game in Yankee Stadium," he said. "In his usual stern way, George told me, 'Tomorrow's game is a *must*-win!' My answer shocked my boss: 'Well, they got Greg Maddux going tomorrow, George. He's pretty good, you know. I figure they'll beat us tomorrow, and we'll take the next three at their place and come back to our own yard and win the series right here.'"

Joe glanced around the table. "You should've seen his face after I said that," he said, then added with a sigh of relief, "I sure was glad when it all turned out the way I said it would."

John's toughest question of the day, in my opinion, was asked by Scioscia. I could tell by the way Mike asked it that he had been thinking about it for a long time. He sounded hesitant. "Coach, who was the most difficult player you have ever coached, and how did you deal with him?"

John was even more hesitant about his answer. It was not like him to say anything negative about a person behind his back. His dad had taught him that, "If you can't say something good about a man, it is best to say nothing." We all waited patiently for John's answer, but I had serious doubts that he would ever say the name.

Sitting next to John, I could see his lips tighten as he struggled to answer Mike's question. I sensed his feelings and concern for the former player he had in mind. At the same time, I could tell that he wanted to return Mike's favor for being so open and honest in telling *his* stories.

Finally, in hardly a whisper, John mentioned the name of one of his former UCLA players. No one would ever have guessed who that player was by reading or hearing anything John had ever written or said about him in the past.

I believe John's response was meant to be confidential. I am not going to repeat the name he mentioned that day, but I will say that it wasn't Bill Walton, who was the main character that caused some concern for John on several occasions. Those stories were highly publicized by the media. The most famous of these incidents, which led to the perception that Bill was a problem, was the day he came to practice with long, scraggly hair. John told Bill he couldn't practice until he got it cut. Bill argued that he had the right to wear his hair the way he wanted. John replied, "That's true, Bill, but I am the head coach, and I have the right to say who plays. Although we would love to have you play for us, we will miss you." Bill quickly rode his bicycle to a local barber shop and made it back in time for practice. Actually, John had told me that Bill was one of the easiest players he had ever coached, and had always given his best effort in practice and in games.

After John had given his surprising answer, Mike asked, "Why was he so difficult for you?"

"At practice, he would do things he knew were not to my liking or in our team's best interest," John replied. "I tried speaking to him privately, and when that didn't work, I criticized his decisions openly in front of the team. Finally, I did what I always did with players whose attitudes needed changing—I dismissed him from practice. That always worked with my players, because they considered practice to be a privilege. They usually returned the next day, eager to do the right thing." John threw his hands into the air. "But not him! I suspended him once for three days, and when he returned, nothing changed. He never did get the message."

Joe wasn't hesitant at all to tell everyone who he had the toughest time coaching.

"Leyritz!" he blurted out. "Jim Leyritz was the toughest for me." Joe didn't mind telling everybody this, because he had told the story about Leyritz before. He described how he had pinch-hit for Leyritz late in the game, and Jim hadn't liked it.

"Leyritz was in the on-deck circle, and began walking to the plate to take his at bat," Joe said. "I yelled to him that I've got someone hitting for him. He stopped, turned around, made a disgusted face, flipped his bat high in the air, and stomped back to the dugout. Everyone in the ballpark saw him. After the game, I called him into my office and told him, 'Don't you ever show me up again!' I told him I never expect a player to be happy about being pinch-hit for—but you don't show up your manager on the field. I told him I'd pinch-hit for better hitters—Jeter, O'Neill, Posada—so I could pinch-hit for him.

"I was real angry, all right, and I made sure he knew it when I ended our meeting. I told him, 'And by the way, Leyritz, after the game, none of the reporters ever asked me why I hit for you.' That's just *one* example I could tell ya about that guy."

When Joe had finished, Coach turned to Scioscia, who had started it all. "What about you, Mike?" he asked. "Who was the toughest you ever coached?"

Like Torre, Mike erupted with his answer. "Jose Guillen! That guy had six different personalities. One was as nice as could be. The other five were all bad." Mike's description brought some chuckles from the group, and a grin to John's face. Mike seemed frustrated just thinking about coaching Jose. "He wouldn't listen—to me, or to anybody," he said. "We paid him to leave us. It was worth it."

At the time, I didn't think I would divulge Jose Guillen's name in this book, for the same reason I chose to keep the name of Coach Wooden's player to myself. However, I later learned that there were plenty of confrontations between Mike and Jose that had been written about in newspapers and magazines across the land. Each of them had thrown uncomplimentary words at each other. After I finished reading, I decided I might as well mention Jose's name, since most baseball fans would guess it anyway.

With those two exceptions—Leyritz and Guillen—both Joe and Mike praised their current players. Although they preferred the toughness of the players who had played in their day, it was obvious that they wouldn't trade their jobs for any other. Joe spent some time telling everyone how much he enjoyed coaching players like Derek Jeter and Mariano Rivera. He, too, knew that Coach Wooden's favorite modern-day ball player was Jeter. When Joe sung the praises of Mariano Rivera, you could feel the admiration flowing out of him. "The guy's just amazing," he said. "He's done everything a closer can do. Nobody works harder."

As soon as Joe paused, I broke in with my first comment of the session. "David Roberts told me that Rivera's move to home wasn't that good," I said. "He thought he could steal second base against him, and he did it twice in key situations."

I liked what Joe said next about his favorite closer. "Roberts made Mariano better with that steal in the American League playoffs," he said. "During the off-season, and in spring training, Mariano worked especially hard on improving his move to first base and speeding up his delivery to the plate. No one ran on him like that again."

Mike asked John another tough question: "Coach, if there's a Dodgers game and an Angels game on television, which game are you watching?"

Torre leaned back in his chair and gave Mike a look that said, "What kind of a question is that?"

As for me, I was thinking, *Wow! He's really putting John on the spot.*

I should have known better; John didn't even flinch. "I'm channel surfing," he said. We all laughed heartily as John chuckled and squeezed my arm again.

I had told my wife and daughter that this affair would probably only last a couple of hours since, at ninety-nine years old, John would not be up for a long party. But when I looked at my watch at 3:00 PM, Coach was still talking baseball and having fun. "John, are you getting tired?" I whispered to him.

He gave me a quick smile and whispered back, "Of course I am, Gary. But I'm enjoying every minute of it."

Finally, about half an hour later, Tony Spino and Angelo Mazzone rescued John from the rest of us. Some of those in attendance, like Scioscia, would never see him again. I would see him one more time after that, and Joe would be one of his last visitors a couple of days before his passing.

As the guests filtered out of the house, it seemed that their handshakes and hugs with coach lasted a little longer than usual. Though he was tired, Coach returned each farewell with his familiar warmth and smile.

"Coach had a great time," Tony Spino told me afterward.

"So did everyone else," I said. "It was a *memorable* time."

TOP OF THE NINTH

These last three chapters are the most difficult for me to write—emotionally, at least. Most of what follows was written within minutes of seeing John for the last time.

Driving from my home in Bear Valley Springs to John's home in Encino takes about two and a half hours. It is a trip I normally dislike because of the traffic in L.A., but this last trip flew by quickly. I was busy reliving our friendship, which had begun in 1959 when I first saw Coach Wooden on the UCLA campus ball field.

Although John had paid a visit to my family's home, I had never been to his condo, where he had lived for thirty-eight years. We had always met at restaurants or at other people's homes, or on the UCLA campus. Coach's loyal friend and devoted caregiver, Tony Spino, had given me directions to the condo. For months, Tony had been spending his days and nights helping to take care of John.

After I parked my truck behind John's condo, I grabbed the book I had brought for him and walked to the underground parking garage less than twenty yards away. After entering the garage, I located the small elevator that would take me to John's floor.

There were no buttons to push outside the elevator doors, only a metal key receptacle. I had no key. I stood there, wondering what to do next. I had come too far to let a silly elevator stop me.

"Does Coach know you're coming?" I turned around and saw a middle-aged man running toward me with keys jangling at his side.

"Yes, sir," I replied, wondering how he knew I was coming to see John. Coach wasn't the only one who lived in this complex.

The man grabbed a key, inserted it into the metal receptacle, and the elevator doors opened. I thanked the stranger and stepped inside.

As I rode the elevator one floor up, I realized how the man knew I had come to see John. I had forgotten that I was wearing my blue and gold jacket with "UCLA" plastered on it. It was then that I realized how nervous I was about this meeting. I had been friends with John for thirty-six years, so it wasn't as if I would be meeting a stranger—what worried me was his physical and mental condition. I had seen him recently, and although he had been frail then, his dry humor was still intact. I remember him saying, "I can't stand on my legs too long anymore, Gary . . . maybe about seven seconds." He had been energetic that day, and his mind was as sharp as ever. Today, I was fearful because of four words Tony had said to me yesterday: "His condition is deteriorating."

When the elevator door opened, Tony greeted me with a wide smile and a warm handshake before leading me into John's condo. It was nothing big and fancy—he didn't require big and fancy. John had grown up in a farmhouse with no running water or electricity. This condo suited him fine.

As Tony and I talked in the living room, I was struck more by what I *didn't* see than by what I did see. There were no trophies, plaques, memorabilia, or awards hanging on the walls or standing on shelves. It was a room just like millions of other living rooms across America, though rather spartan. One thing

that stood out was a coat rack tucked away in the corner of the room, which I would never have noticed if Tony had not pointed it out. The rack had some ribbons draped over its protruding wooden pegs.

"The Presidential Freedom Award that George Bush gave Coach is hanging over there," Tony said. "Several other ribbons are there, too. One is a ribbon and medal that the local Kiwanis Club gave him." Tony shook his head. "Can you believe that, Gary? Coach gets the highest award a citizen of the United States can receive, and he drapes it on a coat rack alongside a bunch of others!"

I would never have guessed that the occupant of this place was a man named by the sports world as "the Greatest Coach of the Century" until Tony took me into John's den, where a collection of team photos hung on the wall facing the entry. These were pictures of the teams that had won ten national championships for UCLA. Tony made sure I noticed that those ten photos were arranged in the form of a pyramid. "Nell placed them that way a long time ago, and John has never changed them."

On the wall next to those photos were shelves that climbed all the way up to the ceiling, holding stacks of books, a wide assortment of coffee cups, souvenir dish plates, and a few souvenir basketballs. In the middle of the room sat a coffee table with a few dozen books between bookends. Alongside the coffee table was John's tan, soft-cushioned armchair, which faced the television, a metal filing cabinet, and the championship photos. This was where John spent most of his time—it was the home plate of his playing field.

John's old-fashioned roll-top desk was against the far right wall, where some framed pictures hung, including one of his Pyramid of Success. On the top ledge of his desk, personal photos of Nell and family members stood alongside a glass cross and a clock. The work area of his desk was cluttered with papers, a cup with a bunch of pens poking out of it, a red porcelain apple, and a couple of books.

As I scanned the rest of the room, I recognized a couple of familiar items—two wooden baseball bats resting against his desk. They were Louisville Sluggers—my favorite model when I played at UCLA.

From there, we proceeded down the hallway to a small bedroom. During the last two and a half years of taking care of John, Tony had spent his nights here, in a room that barely had enough space for a bed. Tony pointed to a baby monitor next to his bed. "That's what I listen to in case he needs me," he said. "I can hear him rustling about, or coughing, or calling for me."

We left his room and continued toward John's bedroom. Suddenly, Tony stopped. "Gary, I want to prepare you before you see him," he said. "Coach might not be himself. He sleeps a lot. He's sleeping now. I think the medication is making him drowsy, and his mind a little foggy. Yesterday, he drifted back to his high school days, when he played baseball."

Tony seemed reluctant to go into detail, but he added, "I went along with Coach's fantasy yesterday, and I asked him if he wanted to play shortstop for his friend, Joe [Torre]. He said, 'Oh, no! I don't want to take Jeter's spot.' Coach thought Joe was still managing the Yankees, so I asked, 'What about playing shortstop for the Dodgers?' He said, 'Yes, I'll play for them.'"

Tony was sure the medication was playing tricks on Coach's mind. "The doctors are working on fixing that," he said. "Coach would still be as sharp as ever if that stupid medicine wasn't in his system. Maybe today we'll be lucky, and he'll be the John Wooden you've always known."

With those words, we entered Coach's bedroom. As Tony said, John was sound asleep, covered up with a blanket and lying on his back on the far side of the king-sized bed. On the near side of the bed, I spotted a framed picture of Nell resting on the pillow where she used to rest her head. The letters that John had written to her ever since her passing in 1985 were missing. Later that day, I asked Tony about those letters. He

told me they were in safe-keeping, but that John hadn't been able to write any recently.

As Tony rounded the corner of the bed, he tried to wake John from a deep sleep. "Gary's here, Coach." This did not rouse John in the slightest, so he spoke louder and closer to his ear the second time. "Gary's here, Coach!"

This time, John stirred and gazed around the room with uncomprehending eyes. Finally, he focused on me, standing at the foot of his bed. After a long, uncomfortable silence, I tried to make a joke. "John, are you ready to play shortstop for the Bruins tonight?" I asked. I knew that UCLA was playing Long Beach State that evening.

John's eyes snapped to attention as he fixed his eyes on me with the intentness I was used to seeing. "You bet," he answered quietly but firmly. "I'm ready."

That old familiar grin told me that *he* was pulling *my* leg, rather than me pulling his. The three of us had a good chuckle at Coach's remark. For Tony and I, our laughter stemmed partly from relief that John was acting like himself. His sense of humor remained intact.

I was still carrying the book I had brought, *The Little Clock Who Had No Hands*. I told John that it was a children's book I had written, much like the children's story he had published, *Inch and Miles*. After I showed it to him, I laid it on the dresser facing the foot of John's bed. "It's only thirty-three pages," I said. "You can read it to your grandkids and great-grandkids when you have some spare time."

After I said this, I remembered that John disliked the term "kids" in place of the more proper word, "children." He always said, "Kids are baby goats . . . not children." But this time, he didn't bother to correct me, although I thought I saw his eyebrows furrow a bit.

"Thanks, Gary," he said. "I didn't know you wrote children's books."

I told him that this was my first attempt.

"I'll leave you two to talk," Tony said, turning to leave the room.

Much of what John and I talked about that day is mentioned in previous chapters, though I saved some bits for these final three. His most memorable words occurred early in our conversation. In a soft, somewhat sad, yet somewhat jesting whisper, John said, "Gary, I'm not going to make it to one hundred." His one hundredth birthday was less than six months away. My heart sank.

Trying to sound optimistic, I said, "Oh, John, think positive. You'll make it to a hundred and even longer."

"No, Gary, I'm ready," he said, pointing a finger skyward. "I'm ready to join my Nellie any day now." He seemed content, almost joyful.

I leaned closer to John so I could hear him better. His voice was weak and had worn thin, probably from the years of yelling to his players and giving hundreds of speeches in front of thousands of people. He talked about his love for Nell, often a part of our conversation whenever we got together. A favorite story of his was one he had told me and others before. It was the story of young Nell's first visit to his farm. On a hot summer day, a couple of John's ninth-grade classmates had driven her quite a distance to visit John, who was working hard in the fields when she arrived. John had liked Nell very much at the time, but, as he told me, "I didn't want to see her."

Although I knew the answer, I asked John, "Why not?" He raised a hand to his nose and pinched it for a second or two. He didn't say a word, waiting instead for me to say it. He knew I had already heard this story. Like I said, he enjoyed telling this story, and I enjoyed hearing him tell it.

"Because you stunk," I said, on cue.

We both laughed, but it caused John to have a coughing spell—not the first he had had since we began talking. The coughs came every two or three minutes, yet he steamrolled through each one. I couldn't help but admire his toughness.

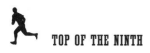

He admitted to me that, as much as he loved Nell, he wished he had treated her "more fairly."

"Why's that?" I asked.

"Well, Gary, she always did what *I* wanted to do," he said. "You name it, if I wanted to do something, she was always okay with it. But I wasn't as good at doing the things *she* wanted to do . . . like dancing. Nell loved to dance. I didn't. I should have danced with Nell more." John glanced away. For an instant, he glanced at Nell's side of the bed, as if to ask for her forgiveness. I told him that if not dancing with Nell was the worst thing he had done, she wouldn't hold it against him.

He tilted his head and creased his lips in an expression that said, "Maybe not."

BOTTOM OF THE NINTH

Shortly afterward, Tony came into the room with a glass of water for Coach. While Tony held the glass, John drank it down with a straw. The water seemed to help ease the cough that interrupted him so persistently. Tony had told me earlier that he was worried about John's coughing, fearing that it might be a sign of pneumonia, especially since they had stopped giving him antibiotics for an earlier infection.

Then, Mike Warren, another of John's former players who had become his close friend, entered the room. I had met Mike before at UCLA events. Tony said that Mike visited John frequently. Mike, with his charismatic, movie-star smile, said, "You two carry on. I'll just wait out here in the other room. I have some calls to make, anyway." When Mike had gone, John looked up at me and said, "That young man had the best basketball mind I ever coached."

We were alone once again, and he asked me if I'd mind if he rolled over to his side. Of course I told him that would be okay. I wondered then if he might have changed positions because of the fear of bed sores which are so prevalent with bedridden patients. When John rolled on his side, I dropped to my knees so my eyes would be even with his.

I thought this would be a good time to tell John the story of my scary meeting with J. D., and how John and I came to share an office. As I finished telling the story, I added, "I've always been grateful to J. D. for giving me the honor of sharing my office with you, and for making it possible for us to become good friends."

John looked at me with a gleam in his eyes I had not noticed until then. Wearing a half-smile, he said, "Gary, you don't know the *whole* story. You see, J. D. first asked me if I would share an office with Gene Bartow [the coach who had replaced John]. I told J. D., 'No, I don't think that is a good idea, especially for Gene.' Then J. D. asked me, 'Well, John, who would you want to share an office with?'"

John smiled broadly before continuing. "I said to J. D., 'My favorite sport is baseball. If Gary would not mind, that would be fine with me.'"

When John finished, I had to take my eyes off of his; I didn't want him to see the tears that had formed in them. *John Wooden chose to be with me*, I thought. I wanted to tell him how that decision had affected my life, but those words never came. I could only manage to whisper, "Thanks, John."

Then, after a deep breath, I changed the subject. I asked him to tell me more about his favorite old-time ball player, Lou Gehrig. John not only talked about Lou, but also included Babe Ruth in his story.

"You know, Gary, I have autographs by Gehrig and Ruth."

I knew about these autographs because Tony had told me about them. But I did not know how John had gotten them.

John explained that the autographs had been scribbled on a local Indiana town newspaper, along with a photo of the two ball players. Both players had signed the newspaper copy while on a barn-storming tour in John's hometown. The man who owned the newspaper had given it to his son, but when the son learned that John loved baseball, and Lou Gehrig in particular, he gave the newspaper to him. John never displayed it in his home for fear that something might happen to it. Coach told me that he was keeping it in a safe place. A few days later, Tony told me, "I think that newspaper is in a box underneath John's bed."

On this spring day, as John and I continued to reminisce, I asked him if he remembered the good times we had had at the Valley Inn.

He looked at me as if to say, "What kind of a question is that?" Out loud, he said, "Of course I remember. That was less than ten years ago."

"Well, I doubt if you remember what I remember about one of those evenings," I replied. "You really shocked me with something you said. The rest of the gang heard it, too, although I've never talked to them about it."

"Really?" John said. I assumed that he didn't know where I was going with this story.

"You were sitting across the table from me when you introduced our waitress. 'Sophia is the best,' you said. She blushed and smiled, and replied, 'Oh, John, I just love you,' then began to walk away. Then you called out to her, 'I love you, too, Sophia!'"

I could tell by the look on John's face that he still didn't know where I was going with this.

"Well, John, more than once you have said that Nell was the only woman you ever loved. I've always wondered why you said you loved the waitress."

He leaned closer to me and said, "What I told you was true, Gary. But you weren't listening carefully enough. I said my Nellie was the only woman I was ever *in* love with. There's a difference."

I am not the only one who has been dazzled by John's attention to detail. His players know about that more than anyone else. He has never been afraid to correct someone, if it means getting to the truth.

"And," Coach added, "Sophia wasn't our waitress—she was the *owner*."

I smiled at him—not so much about what he said, but about how tenacious and feisty he could be when making sure the real truth was known.

I changed the subject. "John, do you know there's a photo hanging on the wall of the Valley Inn with you and about ten of us together?"

He brought his fingers up to his chin. "I know there are some photos of me in there, but I don't recall any with me and our group."

"Well, I doubt you've ever seen it, because it hangs inside the little bar above the rows of alcohol."

"You're right, Gary. I don't recall ever being in that room. But I've passed by it many times on my way to and from dinner." He grimaced a bit, seeming a bit displeased that his photo was inside a bar when he hadn't had a sip of alcohol since that night long ago, when he was a student at Purdue.

Coach changed the subject back to his beloved Nell. "I learned to live without Nell, but I still miss her and love her as much as I did the day she passed," he said. "Not a day goes by that I don't think of her . . . or miss her."

Both of us were silent for a moment before we resumed talking about baseball. Coach remembered that I was a Cincinnati Reds fan, and that my boyhood idol was my hometown hero, Reds pitcher Joe Nuxhall. Although John's favorite teams were the Dodgers, Angels, and Yankees, he admitted that he respected any baseball team that played good fundamental baseball and won with dignity. "That includes your Reds, when Sparky was the manager."

It felt like old times when John began talking about another one of his favorite managers, Smokey Alston.

"Alston got the most out of his players, even though he only had one at bat in the big leagues and struck out on three straight pitches." John knew Walt Alston's history better than I did—and I had grown up only seven miles from Smokey's hometown, Darrtown, Ohio.

John kept up his praise of Alston. "Yes, he had good players," he said, "like Robinson, Reese, Snider, Campanella, and Newcombe—but for a guy who hardly played in the majors, he won their respect. That's not easy to do. But Gary, you know why he was my favorite manager in those days? Because he was a teacher, like me. He taught about the same time I was teaching high school. Smokey coached in the summer, when he wasn't teaching. As you know, I always thought of myself as a teacher first, not a coach."

I asked him if he knew why they called Alston "Smokey." He said, "No, but I hope it wasn't because he smoked."

"When I was fourteen years old," I told John, "I played in a baseball tournament against a pitcher from the state of Washington whose name was Smokey Smith, because he had a smokin' fastball. Maybe that was the reason."

"Alston was a first baseman, Gary," John responded. "Not many first basemen have good arms. I doubt he had a smokin' fastball." I stood corrected.

"Although I did like L.A.'s Eric Karros," John continued, "my favorite *Brooklyn* Dodgers player was first baseman Gil Hodges. He and Alston were both quiet and humble men who worked hard and were intent on doing their best every time they put on their uniforms. That's why they were good managers, too."

John's love for baseball was as evident as a puppy's love for chasing one. His next words did not surprise me.

"Baseball is the greatest game of them all. No two games are ever alike. Even we old people can find something new or surprising in baseball—like that young boy who interfered with the pop-up that cost the Cubs the pennant. Who could have predicted that? And Gary, do you remember the time the Mets won the pennant because the umpire changed his call?"

John gave me no time to answer. "It happened on a pitch that he first ruled did not hit the Mets batter, Cleon Jones, on the foot. When [Mets manager] Gil Hodges showed him the shoe polish on the ball from where it hit Jones, the umpire

changed his mind. Then, with Jones on first base, I think the next batter doubled, and the next homered to win the game. Those Mets ended up winning the pennant."

My knees were killing me as I knelt on the hard floor and listened to John, but I never thought of moving. I was entranced and amazed by his knowledge of baseball history, and his enthusiasm for the game.

"No sport imitates life better than baseball," he continued. "It has its goats in one inning, and those goats can quickly be turned into heroes in the next. A player can make an errant throw that allows the tying run to score in the top of the ninth . . . then he comes to bat in the bottom of the inning, and slugs a home run to win the game. No one even remembers the error our hero made."

John saw me nodding in agreement and quickly added, "But it can just as easily be the other way around—a hero can turn into a goat, just like that. Take the famous poem "Casey at the Bat," for example—he was the hero of Mudville until he struck out to end the game. The good thing about that story, which wasn't written, is that Casey, despite his failure, is loved by everyone who reads that story. They even erected a statue in Casey's honor at the Baseball Hall of Fame in Cooperstown. Only baseball treats its heroes and goats with that kind of love."

He continued, "I think that the Red Sox fans have forgiven Buckner for his error that cost them the pennant. From what I have observed, they feel compassion for him and treat him almost like a hero today." He took a deep breath. "Maybe someday the Cubs fans will forgive the young boy who interfered with the pop-up."

I tried to make a joke. "That young boy might be an old man before that happens, Coach."

He smiled and waved a finger at me. "But in time they will, Gary. That's just the way baseball fans are."

John finished with barely a whisper, and I found myself thinking how lucky I was to be there listening to him. It was obvious that his love for the game of baseball was just as intense as mine. I believe talking baseball took him back to those fond days long ago, when he played ball on the fields of Indiana just for the fun of it.

Coach reminded me of a question he had answered at our breakfast get-together a couple of years ago. "Remember when Jeff Moorad asked me if I would change anything in my Pyramid?"

I nodded.

"Well, Gary, as you'll recall, I told him, 'Not really. For sure I would never replace the cornerstones, industriousness and enthusiasm.'"

"Yes, I remember your answer."

"Well, I was mistaken. You see, the most important word in the world, 'love,' is not included anywhere in my Pyramid. I wish I would have put it somewhere. But now, it's been fixed. It's in our children's book, *Inch and Miles*. The people in charge of distributing it to the schools came up with the idea of putting the word 'love' in all the mortar between every block in the Pyramid. A great idea. The word 'love' is written everywhere."

He didn't need to tell me he was pleased with the idea—his bright smile was evidence enough. But as fast as the brightness had appeared on his face, it suddenly dissipated, and John grimaced and stirred uneasily. I asked him if he was in pain.

Coach strained his neck and pointed at his legs. "My knees hurt, Gary. Sometimes they hurt very much."

"You mean, just lying there, without even moving?"

"Yes. I have put them through a lot over the years."

"Basketball?"

"Basketball and old age." Even with the pain, John managed a quick smile. "Satchel Paige once said about growing old, 'Age is a question of mind over matter. If you don't mind, it doesn't matter.'"

Then he asked me a question that sent me back at least a

couple of decades. "Gary, didn't we talk about the middle innings of baseball being the toughest to play?"

"Yes, John, we did."

Trying his best to make fun, he said, "Well, I'm not so sure it applies to life. These late innings—especially the bottom of the ninth—are real tough."

Hearing those words, I realized that now would be the best time for me to leave. I had promised myself that I wouldn't tire Coach out. During my visit with John, I had never looked at my watch. I knew I had entered his home at 11:00 AM, but I had lost all sense of time as we talked. I guessed that it was nearly mid-afternoon. We had talked about baseball, love, his Pyramid, our choices for the most industrious and most enthusiastic UCLA ball players, our UCLA-American Heroes, and his health. Basketball was hardly mentioned.

I stood up and started to say goodbye. I reached for his right hand and held it gently as he reached across his body with his left hand and put it on top of mine. I bent down and brushed my cheek against his. I felt his warm breath on my ear, and fought hard to keep tears from falling. My heart pounded as I whispered, "Take care, John. I'll see ya later." I was hoping he would say what he always said to me in these late innings: "I certainly hope so, Gary." But on this day, those words did not come. We both knew we would not see each other again in this physical world.

I remember that moment as if it were yesterday. I know I will remember it just as vividly tomorrow, and forever.

As I began walking away from his bed, I saw my book lying on top of the dresser, where I had set it earlier. I picked it up with the intention of giving it to Tony for safekeeping until John would be able to read it. But as soon as I began walking away with it, I heard a hoarse, gravelly voice say, "Gary, where are you going with my book?" It was the first time he had raised his voice during our visit.

I turned, smiled, and laid the book back down. "Sorry,

John," I said. "I was just going to give it to Tony until you had time to read it."

"I'll read it, Gary," he said. "Thank you."

Those were the last words I heard him speak.

When I left his home, I knew this would be our last meeting. Although I tried to convince my heart otherwise, *his* heart was tiring out—its final beat would come only forty-six days later.

EXTRA INNINGS

On Saturday, June 26, 2010, we celebrated the life of John R. Wooden in the basketball arena he had made famous— UCLA's Pauley Pavilion.

I had been to many games in that building, when it was lit with bright lights and filled with screaming Bruins fans. On this day, the building was dimly lit, and over a thousand people sat quietly, as if they were in church giving silent prayer—and many were. I sat between my wife, Sandy, and my daughter, Jessica, two rows of bleachers away from where the "Nell and John Wooden Court" sign had been painted on the floor almost twenty years ago.

The ceremony began with a selection of Coach's favorite songs. In all of our conversations, we had never talked about music. I discovered that some of his favorite songs were my favorites, too. I was especially moved when Louis Armstrong's song, "What a Wonderful World" was played. That rendition holds a spot in my top five favorites, and has always had a special meaning for me.

The speeches given that day were awe-inspiring. Some, like Keith Erickson's, were hilariously funny, while others, like Kareem Abdul-Jabbar's and Jamaal Wilkes's, were a mixture of lighthearted humor and deeply felt sentiment.

On the inside cover of the program was a poem written by Coach, called "Don't Look Back." During John's later years, I had heard him recite this poem from memory. When I read it this time, I could almost hear his voice as I whispered the words:

> *The years have left their imprint*
> *On my hands and on my face.*
> *Erect no longer is my walk*
> *And slower is my pace.*
>
> *But there is no fear within my heart*
> *Because I'm growing old*
> *I only wish I had more time*
> *To better serve my Lord.*
>
> *When I've gone to Him in prayer*
> *He has brought me inner peace*
> *And soon my cares and worries*
> *And other problems cease.*
>
> *He has helped in so many ways,*
> *He has never let me down,*
> *Why should I fear the future*
> *When soon I could be near his crown.*
>
> *Though I know down here my time is short*
> *There is endless time up there*
> *And He will forgive and keep me*
> *Forever in His loving care.*
>
> *May I not waste an hour*
> *That's left to glorify the Name*
> *Of the One Who died, that we might live*
> *And for our sins, took all the blame.*

When the ceremony was over, the guests began to quietly file out of the building. I noticed an extremely tall, athletic

figure walking in front of me, carrying a sizeable chair at his side. I thought it could be Bill Walton because of his size and the large chair—I knew he had serious back problems and reasoned that his personal chair would be more comfortable than the folding chairs and bleachers most of the guests had sat on that day. It wasn't until he had drifted out of the line of people and leaned his chair against the wall that I saw his red crop of hair and knew for certain that it was Bill.

I told Sandy and Jessica that I wanted to say hi to Bill, and dropped out of the procession. I walked over to him as he leaned against the wall.

Looking up at him, I could see that he was feeling the emotions of the day's ceremony. After we greeted each other, I said, "I expected you to be one of the speakers today, Bill, but I think I know why you weren't." He read my mind perfectly and said, "I couldn't have done it, Coach . . . not in this building." His eyes filled with tears. I'd never seen such a big man cry, but I understood why. Of all John's former players, I doubt that any of them loved Coach more than Bill. I doubt that Coach ever had a player who was more like a son than Bill.

I didn't know what else to say to him except what my heart told me to say. "He loved you, Bill."

He looked down at me and said, "He loved you, too, Coach."

When I walked away from Bill, he was not the only one with tears in his eyes.

"John loved everyone," I whispered.

We can give without loving,
but we cannot love without giving.
In fact, love is nothing unless
we give it to someone.
                    —John R. Wooden

ACKNOWLEDGMENTS

A heartfelt thank you to the Wooden family, especially to John's daughter, Nan, and son, Jim, for generously sharing their father with me and countless others over the years. I often thought of the Wooden family as I wrote this book.

Thanks to the UCLA family, especially the late J. D. Morgan, and to all of the Bruins who helped gather facts, photos, and information that were vital to this project—Marc Dellins, Mike Sondheimer, Nick Theodorou, and Alex Timiraos. A special thank you to Bill Bennett for going the extra mile—and whose birthday, October 14, is the same as John's. I know Coach was always proud to share that day with him.

Thanks to Ann Meyers Drysdale. Annie, your "papa" loved the way you played on the court, but he loved you more for the way you lived your life off of it. Thanks for permitting me to make you a special part of this book.

I want to thank Jeffrey Goldman, the publisher at Santa Monica Press, for believing in me and giving me the opportunity to tell my story. It has been a great honor and privilege to work with him on this project. Thanks also to Santa Monica Press's talented editorial director, Kate Murray, for her valuable contributions toward editing and for giving me the liberty to speak freely.

Thanks to Jeff Blank, one of two people who read my first draft of the book. There were many rough spots in that draft, and his handiwork helped smooth it over.

Thanks to the ladies in the Tehachapi writing group— Tanis Galik, Meg Hulbert, Victoria Montes, Tanya Spencer, and Teri Moore. I doubt any of them ever attended a college basketball or baseball game, but that made no difference in the way they contributed to the successful writing of this book. They listened patiently and intently as I read chapter after chapter

to them. I am so grateful for their critical, but wise and expert suggestions that did more than just polish up the book—they made the book special.

To John "Skip" May, thanks for your brilliant ideas and welcome sense of humor that got me started on this project and helped make it such a pleasurable one.

Thanks to Lou Pavlovitch Jr., editor of *Collegiate Baseball Newspaper*, for supplying me with John Herbold's articles from the early 1980s, and also for his continued dedication to promoting baseball on the high school and college level.

A special thanks to the late Buck Compton for sharing his experiences on and off the battlefields and the ball fields. He was truly an American hero.

Thanks to Rafer Johnson for his willingness to be interviewed and for sharing his life lessons, even one of the most devastating—the loss of his friend, Bobby Kennedy.

Thanks to Jim Schweitzer for inviting me to be a part of the "Valley Inn Gang." The lunches and dinners with Coach Wooden in those late innings were indeed filled with great memories. Jim made it possible because of his perseverance and organizational skills. I am sure the rest of the gang is appreciative, also.

To Ken Proctor—you are a man quite similar to Coach Wooden in the way you taught and the way your players respected you. Thanks for sharing your story of the Babe.

Thanks to Ray Smith, my good friend and former roommate at UCLA, whose stories about his relationship with Coach are memorable.

To Chris Krug, thanks for giving me permission to make fun of the famous "error" that put your name into the National Baseball Hall of Fame's record book—and for being a loyal assistant and my best friend.

To T. J. Simers, a writer who really knows how to write from the gut and from the heart—your dedication to helping hospitals raise funds so that they can take good care of our country's children may go unrecognized by some, but it is greatly appreciated by the children and their parents.

To my twin, Gene—you were the first person to read my rough draft. You helped refresh my memory, especially about the events in the late 1950s and early 1960s. Thank you for encouraging me to keep going, instead of telling me to forget it.

Thanks to UCLA basketball players Gary Cunningham, Gail Goodrich, Keith Erickson, Raymond Townsend, and John Matulich for your willingness to tell me stories about your beloved coach. And thanks to all of Coach's players who were so greatly impacted by his teaching. You should know that your impact on him was great as well.

Of course, a huge thank you to Tony Spino for his candid and detailed descriptions of Coach—no one, besides his family, knew Coach better. Tony, I thank you from the bottom of my heart for sharing your memories with me and all those who read this book.

Thanks to my fellow coaches—those I coached with and those I coached against, from the time I was knee-high to a grasshopper to the day I last put on my uniform. You taught me much more than I ever taught you.

Thanks to all of you baseball players who cooperated in making this book complete. I am grateful to those who are mentioned in this book, but I am also thankful for all the players I have ever coached—without you, this book would never have happened.

Thanks to Sandy, my wife of twenty-nine years, for helping with the editing of the book in its early stages and for teaching me how to use a computer. Without your loving technical help, I doubt this book would have been completed in my lifetime.

Thanks to my five daughters, who spent many hours without their dad, without complaining, while he spent his hours coaching.

Finally, a heartfelt thanks to you, Coach. After all the words, there are no words . . .

—GARY ADAMS

PHOTO CREDITS

REFERENCES

Baseball America. May 13–26, 1996.

Blank, Jeff. 2012. *Jeff Blank Baseball Blog.* http://www.jeffblankbaseball.com.

Brown, Joe E., and Ralph Hancock. 1956. *Laughter Is a Wonderful Thing.* New York: A. S. Barnes & Co.

Compton, Lt. Lynn "Buck," and Marcus Brotherton. 2008. *Call of Duty: My Life Before, During, and After the Band of Brothers.* New York: Berkley.

Dohrmann, George. 1996. *Los Angeles Times,* April 5.

———. 1996. *Los Angeles Times,* April 25.

Herbold, John. 1980. *Collegiate Baseball,* April 4.

———. 1980. *Collegiate Baseball,* April 18.

Johnson, Rafer, and Philip Goldberg. 1998. *The Best That I Can Be: An Autobiography.* New York: Doubleday.

Maffei, John. 2002. "The Hustlers." *Baseball World Series Magazine.*

Pavlovich Jr., Lou. 1996. *Collegiate Baseball,* April 19.

———. 1996. *Collegiate Baseball,* May 3.

Proctor, Ken. 2006. *Baseball Memoirs of a Lifetime: 77 Years of Loving the Game.* Self-published.

Purcell, Brian. 1996. *Daily Bruin,* April 19.

Rubinstein, Arthur. 1980. *My Many Years.* New York: Knopf.

Shaikin, Bill. 2010. *Los Angeles Times,* June 13.

Scully & Wooden for the Kids. 2008. Fox Sports West.

Smith, Chris. 2011. *MLB Insiders Club Magazine.*

Steinbeck, John. 1995. *The Log from the Sea of Cortez.* New York: Penguin Classics.

Strege, John. 1976. *Los Angeles Times,* May 12.

Wooden, John. 1998. *Practical Modern Basketball.* San Francisco: Benjamin Cummings.

Wooden, John, Bill Sharman, and Bob Seizer. 1975. *The Wooden-Sharman Method: A Guide to Winning Basketball.* New York: Macmillan.

Wooden, John, and Don Yaeger. 2009. *A Game Plan for Life.* New York: Bloomsbury.

Wooden, John, and Jack Tobin. 2004. *They Call Me Coach.* New York: McGraw-Hill.

Wooden, John, Steve Jamison, and Peanut Louie Harper. 2004. *Inch and Miles: The Journey to Success.* Mexico: Perfection Learning.

Wooden, John, and Steve Jamison. 1997. *Wooden: A Lifetime of Observations and Reflections On and Off the Court.* New York: McGraw-Hill.

INDEX